THE STATES AND THE NATION SERIES, of which this volume is a part, is designed to assist the American people in a serious look at the ideals they have espoused and the experiences they have undergone in the history of the nation. The content of every volume represents the scholarship, experience, and opinions of its author. The costs of writing and editing were met mainly by grants from the National Endowment for the Humanities, a federal agency. The project was administered by the American Association for State and Local History, a nonprofit learned society, working with an Editorial Board of distinguished editors, authors, and historians, whose names are listed below.

Washington

A Bicentennial History

Norman H. Clark

W. W. Norton & Company, Inc.
New York

American Association for State and Local History
Nashville

Copyright © 1976
American Association for State and Local History

Library of Congress Cataloging in Publication Data

Clark, Norman H., 1925
    Washington, a bicentennial history.

    (The States and the Nation series)
    Bibliography: p. 197
    Includes index.
    1. Washington (State)—History.   I. Title.
II. Series.
F891.C57   979.7   76-18284
ISBN 0-393-05587-6

Published and distributed by W. W. Norton & Co., Inc.
500 Fifth Avenue
New York, New York 10036

Printed in the United States of America

For my mother and father
Sadie Ollorton Clark and Leigh William Clark
who helped me find
my home in the
Pacific Northwest

Contents

Illustrations

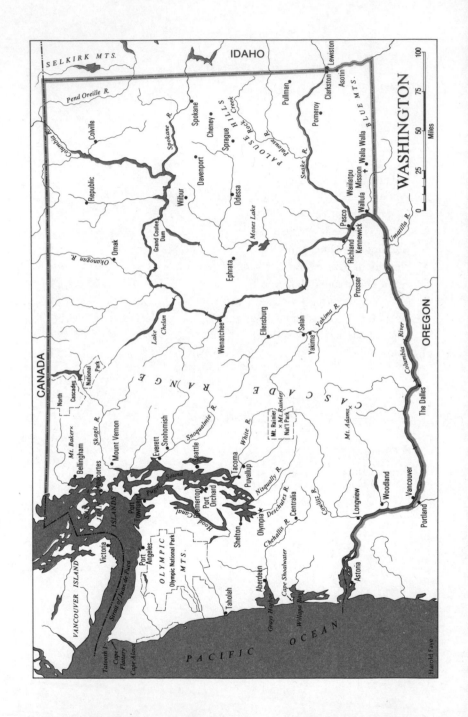

ACKNOWLEDGMENTS

I have completed this book rich in the kinds of debts which follow a period of warmly rewarding friendships. Nancy Pryor and Thomas R. Mayer of the Washington State Library have extended to me a wealth of splendid assistance. Donald Ellegood of the University of Washington Press and Emily E. Johnson of *Pacific Northwest Quarterly* helped me with unpublished materials. Mrs. D. L. Taylor of Sequim, Washington, made a valuable file of newspaper clippings available to me. Kent Richards of Central Washington College, Robert E. Ficken of the Forest History Society, and Albert Acena of the College of San Mateo have graciously loaned me their work-in-progress. My work is better because of their favor.

Then in August 1975, I convened a unique seminar of writers for whom my respect is unbounded. They are also critics of extraordinary independence who would, I knew, be both genial and severe in evaluating my work even while I was in broad daylight stealing theirs. The group included Albert F. Gunns, Raymond D. Gastil, David Stratton, George W. Scott, David Brewster, Roger Sale, Murray Morgan, Richard Berner, and Bruce Mitchell. The critique was conducted by Robert E. Burke, whose friendship and advice I have relied upon through a happy career of teaching and a scholarship. Though these readers could not predict what I might do with their suggestions, I admire their insights as well as their candor, and I hope that each knows that he has helped me write a book that is better because of his good wishes.

I want also to thank other writers whose unpublished work I have pirated, including Paul Thomas, Lawrence Rakestraw, Patrick H. McLatchy, Robert D. Saltvig, Herman A. Sleizer, Bruce Blumell, Fayette Krause, John Rulifson, Howard A. Droker, William Wolman, and Roy O. Hoover. A complete list of the sources I have used in preparing this essay will be published in *Pacific Northwest Quarterly*.

I hope my colleagues and students at Everett Community College understand my deep appreciation of their tolerating my sullen brood-ings about the problems which in writing these pages I imposed upon myself and upon them. If the problems have been in part solved, it is in part because of the superb typing done by Jane Landre. I am, fi-nally, eternally grateful to Kathy Clark for the compassion, patience, and good humor with which she accepted these problems and for her skill in concealing from others the eccentricities her husband sustained in confronting them.

N. H. C.

Invitation to the Reader

IN 1807, former President John Adams argued that a complete history of the American Revolution could not be written until the history of change in each state was known, because the principles of the Revolution were as various as the states that went through it. Two hundred years after the Declaration of Independence, the American nation has spread over a continent and beyond. The states have grown in number from thirteen to fifty. And democratic principles have been interpreted differently in every one of them.

We therefore invite you to consider that the history of your state may have more to do with the bicentennial review of the American Revolution than does the story of Bunker Hill or Valley Forge. The Revolution has continued as Americans extended liberty and democracy over a vast territory. John Adams was right: the states are part of that story, and the story is incomplete without an account of their diversity.

The Declaration of Independence stressed life, liberty, and the pursuit of happiness; accordingly, it shattered the notion of holding new territories in the subordinate status of colonies. The Northwest Ordinance of 1787 set forth a procedure for new states to enter the Union on an equal footing with the old. The Federal Constitution shortly confirmed this novel means of building a nation out of equal states. The step-by-step process through which territories have achieved self-government and national representation is among the most important of the Founding Fathers' legacies.

The method of state-making reconciled the ancient conflict between liberty and empire, resulting in what Thomas Jefferson called an empire for liberty. The system has worked and remains unaltered, despite enormous changes that have taken

xi

place in the nation. The country's extent and variety now surpass anything the patriots of '76 could likely have imagined. The United States has changed from an agrarian republic into a highly industrial and urban democracy, from a fledgling nation into a major world power. As Oliver Wendell Holmes remarked in 1920, the creators of the ñation could not have seen completely how it and its constitution and its states would develop. Any meaningful review in the bicentennial era must consider what the country has become, as well as what it was.

The new nation of equal states took as its motto *E Pluribus Unum*—"out of many, one." But just as many peoples have become Americans without complete loss of ethnic and cultural identities, so have the states retained differences of character. Some have been superficial, expressed in stereotyped images— big, boastful Texas, "sophisticated" New York, "hillbilly" Arkansas. Other differences have been more real, sometimes instructively, sometimes amusingly; democracy has embraced Huey Long's Louisiana, bilingual New Mexico, unicameral Nebraska, and a Texas that once taxed fortunetellers and spawned politicians called "Woodpecker Republicans" and "Skunk Democrats." Some differences have been profound, as when South Carolina secessionists led other states out of the Union in opposition to abolitionists in Massachusetts and Ohio. The result was a bitter Civil War.

The Revolution's first shots may have sounded in Lexington and Concord; but fights over what democracy should mean and who should have independence have erupted from Pennsylvania's Gettysburg to the "Bleeding Kansas" of John Brown, from the Alamo in Texas to the Indian battles at Montana's Little Bighorn. Utah Mormons have known the strain of isolation; Hawaiians at Pearl Harbor, the terror of attack; Georgians during Sherman's march, the sadness of defeat and devastation. Each state's experience differs instructively; each adds understanding to the whole.

The purpose of this series of books is to make that kind of understanding accessible, in a way that will last in value far beyond the bicentennial fireworks. The series offers a volume on every state, plus the District of Columbia—fifty-one, in all.

Each book contains, besides the text, a view of the state through eyes other than the author's—a "photographer's essay," in which a skilled photographer presents his own personal perceptions of the state's contemporary flavor.

We have asked authors not for comprehensive chronicles, nor for research monographs or new data for scholars. Bibliographies and footnotes are minimal. We have asked each author for a summing up—interpretive, sensitive, thoughtful, individual, even personal—of what seems significant about his or her state's history. What distinguishes it? What has mattered about it, to its own people and to the rest of the nation? What has it come to now?

To interpret the states in all their variety, we have sought a variety of backgrounds in authors themselves and have encouraged variety in the approaches they take. They have in common only these things: historical knowledge, writing skill, and strong personal feelings about a particular state. Each has wide latitude for the use of the short space. And if each succeeds, it will be by offering you, in your capacity as a *citizen* of a state *and* of a nation, stimulating insights to test against your own.

James Morton Smith
General Editor

Preface

$\mathcal{O}$N the year of the bicentennial, few Americans will suppose that the purpose of an individual state is to create a singularly meritorious society. Yet many will hope that in their public and private lives the people of each state might enrich the traditions of equality and justice which since 1776 have defined the transcendent purposes of the nation. From the long view of two centuries, how well, we may ask, have the citizens of any state secured for themselves and for all who may follow them the rights of life, liberty, and the pursuit of happiness? To ask this is the Jeffersonian legacy, and at the level of regional history, it is the ultimate bicentennial question.

During the first hundred years, American consciousness of the Pacific Northwest evolved from hazy myths of a fabled river and dreams of Oriental commerce to urgent desires for continental supremacy. This consciousness guided the westward course of empire, but even in 1876 the West was too remote to have presented realistic opportunities for more than a few explorers, fur traders, missionaries, and statesmen. It was the reach of transcontinental railroads, the opening of new lands, and the building of new cities late in the nineteenth century which dramatically refreshed the visions of life, liberty and happiness for hundreds of thousands of ordinary citizens. As they came to make new homes, they were often keenly aware that their first social and political experiences would shape the character of their new states for years to come, and they often approached these experiences with an exhilarating confidence and optimism. As they formed new governments, they quite deliberately extended the functions of democratic institutions. As they developed a sense of community, they offered refuge to many who needed refuge. As they developed an economic system, they presented an expansive range of opportunities to those who could make the most of them. In the same spirit, they were eager to fashion a way of life clearly hospitable to the values of self-reliance, self-esteem, and self-discipline. And because the quality of freedom itself, as Jefferson saw it, unfolds in the dimensions of refuge, of opportunity, of liberation from fatalism, the history of the state of Washington is in many ways consistent with the most noble of American traditions.

But it is also a history haunted with melancholy images. Suppose we could stand together today on the gray-green heights of Cape Flattery, looking out beyond the great waves which break white against the walls of Tatoosh Island. We could contemplate there the fate of Makah Indians, of maritime fur traders, of Spanish and English explorers—and thus would contemplate dark depths of culture and of cultural tragedy, the mystique of adventure, the science of geography, the devious lines of international intrigue, the energies and the aspirations of the new American Republic. And suppose we could drift tomorrow with the Columbia River toward its Yakima confluence. Below Priest Rapids, it moves with current enough to refresh the few salmon which have somehow survived a perilous migration through turbines and over spillways—current enough to urge them forward in their struggle to find again the clear water and clean gravel which are their coordinates of life and death. In a long arch of eight hundred miles and a dozen great dams, this is the state's only remaining stretch of free-flowing water on the Columbia, and as it sweeps broadly around the great White Bluffs it is for a moment a majestic passage, graced on its western shore with the artifacts of lost cultures: walls of an abandoned ranch house made of white river rock; spokes of a broken wagon wheel bleached by a hundred years of rain and scorching sun; mounds marking the forlorn graves of forgotten Indians. The majesty, however, is brief, and our passage would soon edge a bleak lunar landscape now claimed by the United States Energy and Research Development Administration.

Between the broken wheel and the nuclear installations lie the

years which I hope the following pages can in some way illuminate. They are long and complex years for a short book, and the
perceptive reader will identify prejudices which, in this scope, I
can neither conceal nor defend. At the outset, however, I can
state them clearly, and they are, first of all, that serious history
should not serve a society's need for flattery or justification—
that serious history cannot evoke an ennobling vision of a people, past or present, whose lives do not in fact support such a
vision. In such matters, the historian must make his judgments.
In my own system of moral accounting, I list certain vivid
debits: a mindless violence against a delicate ecology; episodes
of racial warfare which denied the spirit of justice; racial discriminations which debased the spirit of equality; attempts to
deny freedom to those who criticized social inequities and
abuses; governments and people who have refused to provide
the kind of welfare—in education, in the care for the aged, in
relief for the unemployed—which is necessary in an industrial
society if individuals are to live with Jefferson's sense of personal dignity and freedom.

There are of course credits, and I shall list many of them, but
what follows now is not so much a deliberately balanced ac
count as it is a personal view of history in which the industrialization of the frontier was at best a mixed blessing. The
rapid economic growth and the cherished economic "developments" of the century behind us were usually good for investors, creditors, speculators, real estate brokers, industrialists,
and building contractors—so good, in fact, that however honorable these men and women may have been, they were quite naturally reluctant to consider the social impact of their windfalls
and exploitations. Their exploitations, in my personal view,
define a central theme, which is that rapid growth and development have always been at the unconscionable expense of those
least able to defend themselves: the Indians before the 1880s;
the millworkers, migrant farm workers, Orientals, and blacks
thereafter. And rapid growth has usually meant a kind of social
pestilence of environmental pollution, rural-urban conflicts, and
political corruption.

On the other hand, of course, the rapidity of economic contraction has usually afflicted the state with the deprivation, the racism, and the radicalism which can be even more fearfully despoiling. A healthy society might reasonably expect the kind of slow and cautious growth which encourages a prudent efficiency and a creative exploration of hidden opportunities, the kind of restrained growth which rewards wisdom more than it does competition, disorder, and exploitation. If this has not been the society of our past, we can hope that it may be the society of our future, and if this be sentimentality, the reader can make the most of it. I would hope, moreover, that the reader will, as I do, want to explore the past for the shadows of ideals we need in the present—ideals such as freedom itself, within the context of individual restraint and forbearance, and racial harmony, and environmental reverence.

This is, then, a limited view; but this is also a limited book. It is indeed a severely limited book, and I can regard myself as among the most acutely sensitive living authorities on what the limitations of space have excluded. Let me insist here, however, that the substance of what remains is carved from realities, not fictions. Let me note also that I have imposed upon myself no formula of balance, no ratios of race, sex, creed, or section. If the viewpoint tilts sometimes toward the experiences of racial minorities, it is because these experiences, in contrast to others, are more revealing and more poignant. If the view seems sometimes fixed on political dynamics, it is because the quality of life is often defined by a political question. This means that what follows is so highly selective that there may indeed be distortions. But it may also mean that it is a carefully limited, biased, but factual view without which the past is often blurred and incoherent. It is a view which focuses not so much upon the group as upon the individual, for without the individual, history has no tragedy, and without tragedy, no spirituality, and without spirituality, no significance.

To approach this significance demands a certain humility. Because the circumstances of our own decades do not always reflect our ideals, we may suppose that in time our flaws, like those of our forefathers, may well obscure our motives, even our achievements, and that however exalted they may now seem, they may by the year 2076 appear as perversions. What I am saying is that I hope my view is a generous one, for I wonder what generosity there may be for us in pages to be written by a tricentennial historian. What difference, he may ask, would it have made to the civilization of the world, to the ability of humans to live harmoniously with each other, with their environment, with their past, present, and future, if there had never existed a state of Washington? It is a stunning question.

NORMAN H. CLARK

September 1975

Washington

1

Ode to White Water

IN the centennial year of 1876, the Columbia River flashed through deep and crooked canyons, its flow so pure and clear and violent that men stood away from it breathlessly, startled by the brilliance and the surging speed. With what fur traders first thought to be a roar of thunder, the northern tributaries dropped into glossy channels of black basalt and tossed small boats through rushes of terror —breaking waves that were twenty feet from trough to crest. Then in its slower descents, the river might pour from dark forests into mirrored depths of sky and sunshine, washing gently past sloping bottom lands where in the black pine and bunchgrass the only sounds might be the muted snorts of Indian ponies. Along the shining sandbars, mining sites had been named by men who had taken their gold to Fort Colville—Six Mile Bar, Twelve Mile Bar— and a few Chinese still worked there quietly sifting through the soft gravel. Yet in even its most tranquil hour, the river was gathering from a thousand creeks and streams the water which would roll white in the next furious plunge toward the sea.

There were men still alive in 1876 who knew the spirit of each steep step through a rock-choked geography—old men, ancient survivors of the generation of French-Canadian *voyageurs* whose language and whose exhilarating respect for power and beauty had since the early years of the century given the river its haunting lore. They were men who in their youth had taken the

3

pace of life itself from images of white-water passages: in Canada, above the Pend Oreille confluence, *Les Dalles des Morts* ("The Rapids of Death") where in pale, hard granite they had scratched the names of companions whose bodies the eddies would not yield; then the raging torrents of *La Chauldier*—"Kettle Falls" to the British and Americans—where the Kettle River entered from the northwest as the Columbia dropped through a narrow channel of jagged rock, then fell into an enormous pool that frothed like a wildly boiling cauldron. A few miles below, the river churned through two elbow turns of Grand Rapids. At Spokane Rapids, the swells broke again into swift white races, sweeping on toward Mahkin Rapids, then Nespelem Canyon, Kalichen Falls, and Whirlpool Rapids, where on a gray day in the 1820s a Hudson's Bay Company brigade had lost eight men.

Where the Wenatchee entered, sun-washed and crystal pure from the Cascade canyons, the river was for a while a perfect water avenue, smooth and broad and deep. There was a cabin there in 1876, a shack where for years restless traders had found a precarious commerce in selling whiskey to the Indians. Beyond the cabin the wide line of water defined the edges of the Great Columbia Plain from which a trader might look west to the snows of the Cascades, south to the majestic Blue Mountains, northeast to the Coeur d'Alenes. But then the steep steps began again: Long Rapids, Rock Island Rapids, Priest Rapids, on toward the flat water where a ferryboat served the few settlers who, after the Indian wars of the 1850s, had entered the Yakima Valley to graze cattle, plant orchards, and, by 1876, to experiment in irrigation.

Beyond the Yakima River, the bluffs of the great plain dissolved into a treeless and grassless desolation of basaltic badlands which had been scorched for centuries by hot blowing sand. At a place which railroad builders later called Hades, the Snake River joined the Columbia with a drainage that reached a thousand miles into the Rocky Mountains and made the Columbia at this confluence one of the earth's great bodies of moving water. Running then in an arch toward the southeast, the Columbia received the Walla Walla near a point where, in 1876, a

boat landing and a stage station, called Wallula, served the people of that valley. This was the former site of Hudson's Bay
Company's Fort Nez Percé, later Fort Walla Walla, built in
1820 from driftwood, and burned by the Indians in the uprisings
of 1855. It marked also the end of a rail line which stretched
east up the valley to a thriving center of stock grazing, flour
mills, and steam-powered threshing machines. To the east and
south the hills rolled in high crests, covered with grass, the
richest and the sweetest on earth. Farmers, coming then from
the depression-ridden coastal ports and logging towns—and
some from California, some from the eastern states—were
planting belts of wheat and series of settlements from Lewiston
to the Blue Mountains, discovering to their amazement that the
deep topsoil was arable without irrigation.

The town of Walla Walla itself—then the largest in Washington Territory, with some thirty-five hundred citizens—had
emerged from the confusion of the Indian wars and to grow fat
and riotous from Idaho gold after 1861. The settlement had
become the principal supply center for the mines, and it had attracted thousands of men and women who intended to get rich
not from mining but from miners: gamblers, bankers, robbers,
murderers, whores, and merchandisers. "Its early history," the
historian H. H. Bancroft wrote in an abrupt understatement,
"was marked by scenes of disorder." [1] With the coming of
farmers, however, the town soon found an enduring stability in
milling and trading, and the disorder was quickly forgotten.

In 1876, boat traffic was common up the Columbia to Wal
lula. However, boat captains were increasingly reluctant to push
against the current through this treeless wilderness where the
steamers burned fifty cords of wood a day. And below the
Walla Walla, at Umatilla Rapids, traffic could be delayed for
weeks by low water. It was in this region, a sandy and desolate
foot of the Columbia Plain, where Americans traveling the
Oregon Trail came to their first view of the river. The young
novelist Theodore Winthrop in 1853 saw it as a "region like the

---

1. Hubert Howe Bancroft, *History of Washington, Idaho, and Montana* (San Francisco: The History Co., 1890), p. 371.

Valley of Death, rugged, bleak, and severe,'' and as he squinted across the vast sheets of basaltic rock to the east and the west, he thought—should there ever be a poet who needed it—that the place might well provide the imagery for an American Inferno.[2]

To the very first American, the inferno was not in the sand-blown rock; it was in the roar of white water. In the fall of 1805, William Clark came upon it like a man from outer space, which, being two years from Virginia, he surely was. He came with fearsome weapons, medicines, and instruments, and with a strange tongue. Yet he had learned to communicate roughly with men who wore white shells through their pierced noses and women who were "nearly necked, wareing only a piece of leather tied about their breast which falls nearly as low as their waste . . . and a piece of leather tied about their breach." He was then a man driven by a fierce determination, possessed by a vision of himself standing on the Pacific shore after two years seeking. Having passed through the Umatilla Rapids, which he called "verry bad," he and Meriwether Lewis could hear the thunder of "the Great Falls" of the Columbia, where the water dropped over a perpendicular twenty-foot ledge. Across a tedious and back-wrenching portage, they helped their men drag the canoes to a foaming pool below. Clark then looked west to a "tremendous black rock . . . high and steep appearing to choke up the river . . . I heard a great roreing." Here approaching its ultimate flow, the Columbia was compressed into a channel no more than fifty yards wide, a fantastic, almost incredible passage. For men with equipment, there was no way around. Showing an impatience which he only rarely recorded, Clark wrote that he was "deturmined to pass through this place notwithstanding the horrid appearance of this agitated gut swelling, boiling & whorling in every direction. . . ." [3]

2. Theodore Winthrop, *Canoe and Saddle,* Nisqually edition (Portland, Ore.: Binfords & Mort, n.d.), p. 182.

3. Meriweather Lewis and William Clark, *The Journals of Lewis and Clark,* ed. Bernard DeVoto (Boston: Houghton Mifflin Co., 1953), p. 264.

To the amazement of the curious Indians, they passed through safely, and rode the sweeping currents on toward the river's great slice through the ridge of the Cascade Mountains—the "Great Shute," Clark wrote, where the white water was "passing with great velocity foaming & boiling in the most horriable manner. . . ." When they emerged finally to the broad and easy tidewater that lapped a thick coastal forest, Mount Hood stood magnificently in view. But after a moment of marveling at this convergence of mountain and river, at this coastal plain where the trees were two hundred feet high and ten feet in diameter, Clark found the underbrush so thick that his hunters could not penetrate it. The river and the tide carried them on toward the ocean, and they slipped quickly and quietly into a gray-green world of soft fog from which the rain came in infinite waves. They shifted miserably through a soggy winter, and their memories of it for years fixed upon the region a bad name.

Their portages were marked by rail lines in 1876, and Portland, Oregon, on the south shore, was a prosperous and stable community, given even to the sophistication which came with new money from railroads, steamboats, fish, wheat, and lumber. Across the river, small towns in Washington Territory sheltered a rail line that ran north and west, passing inside the high bluff where Hudson's Bay Company had for a generation flown the British flag, and to Tacoma on Puget Sound. The Columbia, five miles broad in its final flow, was deep enough for ocean vessels bound for the lumber mills and canneries.

Though this serene expanse suggested that the river had spent its fury, it drifted toward what was yet one of the great terrors of the maritime world: the breakers across the sandy bar where the river met the rhythms of the Pacific Ocean. The breakers had not changed since the spring of 1792 when Robert Gray, out of Boston, raised the sails that would carry his ship, the *Columbia*, into the apparently solid barrier of white water, a prospect so dreadful that some aboard the ship thought him completely mad. Gray, however, crossed in good order and lived to become wealthy from the Indian trade and to claim the river for his new country. But thereafter less fortunate mariners knew the bar as an aggregate of moody and ominous variables, most of which, except for the dreaded low tide, were quite beyond prediction. The bottom shifted from week to week, and what had in January been a certain channel close by the rocks became in February a wedge of graveled sand. The sudden magic, the fluid circumstances of current, wind, and tide, could boil up violent rips and huge breakers that seemed to foam from every direction and crash furiously against the shallow bottom. Harbor pilots, with only slight hyperbole, swore that from the crests of breakers they could see the waves draw up troughs which exposed the naked sand.

And there was here no soft tolerance for arrogance or human error. By 1876—when the combined white populations of the river towns probably did not exceed twenty thousand—a total of sixty-one ocean-going vessels had been dashed against the rocks and sand and had been thrown upon the beaches at a cost of 146 lives. Most of the disasters occurred after 1849 during the years when insatiable markets in San Francisco sent the schooners cruising from the goldfields searching everywhere for the lumber and fish which the river towns could supply with teeming measures—if the schooners could reach them. When the federal government in 1853 finally recognized the desperate pleas for navigational aids at Cape Disappointment, officials shipped materials for a lighthouse north aboard the bark *Oriole*, which sank when attempting its passage across the Columbia bar. When the U.S. Navy commissioned the brig *Peacock* to sound and chart the waters at the mouth of the river, her captain, following his charts carefully, approached the bar on a clear July day and ran her aground at a considerable speed. While the tide flow wedged the hull deeply into the soft sand and silt, breakers pounded her to pieces. The lighthouse, of course, was finally built, but the charts used until the twentieth century were usually meaningless.

North of Cape Disappointment, except for the casual excursions of a few reckless whites, the wilderness in 1876 stood as dense and as pervasive as the Indians had known it in the age of stone and bone. At Willapa—then called Shoalwater Bay—and at Grays Harbor, the shallow and treacherous harbor bars had restrained all but the most determined Americans. During the 1850s a few bold "oyster boys" came up from California to build their cabins at Shoalwater, paying Indians to gather the oysters they sold to the San Francisco trade, living a life of exuberant freedom and boozy leisure. In a short time, however, the newcomers had destroyed the oyster beds, and the area attracted only an occasional sea otter hunter and the most determined recluses thereafter. Point Grenville, surrounded by its shoals of black rock glistening in the soft green light, rose abruptly through the fog like a dark fortress. The Quinault River flowed quietly through rich and unviolated forests. To the north—from Grenville to James Island, from the Quinault to the Quillayute— no whites knew the forests or the rivers or the beaches except as they had seen them from ships passing beyond Destruction Island. No white man of record had ever crossed the Olympic Mountains or knew what might lie at the interior of this vast peninsula. The Quinault Indians were regarded by whites as practically inaccessible, the Hoh Indians as absolutely inaccessible. At Cape Alava, there was no sound or signal to warn the innocent seaman. There were in fact no navigational aids between Willapa and the Strait of Juan de Fuca, where at Tatoosh Island a feeble light swept over the jagged teeth of Skagway Rocks, out to the western sea, then north toward Vancouver Island.

The gray rock and towering green foliage of Cape Flattery in 1876 could be as ominously dark, or as bright and dazzling in the whitecaps and sunshine, as it was when George Vancouver had seen it in May of 1792. And it could be as remote. At Neah Bay, the Indians still hunted whales and seals from their high-prowed wooden canoes, and aside from Governor Stevens, who wanted their land, and James Swan, who studied their language and culture, few whites had ever thought to disturb them. There was no prominent evidence of white society anywhere along the strait between Tatoosh Island and Ediz Hook, where one might have seen not a settlement, but ruins. In 1863, a canyon flood had washed away the customs house and the few buildings that had been called Port Angeles. Around Point Wilson, at Port Townsend, named by Vancouver "in honor of the noble Mar-

quis," there was a muddy clearing and a scattering of cedar
shacks, the new customs house, and a society whose principal
commerce, according to those who investigated it, had usually
been the illegal sale of whiskey to Indians.

Aboard the British sloop *Discovery*—at anchor in eighteen
fathoms off Bainbridge Island in May 1792—George Vancouver was in high spirits from the prospects of exploring
"the promised expansive mediterranean ocean, which, by
various accounts, is said to have existence in these regions."
After directing the repair of his fore-topsail yard, he rejoiced
that his men could go ashore and pick from among the "thousands of the finest spars the world produces." Having also
seen to the brewing of an excellent spruce beer, he pushed his
charts aside and sought to record his impressions of the region
he later named Puget Sound. "The serenity of the climate,"
he wrote, "the innumerable pleasing landscapes, and the
abundant fertility that unassisted nature puts forth, require only
. . . the industry of man . . . to render it the most lovely
country that can be imagined. . . ." [4]

In 1876, the industry of man was obvious in the effluence of
sawmills and logging teams—sawdust, bark, petroleum, often
sucked together in an ugly tide rip that might stretch across a
bay or inlet. The same industry marked the hillsides of Elliott
Bay, where among the raw clearings one tract of wet stumps
and debris was especially prominent—the site of the University
of Washington Territory. The title, however, implied an exalted
purpose of which the campus itself presented only a sad sugges-
tion. The two-storied frame classroom building, like the nearby
president's home and boardinghouse, was prematurely soggy
and faded. And to those who thought about such matters, the
rotting wood and flaking paint reflected a deeply institutional
decadence: there had never been any qualified instruction
beyond the lowest primary grades since classes had opened fifteen years before, and during some of those years there had
been no faculty, no students, and because the public monies for

4. Quoted in Edmund S. Meany *Vancouver's Discovery of Puget Sound*
(Portland, Ore.: Binfords & Mont, Publishers, 1949), p. 128.

its operation had been recently exhausted, the "university" would open no classes at all that autumn. Nevertheless, it had granted its first collegiate degree that June, a bachelor of science diploma to Clara A. McCarty, and however improbable the ceremony may have been, it was not an end but a beginning—a bold assertion of institutional identity and a triumph in Seattle of some real significance.

That college degree could be awarded in a rain-soaked village meant a special satisfaction for two developers, Arthur Denny and the Reverend Daniel Bagley, who during the decade of confusion after the organization of territorial government in 1853 had been the first to grasp the implications of fastening the proposed university upon a hillside near their own land claims. As a legislator, Denny had been a part of the rude scramble for federal favors which followed the creation of the territory, and he had been able to promote a three-handed deal: the capital should go to the small town on the Columbia River called Vancouver, the penitentiary should go to Port Townsend, where it was perhaps most needed, and the university should go to the Elliott Bay settlement, where he himself would donate a site. He was also able to arrange for the Reverend Bagley to receive an appointment as the university's first commissioner, a capacity in which the missionary was legally empowered to manage or to sell the 46,000-acre educational grant provided by the territorial organic act—the gift to the citizens of Washington Territory from the people of the United States who believed, in the words of the Ordinance of 1787, that "Religion, morality, and knowledge" were necessary "to good government and the happiness of mankind."

Moving then with great haste, the new commissioner exercised his powers to identify some of the finest timberlands in the region as the university's. Within a year he had sold most of them to timber companies at the minimum legal price of $1.50 an acre and raised enough cash to clear the hillside, erect the buildings, and operate the classes for a short season. As an academic enterprise, the school at its best gathered a few semiliterate children. But as a political fact, the buildings, the curriculum, even the college degree, however miserable, were signals

that Seattle offered great potential. Bagley thereafter met all
criticisms with the boast that he had not, as some insisted,
squandered a handsome endowment: he had with agility and
foresight captured a brilliant future.

This cheerful perspective in 1876 was but one of the signs of
relief from the stagnation and gloom which had followed the Indian wars and the panic of 1873 to the Pacific Northwest. That
spring as many as five thousand people were in Seattle, most of
whom had come recently by ship. Few of them had ever seen
the Oregon Trail, probably fewer still ever cared to. They were
people eager for a saltwater cargo trade—railroad timbers for
Latin America, raw lumber for Hawaii, fish for California—and
they crowded day and night across narrow, muddy streets to
make their purchases in unpainted stores and to talk at length
with friends and newcomers on the muddy board sidewalks.
That summer the *Daily Intelligencer* reported that the city had
recently grown by five new law practices (there had been only
ten in 1874), six Chinese laundries, seven grocery stores, five
physicians' offices, five restaurants, and, among other mixed
blessings, some twenty-six saloons. During the week of the centennial Fourth of July, *Intelligencer* columns recorded the deliv-
ery of a centennial sermon ("We must stand by our Constitution
and religious principle"), a centennial editorial ("The ship of
state had swept with dizzy speed forward over this hundred
years of its course in the career of empire . . . The shoals of
treason have yawned around her, and the lee-shore of corruption
threatened her with destruction"), and a centennial oration
("We have experienced here much of the same kind of discour-
agements and dangers that were the lot of the first colonies upon
the Atlantic Coast . . . we can look back to the time when the
thick shades of the unbroken forest enclosing the little hamlet
that nestled on the shore of our beautiful bay, served as a cover
to conceal the lurking savage foe. . . .") [5] The days progressed
in lively talk about coming railroads and increasing land values,
and, in the frivolity appropriate to a centennial, there was talk
also of a regatta, a military procession, public fireworks, a cen-

5. *Seattle Daily Intelligencer,* July 7, 1876.

tennial ball. In the course of these festivities, the newspaper's editor carefully noted, officials of the city were compelled to arrest three "Chinamen" for theft and to jail three "drunken Indians."

2

A Commemorative Occasion

*T*HE spirited activities in Seattle in 1876 were conspicuously more newsworthy than those at the southern tip of Puget Sound, where the town of Olympia numbered perhaps two thousand. The early settlers here had come to pre-empt the water-power at the falls of the Deschutes River and had later—despite Arthur Denny—captured the territorial seat of government. For two decades their growing village had been the center of American activity north of Oregon City. In time, however, it was clear to them that steam-powered machines would take from them whatever advantage they had in a small waterfall, and that the railroad, running fifteen miles to the east, had isolated them from the new industries. Their most prominent landmark in 1876 was the Capitol, a sagging, oblong building of two stories, topped by a bell tower and fronted with a narrow portico—a sort of midwestern barn with windows, a front porch, and a watch-tower. It was clearly not in good repair. The secretary of Washington Territory had recently informed the United States secretary of the interior that the building was approaching "a state of utter decay and wretched worthlessness." The wooden-block foundation, he wrote, had rotted, causing the building to tilt precariously at one end. For more than a decade there had been no paint applied to the exterior, which was "a sad picture of melancholy dinginess." Inside, the "faded, soiled, and ragged" carpets could not lend even the appearance of "shabby gentil-

14

ity." The several stoves in the legislative chambers were then a hazard to those who needed heat, and the five committee rooms consisted of "nothing but the naked walls, uncovered with paint, plaster, cloth, paper, or whitewash." Situated on the edge of town and bordering the forest, the building was even then enveloped by undergrowth, and legislators were demanding a meeting place which would not be "a standing reproach" to their dignity.[1]

Under these rather seedy circumstances members of the legislative assembly appointed a joint committee "to wait upon Hon. Elwood Evans" and request that he favor them with a reading of an address which he had delivered during the centennial exposition in Philadelphia, where as centennial commissioner he had represented Washington Territory before the nation. Evans had come West early, in 1851, when he was twenty-five years old. He had married in Olympia, had supplemented a law practice with service as deputy collector of customs and as the governor's secretary. He had influential friends in the Whig Party, but he was ardently antislave, and he led local Whigs into the Republican ranks in 1856. He was himself acting governor during the Civil War and then speaker of the house in the 1870s. Among the most literate of the territorial barristers, his experiences left him with an intense interest in the drama of those early years, and he had already presented manuscripts to the most enterprising historian of the West, H. H. Bancroft of San Francisco. His selection as centennial commissioner was in grateful recognition of his writing and speaking about historical matters for which most citizens regarded him as their leading authority.

When he appeared before the assembly, Evans was a stout and vigorous man of fifty-one, wearing a full mustache and beard, much in the fashion of Gen. U. S. Grant. His address, which he entitled "Washington Territory: Her Past, Her Present And the Elements Of Wealth Which Ensure Her Future," was,

1. Henry G. Strube to B. R. Cowen, U.S., 43rd Congress, 2d session, *House Executive Documents,* 104, Dec. 23, 1874, "Capitol Building at Olympia, Washington Territory."

for the time and circumstances, fashionably elegant and adequately windy, an extended description of both the historical and the physical features of his home—over fifty pages in the printed version—the reading of which must have consumed a full afternoon in Philadelphia as well as in Olympia. Paying his respects to the explorers who had "devoted their earnest efforts to earn fame by adding to the store of the world's geography" and whose efforts "were all-sufficient to invest the region with peculiar historic interest," he naturally reviewed the story of the Greek mariner, Apostolos Valerianos, whose alleged discoveries had evolved into the myth of Juan de Fuca. He gave oratorical tribute to the aspirations of the Spanish during the eighteenth century, then to "the illustrious but ill-fated Captain James Cook" and his futile search for a northwest passage, to the maritime fur traders, John Meares and Robert Gray, and to the more scientific explorations of George Vancouver and of Lewis and Clark. He recounted briefly the disastrous adventures of the Astorian expeditions by sea and by land. Then he focused his personal involvement in the region by reviewing the "Oregon Controversy" of the 1840s between the United States and Great Britain.

From his earlier orations, his Olympia audience already knew that Evans was an anglophobe of the old revolutionary order, always ready with a belligerent outburst of patriotic sentiment against England, its monarchs, and its Hudson's Bay Company, which, he said, had "reduced to subjection" the native populations of the Pacific Northwest and maliciously trained them to favor the "King George" men and to hate the American "Bostons." Evans ignored the validity of any British territorial claims at all when he asserted that the Oregon Treaty of 1846 had been a deep humiliation of American interests. In his youth he had in fact been an emotional proponent of the "54-40 or fight" slogan, eager even then to drive the British from all of North America, and he had again solemnly urged war with England during the petty dispute over international boundary lines through the San Juan Islands, a dispute which the two countries finally arbitrated in 1872.

It was, however, in his recital of "the irrepressible conflict between the settler and the Indian race" that Evans became even more passionate, and he reminded his audience of the "difficulties and dangers" to Americans who had come, as he himself had done, to claim their share of the Oregon Country, to take land, to build a new home. At this point his address became the determined cry of the apologist, and it is precisely here that we must subject Elwood Evans to the revisionism which is probably the fate of all historians. We shall hear him at length:

In preparing Washington Territory to become a future State of the American Union, its pioneers were subjected to the usual difficulties and dangers consequent upon the presence of aborigines, dangerous in their native disposition, but more so when influenced by the presence of two white races quasi hostile in their relations to each other. . . . On the 29th November, 1847, at Waiilatpu, within our present territorial limits, the Whitman Massacre occurred. Dr. Marcus Whitman and his excellent wife (one of the two heroic women who had crossed the American Continent on horseback, in 1836) had established a mission at that place, under the auspices of the American Board of Foreign Missions. Houses, shops, a mill, a school-house and a place of worship for the Indians —indeed, all the accompaniments of civilization had been provided—and there the good Whitman treated the savages as children of our common Father. But the pious missionaries were murdered in cold blood, together with nine other inmates of the establishment. Every white American within reach fell victim to the merciless perfidy of the treacherous Cayuse Indians. A rude mound near the old site, overgrown with weeds, enclosed only by a plain fence, marks the last resting-place of these victims of Indian jealousy, superstition and hate. The Cayuse war was the necessary sequel. [2]

Her father was Judge Stephen Prentiss, a lawyer, miller, distiller, and—in the small town of Prattsburg, in western New York—a prominent Christian. Townspeople remembered him as

2. Elwood Evans, *Washington Territory: Her Past, Her Present And The Elements Of Wealth Which Ensure Her Future* (Olympia: C. B. Bagley, Public Printer, 1877), pp. 1–14.

prosperous, thoughtful, shrewd, and disciplined. They remembered her mother as a large and stern and devout woman who
did not often smile, and Narcissa herself would mature in that
image. But in her youth she was a sandy-haired, blue-eyed
vivacious presence, quick and bright, eagerly gregarious, the
girl and the young woman whose voice rose like a clear bell
through a room full of animated conversation.

She liked most to converse about predestination and redemp-
tion through the sufferings of Jesus, and the reconciliation between God and man in America. As her Presbyterianism developed with her body, she became even more prominently vocal
and emotional. Because she loved to sing and to pray in a full
voice, she drew deep satisfaction from the camp meetings where
under God's clear sky she could weep in open joy when a sinner
came forth to cry aloud his anguish and his transcendence as he
accepted his Christ and confessed to past wickedness. This experience was for her indeed so moving that she often considered
the truly staggering extent of wickness among those who had
never heard of Christ's suffering, and she thought about the
deeply spiritual rewards that might come to those who could—
as she wrote later—carry Christ's message out into the wicked
world for "the salvation of the heathen." At the age of twenty-
six, dangerously on the brink of spinsterhood, she put a bold
question to a visiting missionary who had just preached about
the obligation of God's elect in America to offer salvation to
those who wandered in darkness through the forests of the Far
West. "Is there a place," she asked the Reverend Samuel
Parker, "for an unmarried female in my Lord's vineyard?" [3]

In the Presbyterian vineyards, at least as the Reverend Parker
knew them, there was not, and Narcissa was much depressed.
But she soon realized that in time God's will can be known, and
within a few days there came to her door Dr. Marcus Whitman,
who lived in a nearby village and whom she had known casually
for several years as a Presbyterian elder and physician. He was
then thirty-two years old, a tall, muscular, strikingly handsome

3. Clifford M. Drury, *Marcus and Narcissa Whitman And The Opening Of Old
Oregon,* 2 vols. (Glendale, Calif.: The Arthur H. Clark Co., 1973), 1:109.

man with sincere eyes and a dark brown beard, soft and neatly
trimmed. He was also unpretentious and of sound Christian
habits, ungiven to vanity or frivolity. Having himself been in
the West with the Reverend Parker, he said, he was now volun-
teering his services to the church as a missionary to work among
the Indians, and he was even then preparing to make the long
journey to the Columbia River. He wanted Narcissa to marry
him.

Thus she said goodbye to her home and to a lifetime of orderly expectations, marrying a man bound for the wilderness,
crossing the plains in a wagon, passing through a time barrier of
four months that would forever isolate her from parents, friends,
and fellow Christians. Yet there were, in the beginning, months
of high elation. She was the joyous center at the mountain rendezvous of fur traders in 1836, bright and quick around the
campfires, singing and praying with a Christian certainty, eager
to talk to the fur traders and to the Indians. It pleased her that
the mountain men, in solemn wonder, drew away momentarily
from their indulgences of flesh and whiskey to witness this remarkable appearance of white femininity and evangelical religion. She crossed the Rockies on horseback and entered the
Oregon Country, then occupied jointly by the United States and
Great Britain, where at Fort Vancouver she delighted the impe-
rious Dr. McLoughlin of the Hudson's Bay Company and was
herself delighted by the hospitality, the formality, the aristo-
cratic and barbaric splendor, the civility of this towering British
institution. Word of her warmth and devotion spread to the few
white settlements before she arrived at Waiilatpu, some twenty-
five miles up the Walla Walla Valley from the Columbia, where
Whitman had determined he would build a mission and do the
Lord's work in the vineyard then held principally by the Cayuse
Indians.

High elation soon cooled into early winters of discontent. Al-
though Whitman probably knew as much about medicine as a
person could know in the 1830s, he was no carpenter, and the
brown-dirt adobe shack he built for them that first autumn was
more raw and rough than the southern slave quarters she had
heard the abolitionists describe, more crude than any residence

she had ever seen. She learned to sleep on a bed of cornhusks, to wash her clothes in a barrel, and to roast horse meat. With barely enough space to sleep and eat, she was soon crowded with the coming and going of other missionary families whose impracticalities and sheer incompetence amazed even Whitman. Some sat for weeks or months. Some used wine and smoking tobacco, which were contemptible vices to the Whitmans. And even in their wine, the visitors were a stiffly pious lot, complaining when Narcissa rose to express herself during the long prayer meetings. "The brethern only pray," she wrote to her father. "I believe all the sisters would be willing to pray if their husbands would let them." [4] And there were the Indians— curious and silent, coming and going. Because Whitman did not want to offend them, they seemed to be omnipresent, prowling furtively through the rooms. "The greatest trial to a woman's feelings," Narcissa wrote, "is to have her cooking and eating room always filled with four or five Indians. . . ." [5]

And there was, at least in the beginning, an even greater trial. By what in her secret heart must have seemed a monstrous perversion or miracle of coincidence, she had traveled west with the Reverend Henry Spalding and his new wife, Eliza, and at Waiilatpu she served as their hostess, unable to escape them. This was the Henry Spalding she had known in Prattsburg as the withdrawn and pitiful boy referred to contemptuously by his foster father as the little "bastard," the darkly introspective youth possessed with a burning sense of sin and mission which—in asking for her hand—he had vainly supposed Narcissa might share with him. "The man who came with us," she wrote, "is one who ought not to have come. My dear husband has suffered more from him . . . than can be known in this world." [6] The long winter days became dreary, then tense. She stayed in her room until noon, then sometimes went down by the river to weep in the sun or the wind or the rain or the snow, which became the walls for her private world.

The Spaldings did not linger long before settling at Lapwai,

4. Drury, 1:333.
5. Drury, 1:334.
6. Drury, 1:376.

120 miles up the Snake River near the Clearwater. Then Marcus and Narcissa could make plans for a church and a school, but there were still unimagined frustrations. They wanted to evangelize, but they had no training for it. Whitman himself was not ordained, and he had no deep knowledge of theologies, no key to Indian language or culture. And the Indians themselves—most of them the proud and aggressive horsemen known as the Cayuse, which was their word for horseflesh—sometimes disappeared for weeks and months. They were gone to the Columbia to catch and to cure fish, or gone beyond the Rocky Mountains to hunt buffalo, or gone south to the Blue Mountains to gather roots and berries. They even rode beyond the Cascade Mountains to trade with the Indians of the lower Columbia—or to attack them, carrying back to their lodges near Waiilatpu a bounty of food, tools, weapons, and slaves. Narcissa might even feel relieved when they had gone, for they were to her a fierce and unpredictable people, and even in their absence there was so much work to do—the endless, tedious, physical work of building, digging, plowing, planting, harvesting, preserving, storing, hauling, chopping. The struggle for simple existence was itself often more than she could sustain. They had come to another world to be missionaries only to learn that they had no time for their mission.

Within a year, however, Marcus could manage his doctoring as well as his school, and both he and Narcissa made progress with the language. After 1840 Narcissa had the girls to help her—the children of mountain men she had met at the rendezvous, men such as Jim Bridger, Tom McKay, and Joe Meek, who had thoughtfully brought their daughters to Narcissa to be raised as white Christians. Whitman was then deeply pleased that the Indians seemed eager to learn about farming, and there was thanksgiving around the mission when the valley began to green with potatoes, corn, and wheat. Whitman had become convinced that farming was for the Indians a true road to Christian salvation. The valley in the spring could move one almost to tears—a universe of grass and wildflowers and sun and water, adorned here and there by Whitman's efforts and those of his native students.

They finally completed the new mission house, and it was

more spacious, warmer, more orderly—more like a Christian home. There was an upstairs quarter with private rooms, and downstairs there was a room for mission work, one for Indians, one for cooking, one for talk and hospitality. On unpredictably wonderful days Archibald McKinley came from the Hudson's Bay Company's Fort Walla Walla with mail and news, and with no warning at all McKay, Meek, and Bridger might troop in jubilantly from the Rocky Mountains to see their daughters and talk into the night about what they heard from the United States of America. Though the earth-brown adobe and the rude furniture were indeed a world away from her father's sitting room, life was not entirely without gracious promise.

When she was twenty-nine, Narcissa gave birth to Alice Clarissa. "Her hair is light brown," she wrote to her own mother, "she . . . holds her head up finely." The child became the "treasure invaluable" as she walked and talked to the wide wonder of her parents and the Indians. At the age of two, Alice Clarissa was fascinated by the world of missionaries, natives, animals, hills, and water. Narcissa began to speak in worried tones about the child's irresistible attraction to the river, and Whitman, having thought much about it, revealed a grotesque corner of his Calvinist broodings: deciding then that he must kill the child's sick dog, named Boxer, he determined to drown the animal in the river so that his daughter might have a lesson in mortal danger. The child was forced to watch, then to repeat aloud over and over again, "Alice fall in water . . . she die like Boxer."

She grew through two years and two months, and on a Sunday afternoon when, as always, her parents were reading their books, Alice Clarissa ran happily and busily into the sunshine and disappeared forever. After the vague foreboding, the urgent demands, panic and the hysteria, Indians finally swam under the water and recovered the little body. "Thy will be done," Narcissa wrote, while the bereaved father hammered together a rough coffin.[7]

For Narcissa this was the beginning of a deep desolation. The

7. Drury, 1:223–359.

Indians, it turned out, did not really want a school or a church, and while they surely ate the wheat, potatoes, fruit, and vegetables, they resented Whitman's admonitions that they cease their endless riding around the country and instead tend constantly to their crops. They were increasingly indifferent to their fields, for farming not only distorted the easy rhythms of hunting, fishing, and gathering; it denied them the deep securities they drew from a way of life which had evolved in the mandates of hunting, fishing, and gathering. They knew those mandates, how to raise their children to them, how to relate their spiritual energies to them, how to live and die in them. To be urged into replacing these mandates with those of farming was to be urged into apprehension and confusion, and it was these feelings which they were more and more openly revealing. Whitman was at this time shocked also to learn that the Cayuse were actually a dying race—of the some one thousand Indians in the valley when he had arrived in 1836, almost half had died by 1840 from diseases carried to them by whites. He was alarmed to learn that some Indians were inclined to blame their great grief entirely upon the Americans.

Narcissa then saw her husband—God's white knight in buckskins —retreat into his own broodings and quiet desperation. Carrying with him the ill balanced burdens of a Calvinist contempt for human nature and a typically American belief in progress, he could not conceal his impatience with the Cayuse and their impenetrable darkness. Sensing the scope of man's depravity—the almost overpowering compulsion of most men to dishonor God and their parents, to fall easily into adultery and fornication, to debauch their minds in alcohol and tobacco, to accept a life of lethargy and sensation—Whitman supposed that he saw these evils tenfold in the wilderness, and he shuddered to think of God's wrath. Those who knew the road to salvation must build churches and schools and farms; they must civilize this wilderness with preachers and teachers and laws and regulations. The savages must understand God's mercy in allowing them to exist on this earth even a moment longer, and they must change their lives, demonstrate in some blessed way their gratitude for atonement. To be saved from the enslavement of

Satan's passions, a man must show that he has forsaken indulgence, impulse, and shallow gratifications; he must tend to his fields, and work by the sweat of his brow, and pray for forgiveness in fear and trembling. He must look beyond the impulse of the moment and become clean, chaste, frugal, ambitious, restrained, reverent.

And the Whitmans felt a great urgency, for they had always believed that John Calvin and Martin Luther had begun the great cleansing of the world, the restoration of the gospel, and that the subsequent two hundred years of war, massacre, riot, and turmoil had been necessary steps toward ridding the world of Satan's ultimate deceit, Roman Catholicism. They were thus stricken with a dark anxiety when priests from the Society of Jesus came under the shelter of Hudson's Bay Company to tender their services to the Indians.

The Whitmans learned of startling episodes of mass baptism. Father Pierre-Jean de Smet came to the Columbia doing what he did superbly—telling the story of Jesus, conversing with the Indians, using only a cross, a candle, a bell, and a unique sensitivity to Indian aspirations to transcendence. De Smet was a man of great courage and great adaptability, convinced that God would protect him. He went alone on his errand, living like the Indians on fish and camas root, quite eager to offer his total life for the salvation of the Indians from barbarism and from Protestantism—between which he saw little distinction. In each village he would stay a few weeks, tell of heaven and hell and Jesus, then accept the baptisms, a hundred in one village, two hundred in another—in sum total, thousands—then return the next year to baptize children.

Beyond an attraction to ritual and symbol, however, the Indians' response to de Smet's religion was seldom more than superficial—baptism did not mean conversion, and its promise could wash away in a season. But the Whitmans could not know this, and what they saw as the work of the antichrist brought to them a daily anguish. De Smet's mission was, as they saw it, to tell the ignorant savages that they could become Christians before they had transformed their lives, and this was to place the cross in the hands of the heathen. Whitman himself had been telling the Indians that baptism was not necessary for salvation, that the act alone surely had little to do with being a Christian—but that good works, humility, discipline, and dedication were essential. Baptism was a moment; the transformation of the spirit was eternal. Thus one day, Narcissa wrote, he screamed to the Indians that, cross or no cross, "none of them were Christians, that they are all on the road to destruction, and that worshipping will not save them." And when at the Hudson's Bay Company post he confronted the new bishop of Walla Walla, Augustine Blanchet, recently from Quebec, he spoke bluntly: he did not think Roman Catholicism was right; it was wrong, and he would do everything in his power to protect the Indians from it. Thereafter, like Lyman Beecher, the American theologian who had most influenced him, he foresaw in the American future a bloody conflict between "Christianity" and "Popery," and the terrible vision of it burned at the center of his holy dedication to his mission. Again he screamed to the Indians that "because you have priests among you, the country is going to be covered with blood! You will have nothing but blood!" [8] And it was their blood, not his own that he expected to see, for the militant pietists of his own nation were surely coming to the Oregon Country, and he knew them to be fiercely intolerant of the "barbaric," the unpure, the unholy. If the Indians could reject the life of impulse and embrace a Protestant discipline, he believed, they might survive; as Roman Catholics, they were doomed.

Thus Marcus fought against his vision, and Narcissa gave him her strength, and they lost everything. The Indians ignored their counsel, insulted them, ran horses into their cornfield. When Whitman needed help in digging a millrace for the benefit of the mission community, the Indians refused to help unless they were paid in tobacco, which they knew Whitman would not touch. They laughed at him. They could get tobacco at Fort Walla Walla for furs. Taking furs was a man's work, and at the fort the priests would treat them as men, not sinners. Then they pushed and shoved him, challenged him to violence, ridiculed a

8. Drury, 2:187.

man who would not fight as no man at all, ridiculed—more in
fear than in laughter—a man who told them that to hunt, fish,
eat, and sleep without regret was not the good life on earth
which the earth intended.

Curiously, as the Catholic advance paralleled the approach of
American wagons over the Oregon Trail, the mission house became a babble of controversy, acrimony, and confusion. In the
spring of 1841, Asahel Munger, who had come with his good
wife to the mission vineyard, began to have revelations: God
directed him to take over the mission and to drive out Marcus
Whitman. When he was obviously raving mad, Whitman sadly
sent him away under escort, Narcissa forlornly consoling the
young wife and child. They learned later that at Christmas time
in Oregon City, convinced that God demanded miracles of him,
Munger had driven nails into his hands and burned himself to
death. Then de Smet came down the Columbia again in the
summer, equipped with his cross and firm heart and generous
conviction that Christ's work would not be done in a day, perhaps not in one generation. His conversions were again remarkable—hundreds among the Colville, the Yakima, the Umatilla—isolating the Whitmans, as it were, on their small
Protestant outpost in a wilderness of Popery and barbarism.

These prospects seemed even more dismal when Whitman
learned that the mission board—alarmed by the apparent failure
of Whitman's and Spalding's efforts—had determined to end its
support of the two stations. In the early fall of 1842 Whitman
decided that he must ride to the United States—to Saint Louis,
Washington, D.C:, New York, and Boston. He must explain to
the mission board the desperate character of its difficulties in the
West and plead that the missions not be abandoned. He must
encourage Americans everywhere to migrate immediately to the
Oregon Country and save it and the Indians from the Roman
Catholics, who, he felt, had been sent out to undo the Americans even while they were preparing the Indians for Christ's
kingdom. (He could explain none of this to the Indians, who
were of course puzzled about his sudden departure, and believed—some of them, and not without reason—that he had

gone East to gather American farmers and soldiers who would come out to steal their land and to kill them.)

Thus suddenly the visitors were gone and Marcus was gone, and Narcissa was for the first time—except for a young Hawaiian boy and the children—entirely alone. On October 4, determined to overcome her fears, she wrote that "I believe the Lord will preserve me from being anxious. . . ." October 5, her anxiety rising, she began her letter with, "Where are you tonight, precious husband?" Then on October 6, flushed with terror, after a night of screaming by candlelight: "My Dear Husband, At about midnight I was awakened by someone trying to open my bedroom door. . . . Thanks be to our Heavenly Father, He mercifully delivered me from a savage man." [9]

Thereafter her alien world unraveled in torn pieces. Fleeing to Fort Walla Walla, she learned there that Indians at Waiilatpu had burned the mill and the storehouse behind her, and at Lapwai, Indians were threatening to kill Henry Spalding. She moved under British escort downriver to the Methodist community of The Dalles, but while resting there she was suddenly unable to leave her bed because of a pain knifing deep into her abdomen, a pain for which there was neither relief nor explanation. Then she moved again, to Fort Vancouver on the lower river, where the British physician could tell her that she had an ovarian tumor but could do nothing to help her. In swelling and blinding pain, she became weak and sickly. Her eyesight was then failing, and she could read, write, or sew only with great pain. Limping to friends in Oregon City, where a small community of Christians could care for her, she stayed until Whitman returned in the fall of 1843. By then, as she well knew, her husband was the subject of newspaper stories and magazine articles everywhere—he was praised as the heroic missionary physician, the Christian knight from the mountains, the hero of American-Christian expansion, the vanguard of a mighty westward army of pietist families in the service of country and God. It would for him have been unthinkable not to

9. Drury, 2:13–14.

return to the field of his labors at Waiilatpu. "Dear friends," Narcissa wrote as she prepared for the journey back to desolation, "will you not sometime think of me almost alone in the midst of savage darkness?" [10]

She was thereafter usually in poor health and humor, projecting to those around her the qualities she had earlier seen as faults in the Indians—she became abrupt, proud, haughty, and cold. The unraveling continued. Spalding, deeply frightened by the attempt on Narcissa, demanded that the Indians abandon their permissiveness and accept the discipline of the lash and the gallows. Indian men surrounded him, spat upon him, pushed him stumbling and falling into a large cooking fire, from which he was saved only because of his heavy buffalo robe. Philip Littlejohn, who had come with his wife in 1840 to be a Christian knight in buckskin, began in 1846 to cry out that he too must kill himself, and Whitman again sadly expelled a family to whom he had looked for help and friendship. The impetuous William Henry Gray, when Indians took melons from his vines (were they not the fruit of the earth, and were not the children of the earth to enjoy them?) went out in his field and dosed the remaining melons with a stout laxative so that the natives might learn a dramatic lesson about the sanctity of private property to a true Christian. Unknowingly, the Indians assumed that it was Whitman who had poisoned them. What they learned was ominous: a man who would poison the fruit of the earth must indeed be possessed; all Indians had much to fear from Dr. Whitman. At about the same time, Whitman himself set out meat he had laced with arsenic to get the wolves that got his sheep. When Indians found the meat and ate it, and nearly died, the Cayuse learned from the doctor still another ominous lesson.

If the wagon trains following Whitman's return from the United States seemed to the Indians to be larger every year, and they were, those of 1847 seemed endless. Maybe seven thousand whites crossed the Rockies, more humans than the Indians had ever seen anywhere, passing beyond the Blue Mountains to the Columbia. As the Indians watched the wagons come and go,

10. Drury, 2:98.

they were easily convinced of their worst suppositions. The summer brought disease—from the Americans in the wagons or the Americans in the Willamette Valley, it didn't matter—a devastatingly virulent combination of measles and dysentery which threw the Cayuse into feverish convulsions. And unlike the whites who also suffered, the Indians began to die, child after child, family after family, lodge after lodge. Their rage rose slowly, indirectly, impulsively, without any immediate focus, in wide circumlocutions: grief-stricken and hysterical young men rode out along the trail, striking at American stragglers, especially those innocent enough to have demonstrated their boisterous contempt for Indians. There were words and gestures, then burnings and killings. In the rising fury, Whitman and Narcissa finally realized that when Indians died after taking Whitman's medicine, their survivors might with reason suppose that the doctor wanted their land and had brought them poison. Marcus brooded at length, indicating that he would leave the valley in the spring.

Why wait? The mission needed him. Narcissa could understand this, because "mission" by 1847 meant the white community, not the Indian. That autumn it meant seventy-five whites, half of them children, all of them nearly totally dependent upon Marcus and Narcissa and their strength and their experience. Dropouts from the wagon trains—families, most of them—they were paralyzed by self-pity and the injustice of their fate in an alien world. Though some were simply insufferable, Narcissa tended their children as her own. While Whitman saw to their food and shelter and doctored their daily afflictions, she fed the hungry, nursed the ill, consoled the desperate. When the epidemic came, it was in a sort of crescendo of complaint, grief, and wretchedness from seventy-five souls who followed Marcus and Narcissa around the mission like a ragged Greek chorus, asking daily for comfort and protection.

Thus were the lines of their tragedy clearly drawn: the Oregon Treaty of 1846 had given the valley to Americans, but the eager settlers of 1847 felt uneasy among the open and endless hills and went on down the river to the lush valley of the Willamette, leaving Waiilatpu as a lonely aid station for the physically and mentally infirm. And the treaty, by an unusual compromise, had allowed the Hudson's Bay Company to remain. At Fort Walla Walla, the Jesuits stood in this shelter, naive and imperceptive. The bishop of the Missionary Diocese of Walla Walla, himself only recently from Quebec, in October 1847 assisted French-speaking priests of the order of the Oblates of Mary Immaculate in opening three missions among the Yakima and one among the Cayuse, where the missionaries would thoughtlessly take advantage in Whitman's rising peril. There were no more than a few Protestant Indians in the valley. Most of the Indians were sick; many of them were dying; almost all of them feared and blamed the Americans.

On November 28, Narcissa was up late, for it had been after ten o'clock when Whitman returned home from his doctoring. He was dejected. He had talked with Spalding, who found his own mission untenable, and with a new priest, who reported that some of the Indians were urging that Whitman himself be murdered. Though this was frightening, it was not new—some Indians had for years talked of killing Marcus, but Indian talk was not often plot or conspiracy. Indians would do serious things according to their instincts for the proper time. No one could say when the balance would be tipped toward mad impulse, yet clearly the balance was tipping.

The next morning some of the mission people, as usual, worked on the mission house. Others butchered a beef. By nine o'clock school was in session, but the orderly progression of another day could not dispell an expansive melancholia: some of the mission people were ill, some sat quietly weeping, others worked at their food or their beds without energy, thought, or direction. The bodies of three Indian children had to be buried quickly—there had been six the morning before—bodies brought forth quietly by unknown hands in the depth of the night. Narcissa arose at eleven o'clock and began to bring some order to the scene, helping those she could help and preparing for the noon funeral. After the services, she began to bathe two of the children, urging them to keep their voices low because Whitman, exhausted, sat across the room, grateful for a moment that he could do what he wanted most to do—read his book

without interruption. Narcissa was suddenly aware of an ugly
commotion—Indians in the kitchen, talking loudly to each other
and demanding to see Whitman. She rushed to the door, but immediately Marcus was alert and among them. They wanted
medicine, and he promised it. Taking a bottle from his medicine
chest and demanding sharply that the Indians remain in the
kitchen, he told Narcissa to bolt the door behind him.

The voices rose. She could hear Marcus explaining, his voice
almost lost in the confusion of Indian noise. Then there was the
blunt explosion of a rifle shot behind the door. Transfigured in
fear, she was somehow cooly efficient: she dressed the children,
calmly ordering the adults to take them to the rooms upstairs.
Everyone moved quickly, but suddenly the Bridger girl burst
into the house, choked in terror. "Did they kill the doctor?"
Narcissa demanded. "Yes." There was more rifle fire outside
as Narcissa rushed toward the kitchen. He was on the floor, his
head and neck spilling a pool of blood. She screamed to the
women who returned her screams as they helped her drag him
into the larger room and into his reading chair. When she asked
if she could do anything to stop the bleeding, he indicated that
she could not, and blood seeped over his chest as consciousness
passed from him.

Narcissa looked up as a man fell through the front door,
bleeding in a great gush of red, crying loudly, "I don't know
what the damned Indians want to kill me for—I never did anything to them." One of the girls giggled, expecting Narcissa to
rebuke him for swearing in front of the children. Dazed and
unbelieving, Narcissa stepped to a window to look out into the
world of sunlight, where she saw an Indian man raise a rifle and
shoot. She fell backward with fire in her shoulder, and from the
floor she sobbed, "Lord save these little ones." She then whis-
pered, incoherently, a prayer for her own parents, crying that
surely this miserable death of hers would kill them. Finally from
the rush and the firing and the hysteria she was aware that someone was telling them all to get themselves out of the house and
across the yard, for the Indians were setting fire to the main
mission. Assisted by young Andrew Rogers, Narcissa rose to
her feet, but as she cleared the door, a salvo of rifle fire pitched

her crazily to the ground. An Indian gave a mad yell as he held up her head by the hair and lashed her dead face with a leather whip.

A murder fever rose and then raged for days, passing from one lodge to another. During the first day nine whites were killed, and then a total of thirteen before the madness subsided. Three died as captives before the men came from Fort Vancouver to demand their release; and others told of rape and abduction. When friends could look for the graves of the Whitmans, they found a shallow ditch torn by wolves, the bones scattered a mile across the valley. They dug a deeper trench, covered the bones with an abandoned wagon box, then piled it high with rocks and soil.[11]

The satellite missions quickly collapsed. Spalding, protected by friendly Nez Percé, had been saved from murder, but was for years too hysterical to work among the Indians. Even the Catholics retreated as the Cayuse were pursued relentlessly by volunteer companies of riflemen. Finally starving and homeless, the few Cayuse who had not perished in the epidemic themselves surrendered five men allegedly responsible for the massacre. On the morning of June 3, 1850, in Oregon City, having refused to accept the Reverend Henry Spalding, these five received the sacraments of holy baptism and confirmation from Frances Norbert Blanchet, archbishop of Oregon, who bestowed upon them the Christian names of Peter, Andrew, John, Paul, and James. It was Andrew who spoke, saying, "Did not your missionaries teach us that Christ died to save his people? Thus die we, if we must, to save our people." [12] At two o'clock in the afternoon, Joe Meek, whose daughter had learned Christianity from the Whitmans, used his Indian tomahawk to cut the rope, and Peter, Andrew, John, Paul, and James swung out to strangle before a crowd of several hundred Americans.

Evans spoke in full confidence now, relating the substance of his own experience:

11. Drury, 2:205–365. See also Alvin M. Josephy, Jr., *The Nez Perce Indians And The Opening Of The Northwest* (New Haven: Yale University Press, 1965), pp. 158–285.

12. Quoted in Josephy, p. 284.

The passage of the act of Congress of the 3d March, 1853, endowing the Territory of Washington with separate political life and conferring name and identity, might be regarded as the commencement of the history proper of such Territory . . . The act to organize the Territory of Washington established as the dividing-line between the Territories of Oregon and Washington, the Columbia River from its mouth to the 46th parallel, thence east along said Parallel to the Rocky Mountains, our Territory lying upon the north side of said line. President Pierce among his earliest official acts, appointed Maj. Isaac I. Stevens, U. S. Engineers, Governor. . . . Congress at its session in 1852–3 had made appropriations for the survey of Railroad Routes to the Pacific Ocean. The Secretary of War selected three great lines, entrusting to Governor Stevens en route to the Territory, the exploration from the headwaters of the Mississippi river to Puget Sound. This survey occupied the entire Summer and Fall. By proclamation, September 29, 1853, from the summit of the Rocky Mountains, Governor Stevens announced his entrance into the Territory, his assumption of executive duties. . . . More or less difficulty occurred with the Indians within our own borders, but the efficient service of the few U.S. troops at Fort Steilacoom, and the energetic action of Gov. Stevens, ex-officio Superintendent of Indian Affairs, prevented any general outbreak. At this period treaties were negotiated by Gov. Stevens with the various Indian tribes, by which the so-called Indian title to the lands was extinguished upon the most liberal concessions to the Indians, and with scrupulous regard for their welfare. . . .[13]

Isaac Stevens had in his youth been unhappily deformed by heredity as well as by environment. His body was too short, his head too large, his father a bitter cripple, his mother a woman who had to be restrained from suicide. When he was twelve years old, he worked twelve hours a day in a New England mill. Nevertheless, he had an irresistible compulsion to excel and a quick mind for mathematics, and he went through West Point first in his class. He emerged from the Mexican War with a rep-

13. Evans, pp. 15–16.

utation for intelligence and enormous stores of energy. Among
the rather dull officers of that expedition, his exploits were, if
not heroic, at least highly visible. After the peace, he moved
boldly into national politics. While still an officer in the regular
army, he drew to himself considerable attention when he openly
supported the presidential candidacy of Franklin Pierce. As his
reward he took the governorship of the newly created Washington Territory, for he was eager to fashion responsibility and opportunity in the new West into a base of personal power and
national acclaim.

Stevens was bound for glory in a great hurry. He came west
as a governor facing the problems of organizing the counties,
schools, courts, and the legislature, and he came also with the
authority of Indian agent and as surveyor for a possible transcontinental railroad. Impatient with the new governmental agencies, superficial in his surveys (they kept his name in the news,
but the work itself was regarded by some as more political than
topographical), he gave himself a year to solve all the momentous problems with the Indians, both east and west of the mountains. Though he brought his wife and family with him to Olympia, he was almost constantly in the field, even at Christmas
time, urging speed and expediency, often drinking heavily,
moving even his closest associates—like Elwood Evans—to
wonder about his arrogance, his towering ambition, and his
sometimes ruthless disregard for honesty. He was easily convinced of his own virtue and easily persuaded that what he
wanted was what everyone else needed, especially the Indians.
He wanted the Indians out of the way—out of the way of
railroads, of gold miners, and of white settlers. (It had occurred
to others, many others, that the man who opened the trans-
mississippi frontier might indeed become president.) He thus
approached the most profound cross-cultural chasm in the American experience without a language that could communicate his
ideas or Indian ideas, without any sensitivity to Indian religi-
osity, without knowledge of the Indians' social structure, their
practices of representative authority, or their deeply spiritual
concepts of land stewardship.

Stevens called the Indians "my children" when they pleased

him, but when they resisted his demands he could be imperiously insulting. He told one group that their wise and thoughtful leader was "dumb as a dog." Presenting his demands at Cape Flattery, he ordered the Makah and the Ozette to present one "chief" with whom he could confer. When the Indians could not accept a condition so alien to their traditional practices and expectations, Stevens "appointed" a single "chief" for all these Indians. In other circumstances he urged his agents to use bribery and deceit to get the signatures on the treaty papers, which he could then claim were binding commitments—commitments that apparently bound the United States Government at some times to shoot all those who did not honor them and at other times to shoot those who did. His "scrupulous regard for their welfare" meant to the Indians of Puget Sound that sometimes they faced a drunken governor who forced them to give up their ancestral lands, leave their homes and burial grounds, and confine themselves to areas called "reservations," there to live among other Indian people whose language they did not always understand and to survive as they might where whites themselves, with all their iron and steel could not always have scratched out a decent living. These acts soon convinced most Indians between the Rocky Mountains and the Pacific Ocean that under Stevens not only their land titles but they themselves would soon be extinguished.

In the summer of 1855, Stevens was hurrying to conclude treaties with the inland Indians before they understood the implications of gold discoveries along the Colville River. With open threats and tilted promises and downright subterfuge, he rushed them through conferences and gathered his signatures just as the gold seekers began to stomp across the reserved lands. Even where there had been little subterfuge, there were massive misunderstandings. When Stevens announced the signing of the treaties, white settlers assumed that the land not reserved was up for grabs and began to push aside the Indians. But Stevens had told the Indians that they would not be required to leave the ceded lands until the treaties were ratified by the United States Senate—a matter not of days but of years. Indians resisted the white invasion, and white troops came to punish

them. On other occasions whites assumed that land reserved by
the treaties for the Indians could not be legally closed until rati-
fication—and moved defiantly across it when it pleased them.
Indians understood naked provocation, and they met force with
force, and they understood the calculated deceit of Governor
Stevens. What was abundantly clear to them, from actions and
from words, was that Stevens would not restrict whites, but that
he was absolutely determined to confine Indians. The period of
final protests began.

Evans spoke on, for he remembered these events well.

*In 1855, gold was discovered in paying quantities in the
rivers of Eastern Washington, near the 49th parallel. Miners
journeying to the new gold fields necessarily traversed country
hitherto unfrequented by the white man. . . . Unarmed miners
alone or in small parties, on their way to the Colville mines,
were frequently murdered during the summer of 1855, which
became known in the Fall, by the non-return of the goldseeker
at the time fixed for his return, and by reports of friendly Indians. Emboldened by success in cutting off unarmed travellers,
at last the Indians became more defiant. In the Fall, in cold
blood, attended with most shocking barbarity, they murdered
Andrew J. Bolon, a U. S. Indian Agent, one of our best citizens,
one who had been selected for his justness as a man, his friendship and influence with the Indian race. Maj. Haller, U. S.
Army, with a small detachment of troops, was sent to arrest the
murderers. . . .*[14]

As the inland Indians began to talk among themselves and
with leaders from Puget Sound about what they should do to
keep whites from their land, and as the Yakima sent men into
the passes to warn whites to stay out of the Yakima Valley,
Catholic priests in the region warned Stevens that Bolon was ignorant, bigoted, and insulting. The agent had in great anger
recently threatened to bring troops into the Yakima Valley—
defined by treaty as reserved for the Indians—if the Indians in

14. Evans, p. 17.

any way molested white gold seekers. Advised by friendly Indians to leave the area, Bolon set out for The Dalles. But to the disgust and then the distress of Indian leaders throughout the interior, he was overtaken by two impulsive young men. The murderers, related to Indians recently killed by whites, felt obligated to some bloody revenge, and found Bolon an easy victim.

The Indian war known as the "Oregon-Washington Indian War" was the necessary result of these repeated outrages. It continued from November 1, 1855, till the close of August, 1856. Its history cannot be given in detail. But in its inception, its causes, its progress—the people of Washington Territory have no cause for reproach or shame. In no respect were they aggressors—no act of theirs provoked its commencement—they were innocent of every justifying incentive for its being forced upon them, save their lawful presence in the country. That war was prosecuted solely with a view to secure peace within our borders. [15]

Territorial newspaper editorials were then calling for the extermination of all the Yakima people, and that fall an army unit went into the valley, not to apprehend murderers, but to fight what the officers called war. When they were driven back by the Indians, a call from the governor began to draw into rowdy musters the men around the settlements of Washington and Oregon who were eager to join a volunteer militia and were often fascinated by the thought of murder and plunder. Though there were surely some responsible and thoughtful men among them, they moved up the Columbia on whiskey and in riotous disorder. Under elected "officers," several hundred of them approached the people of the Walla Walla, whose leader Yellow Bird (Peopeo Moxmox) was reputed to be sullen and bitter about the terms of his treaty and probably hostile, probably in league with the Yakima. Shooting any Indians they saw as they rode toward Waiilatpu, the militia officers brought Yellow Bird himself into conference under a flag of truce. Though they

15. Evans, p. 17.

learned that he had no thought to wage war, they seized, bound, and later murdered him. During the attack that massacred many Walla Walla Indians, volunteers amused themselves—as they later told the historian H. H. Bancroft—by mutilating the body of the dead chief, "cutting off bits of his scalp as trophies . . . the assistant surgeon of the regiment cut off his ears." Others took fingers, and still others said they skinned the body "from head to foot and made razor-straps of the skin." [16] Volunteers then drove off the Indians' horses and cattle, which to many of them was what the "war" was all about, and as they returned to their homes they fought angrily among themselves over who would get what plunder. Governor Stevens praised their patriotism. When Gen. John Wool of the regular army tried to disband the militias and to have his regular troops protect the Indians from them, he was relieved of his command. This regard for Indians, however, was not thereafter an army rule. When the Yakima leader Kamiakan in desperation sent a note begging for a truce, Maj. Gabriel Rains wrote in response that "The river only will we let retain this name, to show to all people that here the Yakimas once lived. . . . We are thirsting for your blood." [17]

Synchronously with these hostile acts east of the Cascade Mountains, that brutal massacre accompanied with all the horrid evidences of Indian hate, took place on White River, on the shores of Puget Sound, developing the fact that an extensive combination of Indians had been formed to wipe out the white settlements of the Territory. . . .[18]

Among the Nisqually people the substance of history rose from the intangibles of feeling and memory, from tales recalled in the light of burning embers and lifted delicately into the song of the moment and the dance of the night. Thus we know less about Leschi's life than about the circumstances of his death, which are recorded in the hard documents, papers and books of

16. Bancroft, pp. 106, 141.
17. In Josephy, p. 357.
18. Evans, p. 17.

the white society. These, unlike the songs and the dances, exist today in libraries, but they describe the man only as whites knew him. They forever deny us the man as he knew himself or as his people knew him—a bright thread in the torn and ragged fabric of their total existence.

We know that his father was honored among the people who lived along the Nisqually River before the whites came there, and that his mother lived in the valley of the Klickitat, where her language and customs were much like those of the people of the Yakima. This union of a man and a woman whose homes were separated by the mountains, we know, distinguished the families whose lives were graced by mobility and wealth and social prominence. We know that as a man Leschi had several wives and several slaves and was therefore regarded as among those most worthy of admiration and respect. We know that he stood tall with dignity and authority, and that some whites saw him as compassionate and intelligent, a valuable and reliable friend. On the treaty which Governor Stevens presented at Medicine Creek, there were the marks of sixty-two Indians identified by the governor's aides as leaders. The third among these was recorded as "Lesh-High" of the Nisqually, in whose valley they were standing then on December 26, 1854. That mark—which he later insisted he had never made on any paper—was for Leschi the beginning of a long anguish which the substance of white history can only dimly reveal.

As he came to understand the treaty, he learned that it meant the Nisqually people could no longer live where they had always lived, that they must move away for a promised few thousand dollars. Stevens had "reserved" certain lands for them—lands which were not good lands, and lands which, even so, they would have to abandon whenever their moving might please the white governor. Much of the governor's talk had been vague, most of it had been rushed, and the marking of the treaty by some of the Indians came only because they had always helped the white people, because they did not like to refuse, because indeed they were willing to say "yes" to almost anything if it meant they could live peacefully. Leschi learned of the hurried imposition of similar treaties and similar forgeries

upon other groups—at Point Elliot on January 22, at Point No
Point on January 26, at Cape Flattery on January 31. When he
later came to talk with other men who had been persuaded by
the governor to act for their people, he opened his feelings to
them, and it was soon clear that they all felt intimidated and
humiliated because the governor had caused them to serve their
people so poorly. Thereafter when others asked him for his
judgment of the governor's papers, Leschi voiced his contempt,
his distrust, and his deep apprehension.

Because he often crossed through the pass to visit among his
mother's people, he was eager to learn of their experience, and
we know that when he rode there that summer he found leaders
of the Yakima who shared his sense of apprehension. He may
have spoken at length of the distrust among Indians everywhere—and of their sorrow and their humiliations—and it may
have been that these darkly moody discussions inflamed the
quick and thoughtless young men who followed and then killed
the agent Bolon. When later they knew of the murder, the talk
was about what had happened to the Cayuse after the Whitman
massacre and how army troops, unless Indian people could stop
them, would probably come to kill them. The difficulty was that
Indian people could never unite their diverse, polyglot cultures
into any directed action. It was, indeed, almost impossible for
any leader to convince the people of the Nisqually that they had
much in common with the people of the Walla Walla or of the
Yakima when, except for the rudimentary and simplistic Chi-
nook jargon used for trading, they did not share a common language. And among all the groups, nobody—not even men so
highly regarded as Leschi or Kamiakan—could actually give the
kind of orders necessary for unity: men might talk and warn and
advise, but each individual held inviolable his right to respond
to the urgings, ridicule, or promises of the leader who could
best persuade him.

Leschi returned home in the fall to find disorder and panic
sweeping through the valleys of the Puget Sound country. Following the death of Bolon and the mounting of army companies, volunteer "rangers" around Olympia had formed armed
units in fear that Indian unrest would spread across the moun-

tains. One group of them was even then searching for Leschi himself, intending to hold him hostage. At the same time groups of Indian young men were convinced that with the treaties they had been cheated and treated as fools and that the whites planned to steal their homes. These young Indians, humiliated and fearful, were agitating themselves toward a murder fever with surly and boastful declamations. Leschi sought out his friends Tenaskuet, Kitsap, and Sugieu, and found them with others along the White River, where the fever was already upon them. They had made their boasts and promises, and they told Leschi that whatever his plans may be, their determination was to drive whites from the valley. We have no clear evidence of what Leschi himself determined: he may have chosen not to leave his friends, or perhaps persuaded that theirs was the only course, he may have gone with them. Some of the children were spared, but on October 24, 1855, they moved quietly from cabin to cabin, murdering three families, leaving in their wake the crudely butchered pieces of eight white bodies.

Panic then became hysteria, and more ranger groups rode off separately to kill Indians, often those who had hurt no one and intended to hurt no one and who, like so many white families, pleaded desperately to be saved from this madness. Then marauding Indians, each group answering to its own fury, struck without plan or direction. Leschi at some time did try to bring them together, and he induced his cousin, Qualchan of the Yakima, to bring men through the snow of the passes to help the Puget Sound Indians who, in January 1856, allegedly made their attempt to destroy the village of Seattle.

When word came through friendly Indians—there were many of them—that the attack was being discussed, whites abandoned their homes and went to the blockhouse, which was secure under the protective guns of a naval vessel in the harbor. When word came that Indians were approaching through the woods from the east, some said there were a few hundred, some a few thousand, and no one today knows what the number was because whites saw too few of them. When Indians fired upon the blockhouse, killing two whites, they received fire in return, but no one saw any Indians who were wounded or killed. When Indians began to burn the cabins beyond the blockhouse, naval guns drove them back in among the trees. When Indians then tired of this futility and disappeared, Leschi sent a message to the naval commander to say that he would yet someday drive the whites from the land. No one knows why he made this gesture or what it did for him or the Indians.

Again in March, Leschi called upon Qualchan when soldiers were pushing through the White River Valley and might have overtaken the Indian women, the old people, and the children. After two fierce battles Leschi realized that there would always be more and more troops, and he knew then that unless he found peace, all his people could be massacred. In great suffering, most of his followers and their families followed him through the snow to find at least a moment's refuge in the Yakima Valley. It was then clear to them that they had more to fear from the mobs of volunteers, who wanted murder, than from the regular army officers, who would indeed wage a war but would also negotiate a peace. By 1856, army officers were, they knew, trying to stop the killing and were sometimes protecting helpless but friendly Indians from the rangers. Leschi knew that the army was then seeking the surrender, not the extermination, of the Yakima, and after much talk, he and his friends rode together to Col. George Wright. They pleaded before him, saying that they wanted no more fighting, but that they would surrender only to him. Though Wright was an officer who pursued his career sternly, his goal was peace and quiet in the territory, and he was willing then to act honorably with men of war who would promise to quit war. In doing so with Leschi and his followers, he granted them total amnesty. In this matter, the substance of white history reveals what we need to know, for Wright wrote in March 1857—as recorded by the *Olympia Pioneer and Democrat*—that "the assurances I gave all the chiefs who submitted, including Leschi, were full and complete, as far as military authorities were concerned, as to their personal safety."

But because Governor Stevens had already sent word to the Indians that he must punish their leaders, he was furious that the army should frustrate him. (He was also himself humiliated now because "war" had erupted in his territory just when he was telling the nation how quickly and effectively he had solved all the problems between whites and Indians.) He first demanded that the army capture and deliver to him five Indians, including Leschi, whom he intended to hang. Colonel Wright refused, for he would not violate an honorable agreement, and he would not provoke more war to please the governor. He was thereafter among those who deeply detested Isaac Stevens.

The governor then ordered territorial officials to make the arrests, which he accelerated by offering a bounty of $500 for Leschi, dead or alive. Leschi quickly fled from his valley and rode to the Yakima, where, to his great distress, he found himself feared and shunned. The Yakima had their peace, and they were afraid of further trouble; they were convinced that if they offered any offense to Stevens, then surely the fate of Peopeo Moxmox and the Walla Walla would fall upon them. They would harbor no refugees, and they expelled their former friend. Leschi then returned to his own river, and in October, desperate, homeless, and hungry, he approached a white he had known as a faithful friend even before there were any Americans in the region—old Dr. William Tolmie of the Hudson's Bay Company post near Fort Steilacoom. According to Tolmie, who later wrote his recollections, Leschi wanted some trustworthy white to tell the Americans that he would, should it please them, gladly cut off his right hand as a promise never to fight, if he could surrender to army officers and not to rangers.

Tolmie learned that officers at the fort could not vouch for the Indian's safety, and that they believed he would be more secure in hiding. Leschi went again to the woods, where in a few days he was seized and bound over to Governor Stevens by two of his own people, who perhaps wanted peace or perhaps thought only of the fifty blankets which $500 represented. Locked in a cold jail cell, Leschi learned shortly that his brother Quiemuth, who like himself had been hounded, had surrendered to Stevens in Olympia for safekeeping and trial but had been murdered with a knife—"by persons unknown"—while he was in the governor's office. Brooding through a gray November in isolation from his wives, his friends, his children, Leschi may have realized that he would never again experience the personal freedom which was central to his life and to his very existence.

Stevens's charge was that during the skirmishes which followed the White River Massacre, Leschi had murdered the volunteer soldiers A. Benton Moses and Joseph Miles. This assertion disturbed army officers at Steilacoom, who were quite naturally uneasy about any effort to bring the word *murder* into discussions of what they insisted were acts of *war*. They pointed out that Miles and Moses had not been out on a picnic, that they had indeed set out to kill Indians, and that Leschi, for whatever he had done, had since been properly pardoned. Moreover, a young lieutenant (later a general) named August V. Kautz, who had himself been wounded in an early engagement, took a keen interest in the case when he detected what he believed to be false testimony from the principal witness. Kautz thereafter made a careful study of the terrain of Connell's Prairie, where the Moses party had been ambushed, and he demonstrated to the satisfaction of many people that from the point where the witness swore he had seen and greeted Leschi, no Indian could possibly have ridden on to the site of the killings in time to be a part of the action. At the trial on November 17, 1856, this evidence convinced several men like Ezra Meeker, a settler and later a famous pioneer, to vote insistently against a verdict of guilty. Meeker thus split the jury, but Stevens pressed quickly for a second trial, and in March 1857, Leschi was sentenced to be hanged.

An appeal to the territorial supreme court by Leschi's defenders delayed the order of execution, and for two years while Leschi lay sick and lonely in a military prison, the arguments raged over his fate. Those who had come in the 1840s knew Leschi was a friend who had helped them survive in a strange country and were proud of that friendship—some had taken his daughters; those who had come in the 1850s knew him only as an Indian. Thus in the futile arguments, it was settler against settler, regular against volunteer, perhaps even Indian against Indian. Meanwhile Governor Stevens himself resigned his office and went home to the nation's capital, where he would represent the territory as congressional delegate. The new governor, Fayette McMullin (an official distinguished, according to the usually generous historian H. H. Bancroft, by his eagerness to rid himself of one wife and to acquire another) denied a request for a stay of execution, and in January 1858, Leschi was marched to the gallows. His friends, however, had not been idle, and before the sheriff could perform his duty he was arrested by a United States marshal on a charge of selling whiskey to Indians. In the farce and consternation and confusion that followed, the hour passed, and Leschi was marched back to his cell. Thereafter drunken mobs—called "citizens' meetings"—began to form nightly in Olympia, where they threatened Lieutenant Kautz, Dr. Tolmie, and other friends of Leschi by hanging them in effigy and demanding a real hanging. This agitation moved the territorial legislature to pass a law requiring a special session of the territorial supreme court and ordering the court to expedite the execution. While the governor's friends conveniently removed the U. S. commissioner who had earlier issued an arrest warrant for the sheriff, Leschi was again sentenced. The army officers had then quit their protest, and they surrendered Leschi to a posse on February 19, 1858, at Fort Steilacoom, from whence he was led to a scaffold on the flat land where the Nisqually River enters the waters of Puget Sound. Then old in face and broken in hope, he impressed some of those who witnessed that day as a man who might welcome any end to a wretched existence. Without drum or command, he was in whispers dropped and strangled.

For Ezra Meeker, the juryman who had steadfastly spoke for Leschi's freedom, the hour burned in his memory. In his old age he wrote that the Indian had, like Christ, been willing to die for others, and he remembered the hangman saying, "I felt I was executing an innocent man." [19]

On the 16th of May, 1858 [Evans noted], *a hostile combination of Spokane, Pend Oreille, Palouse and Coeur d'Alene Indians surprised and badly whipped the command of Colonel*

19. Ezra Meeker, *Pioneer Reminiscences of Puget Sound: The Tragedy of Leschi* (Seattle: Lowman and Hanford, 1905), p. 452.

Steptoe, U. S. Army . . . in eastern Washington. Gen. N. S.
Clarke . . . sent Col. Geo. Wright to chastise those Indians
. . . he administered severe punishment.[20]

In a final if pitiful effort, Indians had chased Steptoe's 130
men back to Fort Walla Walla. Colonel Wright, who had supposed that his conferences had brought peace, was then furious
that the inland Indians had defied him, and he was sternly determined to put an absolute end to Indian protest and resistance. In
the summer of 1858, his search-and-destroy missions swept
through the interior, seven hundred soldiers burning villages and
supplies, killing Indian horses, seizing hostages, hanging them,
seldom asking or even wondering who they were or what of-
fense they might have done. At Spokane Plains, Wright had his
men slaughter nearly a thousand Indian horses, thus destroying
the Indians' mobility and condemning them to starvation. Then
using prisoners as an instrument of total terror, Wright hanged
several arbitrarily before he hanged the Spokane leaders whom
he could identify. From the site known thereafter as Hangman's
Creek, he moved south toward Fort Walla Walla. Meeting a
band of Palouse who had taken no part in any uprising, Wright
seized and hanged several of them to set a proper tone for his
message: he would return shortly with a treaty, and if they did
not sign it, he would hang all of them—men, women, and
children. To emphasize his words, he ordered several more men
seized and hanged while he spoke, forcing the Palouse to watch
while their fathers and brothers and sons strangled before them.
When he later arrived at Fort Walla Walla, Wright hanged the
four prisoners he had saved for this triumphant occasion. The
Indian "wars" were indeed at an end.

The loss of the Indians was severe [Evans emphasized his
point] *among whom were two of the principal chiefs. This
quelled the outbreak and peace has since continued throughout
the territory.*[21]

20. Evans, p. 17.
21. Evans, p. 17.

Of the few Americans who mourned at all for Leschi, most were among the earliest settlers, and few of these had more to grieve than George Bush. His life, like that of his Indian friend, haunts us with mysteries: his origins are obscure, yet he had traveled widely, prospered financially, and lived fully. He perhaps knew more about American society and the Oregon Country than any man then in the territory. Among Americans of the 1840s he had been an essential source of strength and wisdom without which many white citizens could not have survived. Yet survivors regarded him as neither white nor citizen.

Because we cannot with certainty trace his racial antecedents, we can record as fact only that he was unusually lightskinned for those enumerated in the census reports as "Free Colored" or as "Black or Mulatto," which was the way he knew that others saw him and his children. There were thirty-one such individuals in the territory in 1860, and among them George Bush was extraordinarily distinguished. Born probably about 1790, he had lived in Pennsylvania and Tennessee, had served, it was said, with Andrew Jackson at New Orleans, had traded among the Indians of the Oregon Country in the 1820s, had raised cattle in Illinois in the 1830s, had farmed in the 1840s in Missouri, where he had taken a wife of German ancestry and raised a family of five children. He was a devout Quaker, a pre-eminently successful farmer, a man who had land, animals, and money. It was said that his father had married the Irish maid of his wealthy New England employer—or master—and had in the course of his service inherited part of a shipping fortune, which in turn he had passed on to his own son, George. It also was said that when George Bush came West, his wagons (he had six of them) rolled with a heavy ballast of silver coin.

He was then six feet tall, a broad and muscular man with black eyes, a black beard, and the imposing presence of physical and moral strength and maturity. Fifty-four years old, he was sick of the slave and racist society of Missouri, which must have rudely abused his dignity. Confident that he had enough years before him to find real freedom for himself and his children, he sold his land and cattle, prepared himself carefully, and joined an emigrant party of eighty wagons that crossed the mountains and visited with the Whitmans in 1844. From the Americans along the river he learned that people in Oregon City had recently passed through the legislature of their provisional government a "Law Against Slaves, Negroes, and Mulattoes," which they hoped would prevent the problems of slavery and of a biracial society from ever becoming their problems. Slavery was prohibited, and "free colored" persons were excluded from the Williamette Valley under pain of repeated floggings. Thus George Bush looked to the north—where he may in his youth have paddled canoes with a Hudson's Bay Company brigade—and to the British outposts on Puget Sound. With five families from the wagon train who had learned that Bush and his close friend, Michael Simmons, were the men to follow, he settled near the Hudson's Bay Company post of Fort Nisqually in 1845, at a time when few people ever supposed that the Puget Sound region would ever become American. They built cabins in November and lived through the winter because Bush and Simmons found favor with Dr. William Tolmie, who extended them supplies and credit, and because they learned survival from the Nisqually Indians.

During the next few years members of the Bush party fixed themselves securely around the falls of the Deschutes River, erecting a gristmill and a sawmill which equipped them for more gracious living and for the cash markets of California. George and Isabella Bush prospered again in their strong middle age, this time on their own terms. On "Bush Prairie" they had taken the 640 acres which all American families in the Oregon Country assigned to themselves, and they raised their buildings, bred their stock, planted their fields, and educated their children. Following the advice of Dr. Tolmie, they employed Indians, worked with them, taught them while they learned from them. They learned also to speak the language of the Nisqually, and they gave to these people the assurance that Indians were always welcome to hospitality, dignity, and respect at the Bush farm. Leschi himself was a frequent guest and teacher. When Isabella gave birth to her last son, they named him Lewis Nesqually, and the boy never wore shoes before his twelfth birthday. He grew to maturity speaking two languages, moving at ease across broadening horizons set by his large family and his growing number of white and Indian companions.

The family farm became a sort of cross-cultural community, rich in vital experiences, emotional securities, and material abundance. Bush bought even more land. He hired a tutor for his children. He grazed beef and dairy cattle, horses and oxen, swine and sheep; he cultivated wheat, hops, vegetables, fruit; he kept chickens and turkeys. From the countryside, the bays, and the river, he took oysters, clams, salmon, trout, berries, and venison. Each Sunday he invited a nearby clergyman to hold services in the schoolhouse, and at Thanksgiving Isabella might serve roasted turkey to two dozen or more friends and strangers. During most weeks of the year, Bush's yards were alive with children, friends, Indians, and visitors. Because his home was along the line of travel between the sound and the Columbia, there were often guests for a meal, a day, or longer. Settlers came to learn his farming techniques, to borrow food or supplies, or simply to marvel at his mastery of so many skills. Each visitor—whether traveler or distressed settler in need of food for a bad winter—was the object of warm and lavish generosity, for Bush had apparently discovered that the freedom central to his new life was the freedom to give openly and with dignity, to share his life and talents and abundance with those who would in dignity accept them. He became the patriarch, a soft-spoken baron, honored and respected for his grand existence. Yet the developing society of Washington Territory would quickly threaten his proud identity.

The boom years brought more and more whites to the sound communities, which increased in population from twelve hundred to twelve thousand during the early 1850s. Few of these new people could know George Bush as the early settlers had known him. With government came the new political divisions, and with growth came the official taker of the census—he was Joe Meek from Oregon City, who with oddly opaque sensitivities, casually listed Indians, half-breeds, Hawaiians, mulattoes, and blacks all as "Free Colored" persons and so enumerated Bush and his children. This was for Bush a matter of severe distress, for in 1850 Congress had passed the Donation Land Act, which validated the land claims in the Oregon Territory for "White Americans." He lived then in anxiety until 1853, when the first legislature of the new Washington Territory memorialized Congress to grant special privilege to "George Bush, a free Mulatto . . . exemplary and industrious" in his habits, a man who "by a constant and laborious cultivation of his said claim, and by an accommodating and charitable disposal of his produce to emigrants . . . has contributed much towards the settlement of this Territory, the suffering and needy never having applied to him in vain. . . ." [22] Congress honored this memorial in 1855.

But Bush had peace for no more than a moment. A full third of the newcomers were from slave states, and as they began to cross frequently over the prairie and to take seats in the legislature, the Bushes felt again the sharp edges of racism. When friends tried to persuade the legislature to grant citizenship and the franchise to George Bush, the bill was stopped by men from the South. When these same men attempted thereafter even to exile Bush with a law echoing the Oregon exclusions, their law was then stopped by Bush's friends. But the legislature was thereafter dangerously divided, and Bush could know no end to apprehension. There was an early incident which would be unfair to characterize as bigotry but which is nevertheless worth noting: when Isaac Stevens came across the prairie in 1853 and stayed for a meal, the governor's presence pleased Bush immensely and brought him as a host to his gracious best. But Stevens wanted to pay—a gesture which, as a matter of dignity, Bush would never allow. In taking leave, however, Stevens slipped a goldpiece under his plate, where it remained unnoticed by Bush until later in the day, when his reaction was not recorded. (Our record of this is a family story, which, like all of the Bush family stories, hints at no bitterness.)

The Indian wars erupted to the great distress of those who, like Bush, had come in the 1840s. We have again no record of

22. Washington Territory, *Journal of the Council of the Territory of Washington, 1854* (Olympia: George B. Goudy, Public Printer, 1855), pp. 20, 187–188.

his anguish, but we know that his sons refused the call for volunteers from Governor Stevens. Owen Bush explained later that Leschi "was as good a friend as we ever had . . . I wouldn't raise a gun against those people who had always been so kind to us when we were so weak and needy." [23] Leschi himself came to Bush to promise safety, and the Bush family was safe, but the turmoil destroyed the grand and good life of abundance and harmony. There were miserable months of troops marching, rangers raiding, Indians butchering, then new governors, massacres, gunboats, hangings, new people, a new and alien society which had no respect for a "mulatto" who might also be a friend of Indians.

After the hanging of Leschi, there were the gold rushes and Civil War. (Isaac Stevens, people learned in Olympia, had returned to the army, and as a Union general been caught in a trap by Stonewall Jackson at a place called Chantilly near Bull Run, Virginia. As the musket fire devastated his command and while some ran for their lives, Stevens rushed to the front ranks, where he lifted his staff and colors from a dead soldier. The words on his lips were "Follow your general!" when he fell with a bullet in his brain on September 1, 1862.) In these years, George Bush was less often the landmark, less often the source of moral strength in a colonial society. He had always been a cautiously nonpolitical man, resisting all efforts to trap and tear him in social controversy. And while the issues of slavery and race tore at every part of the Union, he retired more and more to the privacy of his own reflections, the direction and the depth of which he kept forever closed to others. He was then also an old man, his beard laced with silver, his confidence more and more dependent upon the strength of his sons. He had lived at least a good measure of his 73 years in the spirit of freedom essential to his great sense of living with dignity—a freedom to share the abundance which flowed from his touch, to share it even with those who might deny themselves the abundance of his wisdom.

George Bush died in 1863, Isabella in 1866, she passing still two years before the Fourteenth Amendment to the Constitution

23. Meeker, *Pioneer Reminiscences,* pp. 208–209.

of the United States would have conferred upon her husband the rights and dignities of an American citizen.

Obligated, he felt, to span the full chronology, Elwood Evans read on:

A large population was attracted to South Eastern Washington by the discovery of gold in 1861–2, known as the "Salmon River excitement." As a consequence, on the 3d March, 1863, the Territory of Idaho was cut off from Washington, and the Territorial area of the latter diminished to its present limits. By the great influx of population to Puget Sound, consequent upon the Fraser river excitement, American settlement on San Juan Island . . . had largely increased. In the summer of 1859, the exercise of criminal jurisdiction by a British Magistrate against an American citizen, threatened serious consequences . . . For weeks a conflict between the two forces seemed unavoidable . . . This state of affairs continued until Emperor William in 1872 . . . decided that the Canal de Haro was the "main channel separating the continent from Vancouver's Island" . . . Therefore, in the year 1872, all foreign claims having been effaced, Washington Territory became in truth and in fact an American Territory.[24]

Emory C. Ferguson grew up in the Scotch-Presbyterian culture of Westchester County, New York. In 1854, when he was twenty-one years old, he thought that the world awaited him in El Dorado County, California, so he abandoned his carpenter's apprenticeship and set out to sluice and wash the gravel along the American River, where his brother told him there simply had to be gold. But there didn't have to be anything except gravel and sand, and after two years, Emory took his meager stake and bought a small general store. There was little gold there, either, and with a severely diminished stake he bought a steam-powered saw to cut timbers for people who wanted to leave the diggings and build stores.

In 1858, when few people needed cut timbers to build stores,

24. Evans, p. 18.

Ferguson was possessed again with the vision of real bonanza. He sailed with a lusty crew for Bellingham Bay, Washington Territory, and from there went overland to the Fraser River, and by canoe to the new diggings. But the autumn snows were already covering the gravel bars, and the diggers were leaving in fear of being snowbound on the high plains of British Columbia. Joining the exodus with enough money to take him as far as Puget Sound—some of his fellows made it to Bellingham, others to the San Juan Islands—he located at Fort Steilacoom, where people needed houses and would hire a poor carpenter.

That winter Ferguson heard rumors of a proposed army road to connect Steilacoom with the post at Bellingham Bay. After carefully studying a map, he decided to stake a squatter's claim on the north bank of the Snohomish River by hiring a steamboat to take him there with the portable shack he built for that purpose. Chugging north through protected waters, the Olympics rising to the west, the Cascades to the east, the boat carried him into an estuary choked with snags and fallen trees, which he and the boatsmen had to cut with axes. For miles the trees grew out over the water with strings of moss so heavy that they shut out the sun. But at length the sloughs came together, and there was a fine river, swift and smooth in its flow through the foothills, an easy access to the mountains and to Puget Sound at Port Gardner Bay. Confident that as the first white man there he could capture a ferry franchise, open a store, file a homestead claim, and make a good living on military traffic while a town grew around him, he sledded his shack from the boat deck and unloaded his equipment.

Though it did pass Ferguson's store, the road was never more than a blazed horse trail for which the civilian builders could not even be paid before an army inspector had verified that it could actually serve wagon traffic. With Ferguson's assistance, the contractors disassembled a small wagon and packed it piece by piece on horseback, carried it over the trail, assembled it in Ferguson's yard, then called for the inspector, who came by canoe and asserted that he had indeed seen a wagon that had traveled the road all the way to Snohomish—as Ferguson then called his store and claim. The contractors received their money, but there was none for Ferguson, and shortly thereafter the army abandoned both the posts at Steilacoom and Bellingham.

In the spring of 1859 Ferguson packed into Canada again, this time selling clothing and hardware. With a modest profit, he returned in the fall to open a saloon next to his store in Snohomish, where in the woods and along the river there were maybe fifty white settlers and an uncounted few Indians. The whites were at best a grubby lot—most of them in their thirties, refugees from the gold diggings, newcomers to the territory, none of them with families. They kept alive by taking trees from the public domain, picking berries, and growing vegetables, which they rowed over to Port Gamble, where the Puget Mill Company employed about two hundred millhands. Most of Ferguson's white customers kept Indian women, called in the jargon *klootchmen,* who welcomed these arrangements —according to one settler—not because of "the violence of their passion" but because an Indian woman who had learned to cook and to sew from a white was later more highly esteemed by Indian men. The arrangement, according to established rumors, had brought solace to such whites in the region as Capt. George Pickett and Capt. U. S. Grant. Indian men, though they were then confined to a reservation north of the Snohomish estuary at a bay called Tulalip, came to Ferguson with fish, berries, and hides to trade for cloth and whiskey, and to sit around the store and saloon, sometimes for days. They often fell into drunken orgies of such violence that most whites were constantly armed with knives and pistols.

This was at best a gloomy business, but it was something of a living, and on July 4, 1860, Emory C. Ferguson stood proudly in front of his log cabin-store-saloon, ready for prosperity. Though the morning brought no customers to Snohomish at all, the moment elated him: he was free, he owed no man a dollar or a grudge, he had in twenty-seven years become master of his own destiny and captain of his Presbyterian soul. He thought that day of his grandfather, who had been at Valley Forge, and he took from his wall an old musket, stuffed it with powder, and fired it time and time again, shouting salutes to George

Washington and to Lafayette. He wanted to signal his own independence, and he did—a shouting, cheering, hooping afternoon of cheers and explosions, a celebration in which he was
the only participant.

By August, Ferguson's own appetite had sharply reduced his
supplies, and his trade was bringing him more leisure than
profit. He heard then from the canoe men that gold had been
found high on the tributaries of the Columbia, especially around
the Okanogan River, and that thousands of diggers were making
their way up the Columbia to claim it. He reasoned that the
Okanogan was really just across the mountains from his store,
and that if he could find a pass, he could easily convince miners
to go to the fields via the Snohomish River instead of the Columbia. With a friend and an Indian guide, he packed almost all
of his store of clothing and hardware on four horses and followed the river into the mountains.

It was a terrible ordeal—they had to cut the trail with axes—
but they did cross the summit and find a way down to the
Wenatchee River. Going down was even worse than going up—
they had to swim the horses at almost every crossing—but they
finally reached the Columbia and pushed up the plain to the
Kettle Falls, where the excitement seemed to center. But it was
by then late autumn, and they found only a few miners, most of
them profanely disconsolate. Ferguson returned slowly to Snohomish, where he had no valid claim to the land, no trading
goods, no money, and no customers.

He then sought a more sedentary approach to prosperity.
Having for several years kicked against the Democratic domi-
nance of the territory, he was not ignorant of the opportunities
open in 1860. He became an outspoken advocate of Abraham
Lincoln, and after the inauguration of a new president, he urged
the new territorial governor—then a good Republican—to form
a government for Snohomish County, to be carved from the
older Island County. The subsequent reorganization of lines and
jurisdictions left all the Democratic settlers in Island County and
established Ferguson as the "king of Snohomish." He was then
prepared, as a bartender and saloon owner to serve food and
drink, as postmaster to hand out the mail, as justice of the peace

and probate judge to dispense justice, as county commissioner
and auditor to transact official business, as legislator to discuss
the affairs of the territory. He also found time—in a clearing
where there was little public business and no children—to serve
as notary and as superintendent of schools.

Everybody seemed involved during these years in logging.
Men usually worked in small groups, with only a boat, a team
of oxen, and axes. Dropping trees near the beach, they built
skidroads from logs, greased them with fish oil, and dragged the
timbers—some as large as twenty tons—to the water, then
towed them to the nearest mills, whose owners were quick to
find full advantage in the Homestead Act. Staking storekeepers
in the various logging colonies and establishing them as company agents to buy up homestead titles, the company taught the
storekeepers to help "entrymen" through the legalities of filing
a claim, paying the fees, and herding the necessary witnesses
before a notary and a county auditor. Using company funds,
these storekeepers could pay the first taxes on the land, validate
the titles in the territorial capital, and then buy them for the
company, for about a hundred dollars. Entrymen moved through
the Blue Eagle Saloon in number and often bought lots from
Ferguson with a part of their one hundred dollars.

This perversion of the homestead ideal brought many foot-
loose entrymen to Snohomish, where Ferguson's fortunes were
so admirably suited to serve them. Ferguson soon had a larger
store. He married and raised a family as his city was growing to
include maybe a thousand people, a church, a newspaper, a literary society, a Masonic Lodge, and hopes for a railroad. Perhaps when in 1873 Masons solemnly resolved that members living in adultery with either white or Indian women were guilty of
"gross un-Masonic conduct," his city found at least a part of
the identity that Ferguson had hoped for on an early Fourth of
July.

*This year 1872, of happy memory, was also marked by the
commencement within its limits of the consummation of that
grand enterprise, which will utilize and benefit not only our own
people, but add great wealth to the nation. Forty miles of*

*railroad, a section of the great Northern Pacific, were built and
in running operation. . . . With a population now numbering
40,000—a country gifted with an infinite variety of resources—
large areas of good cultivable soil, genial and healthy climate,
an industrious and enterprising people loving the land in which
their lot is cast—such is the status of Washington Territory in
1876—may it prove the guarantee of a glorious future.*[25]

James N. Glover was twelve years old in 1849 when his
parents, then prosperous Missouri farmers, determined to rid
themselves of their seventeen slaves and remove to the Willamette Valley in the territory of Oregon. They "crossed the
plains" and settled near Salem, taking a claim on 640 acres. In
a family of eleven children, six of whom died before he was an
adult, Glover worked with his father on this acreage, building,
farming, woodcutting, until he was attracted to ventures of his
own in 1857.

That year he took a load of apples to California, a commercial prospect then regarded as promising by many Oregonians.
The problems of sale and distribution, however, defeated most
of them. While the apples rotted, Glover opened a fruit store,
and demonstrating his talents for merchandising, began to buy
out the stocks of his desperate friends. He returned later to
Salem with substantial earnings, which he used for mining ventures near Lewiston. Because of his father's wisdom in remov-
ing to Oregon, he could avoid the terrible slaughter of the Civil
War, and by 1870 he had saved more than $15,000, which he
invested again in apples and in a Willamette River steam ferry.
With precisely the right intuitions, he sold both ventures just
before the panic of 1873.

When the sudden depression which followed stopped most
entrepreneurs in their tracks, Glover set out with undaunted confidence to find a place where he could establish a city to call his
own. Such dreams were possible, depression or not, especially
for a man who had thought about railroads and who carried with
him vivid memories of the rich grasslands and the cool pine

25. Evans, p. 18.

groves of the Great Columbia Plain. He took the riverboats
again to Lewiston, where he bought horses and provisions and
listened while the old Presbyterian missionary Henry Spalding
told about the advantages of friendly Indians and water power at
the falls of the Spokane River. What the old man described
sounded to Glover like the most nearly perfect combination of
happy circumstances, and with a vision of development still
evolving in his mind he rode buoyantly north through the hills
and valleys of the Palouse. Only occasionally did he come upon
a few settlers—a tent, a log cabin, a lean-to in valleys—and for
days he saw no white people at all. Blue sky and infinite grass
opened the world for him, and the crest of each rolling hill was
a glorious adventure in freedom and independence. He was a
large man, stout and broad-shouldered. His hair grew long and
straight, and his eyes sparkled with a courage and ambition
always more thoughtful than impetuous. Then thirty-six years
old, he knew the shining hours of his life, days he would recall
moment by moment in his old age, days of unlimited energy
and bright expectations.

Approaching the sound of the falls, he was moved to a deep
emotion by the water, the wild life, the grass, the pine-covered
hills, the cautious but apparently genial Indians, and he was
convinced that the old missionary had been absolutely right and
that his own instincts had again been rewarded. But there were
suddenly problems. Below the falls he found buildings, obviously built by whites, and around a small sawmill he met J.
Downing and S. Scranton, as they introduced themselves, who
had clearly intruded into the center of his vision by staking the
choicest land as their own squatter's claim. However, since they
explained to Glover that they were "former cattle dealers"
eager to return to Montana and that they might be induced to
sell the suspiciously inefficient sawmill which was the substance
of their "claim," Glover's hopes revived quickly. He soon had
reason to regard his new friends not as cattle dealers but as
cattle rustlers, and he learned that territorial marshals were, in
fact, on their trail. Under urgent circumstances, Glover moved
quickly to acquire the dubious "title" to an illegal "claim."

His hopes then leaped forward: official surveyors would soon come to lay their baseline, and thus open the valley to legal homesteading, and the Northern Pacific Railroad would soon come out of the mountains, down to the falls, and there *not* claim Glover's homestead as part of the forty square miles of public land granted to it by the federal government for each mile of steel track it would build across the territory. These seemed at the time reasonable hopes, and with two partners from Oregon, J. N. Matheny and C. F. Yeaton, he bought out the fugitives, brought in a millwright and a real sawmill, and opened a general merchandise store for some cautious trading in blankets and hardware (he hid the rifles and whiskey) with the Indians.

If he were indeed to have a town, he must have the settlers, and Glover's promotion was to offer generous portions of his riverfront "claim." In this way he found a missionary-school-teacher, a veterinarian, an attorney, a miller—maybe a dozen or so enthusiastic dreamers who wanted a pioneer's share of the promised railroad bonanza. Slowly Glover's store became a community meetinghouse, a church, a school, and a potential fortification. In 1874 Glover paid private surveyors to estimate the baseline, and he was reasonably certain thereafter that he had settled on the right section. Yet the depression lingered, and dreams soured, and the hills seemed forever without any sign of civilization, and no official survey teams or railroad scouts came out of the mountains. In the summer of 1876, the two partners, Matheny and Yeaton, giving up hope that the railroad would come in time to save them, sold out to Glover. Then the miller needed to borrow money to build what he wanted to call his Centennial Flour Mill, but Glover was flat broke and could not help him.

Nevertheless, Glover invited people from as far north as Canada to come down for the Fourth of July that year—they could talk about railroads and business and water power and commerce, take fish from the river, game from the hills, and perhaps tap the keg of hidden whiskey. On the morning of the Fourth, Glover hoisted a homemade American flag from a rough pole in front of his log cabin-store and welcomed his guests to begin a three-day celebration. There were maybe two dozen families in all—enough to make an enthusiastic audience for the oration, enough to make lively dinner parties in the shade, enough to dance in the evening under the pines. Still single and sober, Glover was also methodical and orderly. He was happy that his friends were happy. Though the bunchgrass was knee-high in front of his store, he was determined to endure.

In Olympia, the hour was late, but Evans had not reached his peroration. He had yet to offer a promise of golden opportunity and an invitation to share the abundant resources which Americans of his generation saw as their special inheritance, and he told his listeners that the Northern Pacific Railroad, like a miracle ordained for their special destinies, would soon unlock these inestimable treasures. Come and join us, he was saying, come to the West and we shall together drive a steel wedge into the dark fabric of wilderness and open the princely fortunes which God has reserved for men of courage and patriotism and ambition. It was the will of Infinite Wisdom that the treasures should be opened for this generation. When he finally alluded thus to Divine Providence, it was with a short prayer to the "Father of light, liberty and law" that He might protect the glorious future of the United States and the territory of Washington, where to the "western verge of the broad continent" had been carried "the spirit and teachings of 1776."

Then it was done, and in the territorial newspapers the editorial response to Evans's remarks was a call for the public printing and distribution of his centennial address. The legislature complied by ordering five thousand copies, and it was clear that of the centennial sentiments then floating around the Pacific Northwest, Evans's were certainly the most popular and the most eloquent. He had described the past as his contemporaries wanted it described, he had served their need for a historical identity, he had defined for them a satisfying role in an apparently heroic and divinely ordained mission to "subdue," as he had said, the wilderness of the Oregon Country and to "dedicate it to American civilization."

3

Building the Good Life

WITHIN two decades following the centennial, the territory became a state in which there were thousands of people in
places where Elwood Evans had known only a few dozen. And
the frontier communities Evans had so lavishly praised—their
social structure, their inclinations, their expectations—quickly
lost their essentially pre-industrial, colonial character. The new
railroads imposed iron mandates and alien alignments from
which there was no escape; and they brought the new industrial
realities—steam-powered logging engines, sawmills, shingle
mills, canneries, mining machinery, smelters—from which
there was no retreat. As the frontier was quickly industrialized,
the people, by the hundreds of thousands, came to find places in
a new society which in the explosive pace of its growth soon
overwhelmed almost every earlier social predisposition.

Even from their railroad car windows, those who came in the
1880s could look out over marvelous fields of opportunity. For
the poor farmer, there was a cheap rail ticket and cheap land,
credit easy to come by, friendships easy to make, bankers,
merchants, and neighbors eager to help him "get established."
In 1889, a farmer from Nebraska bought one hundred acres of
railroad land near Colfax and planted his wheat. With the harvest of one season—and his experience was not uncommon—he
paid for his land, fencing, sowing, hauling—everything, and
still had $98 to put in the bank. For the urban worker, there

were new mills and factories opening every day, new construction projects, work almost wherever he wanted it. A man might earn wages for a year, then own his own shingle mill or logging outfit. In 1901, a wage earner who brought his family from Minnesota settled in Everett, where he worked in the Weyerhaeuser mill. After two years, he took jobs as a carpenter, and within a decade he had become a prosperous building contractor with extensive investments in farm land and city real estate. For the European immigrant, there were urban neighborhoods of predominantly Scandinavian or German or Italian or English antecedents where the native-language church, the fraternal organizations, and the national social clubs embraced the newcomer and carried him into a rich fabric of new associations. If a man came West with real money for investment, or if he could attract the attention of eastern investors, he might organize a railroad company, build a lumber mill, a cannery, a brick factory, a land company, or even found a city.

But when financial panic swept over the nation in 1893—at first a panic among eastern investors, a panic of lost confidence—it swept west on the mainlines of the railroads like the very spirit of destruction, and for a while it tore at the very foundations of the new and yet incohesive frontier-industrial society. Investors withheld their promised funds. Financiers like John D. Rockefeller actually withdrew from major enterprises around the industrial ring of Puget Sound, abandoning their sinking companies and corporations and collapsing highly speculative developments in places like Everett and Snohomish. Land companies disintegrated, newspapers failed. Wages, for those who could find them, fell as much as sixty percent, and wage earners were faced with destitution on an urban frontier or with somehow returning to whatever place it was from which they had so recently come. Farmers could not sell their wheat at high enough prices to pay their expenses; bankers stopped making loans. The Northern Pacific, even with its government loans and land grants, went bankrupt, an event shattering to the nerve of the most stubborn optimist. Construction halted everywhere, and the market for timber and lumber simply disappeared.

It was a hard time and a bad time, erupting in labor troubles, radical rhetoric, and physical violence as the old Knights of Labor made their last feeble efforts to assert an integrity for their dying union. Most ominously in the coal towns southeast of Seattle, where hundreds of blacks had been recruited from other states by coal mine companies desperately trying to compete with companies in British Columbia employing Chinese labor, protests exploded from street meetings into ugly riots. In 1894 over a thousand men joined the Puget Sound regiment of Coxey's army, boisterously bound for national protest against wage cuts and unemployment. At their Puyallup rendezvous, Governor John McGraw spoke to them personally and pointedly, threatening to call out the National Guard if they refused to disband. Luckily the governor did not have to make good his threat, for Eugene Debs's American Railroad Union was on strike, and some guardsmen were even then refusing to ride on nonunion trains. But later McGraw did successfully call out the guard to protect citizens at the mouth of the Columbia, where net fishermen from Astoria, Oregon, were at war with the men who worked fishtraps on the Washington side of the river. While armed Oregonians destroyed the traps with steam-powered snagpullers, violence was extensive, all of it complicated by a cannery strike and by hostilities among the net fishermen on both sides of the line. Twenty men were killed before the governors could bring that conflict to an end.

In Spokane in 1894, when a strike-breaking crew ran a train into the city, a mob of three thousand rambled into the railyards to push the cars from the tracks. That year many farmers in the state went into a fury about unregulated rail freight rates, interest rates, and wheat prices. There emerged then in state political life a disparate fusion of protesters: almost all of them wanted to stop immigration and to expel Orientals; they criticized railroad monopolies and demanded state regulation of freight rates; some wanted outright public ownership of railroads, utilities, banks, and all natural resources; others demanded a single tax; many were asking for the initiative and the referendum as political tools with which the people themselves could abolish corruption. Hard times can breed not only hatreds but fantastic fears of conspiracies, and some people cheered every sneer at wealth and privilege, or at blacks, or at the foreign-born, especially those who happened to be Roman Catholic. Among the sweeping critiques of government and of the entire social system, it was easy for sensitive people to hear the symptoms of a society on the brink of insurrection.

Yet the tentative nature of almost everything about the new society allowed it to avoid the social convulsions which occurred in Illinois, New York, and Massachusetts. And when the lean years ended, the process of frontier industrialization began again at a breathless pace. It seemed to most people that bad times disappeared almost overnight in 1898 when everyone was talking not about strikes and riots but about gold in the Klondike, war in Cuba, silver in the Coeur d'Alenes, real estate in Seattle, banks in Spokane, wheat prices in the Palouse country, and a national building boom that would lift the lumber industry out of its distress. And behind it all was the expansive vision of James Jerome Hill, who out of the wreckage of the depression had brought together both of the transcontinentals—the Great Northern and the Northern Pacific—and negotiated the greatest timber deal in history by transferring vast acreages from the railroad land grants to Frederick Weyerhaeuser.

This resurgence of prosperity and confidence was not the result of any single or sudden circumstance—though war and gold discoveries surely accelerated it. It was more a reflection of the range of opportunity presented to Americans by the treasures of the Pacific Northwest when the railroads did indeed unlock them. J. J. Hill, for example, looked to revenues from his mainlines, and to generate them he needed mills, factories, farms, canneries, and people to produce the freight his lines could haul. His agents were taking samples of soil and wheat to the cities of the United States and Europe, offering low rail fares and low prices on land, encouraging another great wave of immigration. For most people, the Pacific Northwest was not opened by a few mountain men trapping furs or even by pioneers shooting Indians; it was opened by the railroad companies which made it easy for a farmer or a farm hand to get to Spokane or a wage earner to reach Seattle or Everett or Tacoma or Aberdeen where there were jobs for the asking. There had been nothing like it in American history since the opening of the Louisiana Territory—golden years when no personal ambition, however grandiose, seemed at all unreasonable, when it seemed that every venture might prosper and every family might share in the nobility of wealth because of the democracy of profit.

And in the excitement, the inevitable disorder, the confusion, there were sometimes quiet moments when at least a few people looked thoughtfully beyond the turmoil of population growth and economic expansion to public gestures which might transcend the materialistic center of their daily lives. For example, from the business district of Seattle in the 1890s a car on the Yesler cable line left every four minutes for Lake Washington and the delightful "pleasure ground," as it was then called, where people could yet walk in the forest, picnic on the beach, or, on a Sunday afternoon, listen to a band concert. The ground was called Leschi Park. When it was so dedicated in 1891, there were no protests, and hardly anyone alive then could recall the heat of rancor and bitterness evoked by that name in the 1850s. And on July 4, 1895, the surviving few Nisqually joined hundreds of other Indians from several reservations on a train of rail cars chartered for an extraordinary excursion. Amid rituals both solemn and festive, they exhumed the remains of Leschi from the rude grave in the delta and reburied them near his birthplace beside the swift waters of the upper valley. Then in Walla Walla in 1898, an association of citizens who joined with classes from Whitman College acquired the old mission site, where they opened the graves and removed the bones to a new clearly honored sepulcher.

That year James Glover, having made and then recently lost a fortune, lived quietly in Spokane. Two decades before, two men had saved him by taking half of his uncertain squatter's claim for fifty dollars of a promised five-thousand-dollar payment. This was, at that time, enough to avert disaster, and within months he was again fully confident that his dream of founding a city would come true. The whiskey keg came out of hiding again when survey crews for the Northern Pacific finally did come down from the mountains, and in 1882 the first locomotive passed in front of his store. Glover acquired legal title to his homestead, then richly adorned by the hydroelectric potential at the falls and by the right-of-way of a transcontinental railroad. He could serve the people who rushed to buy whatever land he would sell, and his town began to take a satisfying form and substance. He married a neighbor's daughter, Esther Emily Leslie, and he incorporated the First National Bank of Spokane Falls. As banker, investor, developer, husband, and town father—he was elected mayor in 1884—he settled comfortably into an affluent middle age.

And these were years of almost incredible developments. After a zany colony of atheists had discovered gold in the Coeur d'Alenes, the diggings turned quickly to rich lodes of lead and silver, which, with the railroads nearby, could be heavily capitalized for industrial extraction. And it was a capitalization which men in Spokane, the bankers and investors and developers, could manipulate. Glover's share came mainly through his bank and through the Spokane Falls and Northern Railroad, one of the dozens of rail companies organized in the 1880s and one of the economic lines from the hub of wealth which Spokane was becoming. Then the wheat farmers came, hundreds of them each week—Spokane was growing at the rate of five thousand people a month—most of them eager to borrow money, to buy supplies and machinery. Their predictable demands began to transform a town of street stores and shops and saloons and bawdy houses into a city of staid and stable mercantile institutions. The new industrial and commercial base spread conspicuously across the valley in railyards, brick ovens, machine shops, warehouses, lumber mills, assembly plants, grain storage facilities, retail centers, and Glover often loaned money to their owners, or he himself invested in the newest ventures, which always seemed to be the most promising.

And there was plenty of money for pleasures, invitations to high living unprecedented in the history of the territory. When Benjamin Kizer—later among the state's most prominent attorneys—came in 1890, he was a boy only weeks away from his father's grocery store in Ohio, where he had spent his days haggling for as little as a penny, he said, in the price of a pound of butter. In Spokane he saw men casually matching five-dollar gold pieces on the street, men who could buy a lot for $500 and sell it within a month for $1,000. Glover himself knew a lawyer whose annual income was at least $50,000 and who spent every cent of it on servants, restaurants, gambling parlors, and other indulgences, including extended vacations. Glover's own tastes, however, were less expansive. Though he did put $100,000 into the Tudor mansion he built on a bluff with a broad view of the entire valley, he also built the First Episcopal Church and supported his wife's favorite charities, doing indeed very well by his wife and less fortunate relatives and friends. He was for a while the smiling millionaire mayor known for his enthusiasm for investments, his easy generosity, and his characteristically uninspired byword, "What's good for Spokane is good for me."

The panic of 1893, however, brought waves of catastrophe, which for a while washed away the eastern money that had supported a decade of fantastic growth and diversification. Glover's bank eroded rapidly, and to desperate depositors he paid out over a million dollars of his own savings before he was, in the euphemism of the day, "obliged to suspend." He was also obliged then to mortgage his home with another banker for $30,000, which for years was the only money he had. When his associate foreclosed this mortgage in 1897, the financial substance of Glover's Spokane dream was but a few pieces of real property, drearily unproductive. He was then sixty years old, done forever with loans and investments, never quite in destitution but never safely above it. He was thereafter the observer, never the participant, in the events marking the great migration after 1900. As an aging pioneer, a sort of honorary member of the elite, he watched the city grow from a population of twenty thousand at the time he lost his money to more than one hundred thousand by 1912. He lived comfortably with Esther Emily and was everybody's favorite relative, the uncle who would give a child a dollar for memorizing a poem, the old man surrounded by brothers, sisters, nieces, nephews. In his last year, 1921, he would sleep only in his high-backed chair, afraid that if he went to his bed he would not ever again be able to rise and look out the window across the broad valley of the Spokane.

Spokane was, of course, not long in panic, for its unusual potentials in wheat, ore, land, and water were still there, and the people who had the money soon realized that they needed Spokane's potential for growth as much as Spokane needed their investments. Though early farmers cursed what they called "Jim Hill mustard," a mean weed that sprouted across nearly every field and seemed to threaten their future, they were soon aware that the weed could be controlled and that around Spokane Falls, especially to the south, lay some of the world's finest wheatland. The railroads were eager for them to develop it. There was a fabulous fertility in the soil—wheat at forty to fifty bushels an acre—which some said was like the volcanic ash of Sicily, practically inexhaustible. To help the farmers find its maximum use, the state college at Pullman began a program of basic research into soils and climates. With the railroad companies, the college conducted farmers' institutes and farm demonstrations which brought lecturing agricultural scientists and the latest farm machinery to the crowds that gathered around the rail sidings all over what was coming to be called the Inland Empire, of which Spokane was clearly the center.

There were soon dozens of towns numbering from a hundred to a thousand people—towns like Davenport, Odessa, Ritzville, Cheney, Colfax, Pomeroy, and Asotin—each with its small bank, weekly newspaper, grain warehouse, and railroad station; each peopled by men and women proud of its possibilities or certainties for endless growth and prosperity. These were in many respects like midwestern wheatfarm communities, for indeed most people in them had arrived from Iowa or Nebraska, the Dakotas, Wisconsin, or Minnesota. Yet there were differences: while there were indeed many foreign-born newcomers, most had lived in other states, and there were in the Inland Empire few communities which had any distinct ethnic or cultural identities. Almost all of the migrants were eager to lose the more obvious indications of their national origins and to melt down into the vigorous boosterism and conspicuous Americanism central to their sense of community.

When the journalist Ray Stannard Baker visited the state in 1903, he was amazed to note that everything "seems to have happened within the last ten years," and he was himself swept up in the excitement of refreshing change and growth. Everyone seemed full of hope and pride and even friendship, welcoming newcomers not as rivals but as developers who would contribute to—and share in—a common destiny. As the crops of wheat and hops and the yields of coal, lumber, and fish attained national prominence, thoughtful entrepreneurs looked toward the opening of the Panama Canal, the easier access to world markets, and the end of railroad monopolies—a view of the future which kindled even the most cautious imagination. Thus people worked together without feeling threatened, and they expressed their confidence in the parades, street fairs, public meetings, and community projects which amazed Ray Stannard Baker, because he knew of eastern towns and cities where there had been no examples of such public activity for generations.

He delighted in the bustle and hustle of a chamber-of-commerce society. Most people he met belonged to several interlocking organizations—Eagles, Elks, Masons—and they were intensely involved with the boasts, predictions, and friendly rivalries of boosterism which in more settled communities would have seemed absurd, or at least insignificant. Was Seattle better than Tacoma? For investment, residence, culture, education, wages? Was Spokane the greatest railroad city in the West? Should the mountain be called Rainier or Tahoma? Was the future brighter in Sprague than in Colfax? Was the high school football team at Wenatchee the best in the nation? These were considered serious questions.

The goal of a chamber-of-commerce society, Baker understood, was *to develop*—which was to capture whenever possible the many pearls of economic and industrial expansion. Thus a town acquired a new railroad or real estate company, or a new mill, plant, factory, or store, all amid general rejoicing and speeches about community achievement. In 1909, for example, Seattle's brightest pearl was the Alaska-Yukon-Pacific Exposition—and the federal monies poured into it. An editor of *Harper's Weekly* commented that this was not an exposition to commemorate anything because there was in Seattle nothing to commemorate: it was rather an exposition to celebrate the fact that "in the story of civilization there is probably no record of more astonishing growth" than had recently occurred in the region around Puget Sound.[1]

Another writer for the same magazine, inclined to ridicule the braggadocio of places like Yakima, stopped there one day to discover that barren hills and sagebrush had indeed become the base of a prosperous and even beautiful community. Where cattle had starved to death a decade before, farmers were tilling a magnificent topsoil twenty to a hundred feet deep. Diverting water from the Yakima River across the valley, they had opened opportunities that were positively lyrical: twenty dollars would clear an acre of sagebrush and provide it with ditches, and for the man who would cultivate it diligently, it could in two months yield a cash crop of vegetables or alfalfa; in a season, a bounty of hops, wheat, or grapes; in two years, peaches like the nation had never seen; in three years, apples and pears that would have brought distinction to orchards anywhere in the world. Where dust had only recently risen from whirlwinds around Indian ponies, a man could harvest eighty tons of sugar beets from two acres. The writer found a city of shaded lawns, handsome homes, and new stores. Every house, he wrote, stood proudly by itself "embowered by fruit trees, in yards green with grass or gay with a riotous growth of roses." [2] Each quiet street had its irrigation ditch for home gardens; and in space, pride, abundance, peace, and fertility, the city presented a face of harmony amid plenty. One could see Yakima indeed as the goal of much American experience. It was new and optimistic, firmly structured to shelter the values of ambition and discipline and self-reliance and to offer opportunities which were perhaps without parallel.

Thus the widowed mother of William O. Douglas moved there in 1905 and built a comfortable five-room home for six

1. "The Wonderful Northwest," *Harper's Weekly*, April 3, 1909. Quoted in W. Storrs Lee, ed., *Washington State: A Literary Chronicle* (New York: Funk & Wagnalls, 1969), p. 411.

2. Kirk Monroe, "Eastern Washington and the Water Miracle of Yakima," *Harper's Weekly*, May 19, 1894. Quoted in Lee, p. 384.

hundred dollars. Though she was often nearly penniless, she kept a garden and a cow and could stay in her home to rear a distinguished family. While the boys worked for the money the family needed—tending yards, sweeping sidewalks, delivering newspapers, picking fruit and berries—the mother patched their coats and trousers, scrubbed them for church and school, and faced the community with dignity and pride. The boys yet had the kind of leisure and liberty which allowed them a wholesome progress toward manhood while they roamed in perfect security throughout the city. At the age of eleven, Douglas could go off into the mountains for weeks at a time without adult guidance or supervision—go off to learn from an Indian how to find berries and roots, how to catch fish, how to find a sense of confidence and maturity in coming to terms with himself and with an uncorrupted environment. At Yakima High School, even though he was working for wages during most of his out-of-school hours, Douglas received a superior education. When he was graduated in 1916, he was sensitive to music and poetry, familiar with literature, fluent in Latin, knowledgeable in biology and physics, a young man admirably literate and articulate, the classical poor-boy valedictorian. A scholarship to Whitman College carried him forward to a gloriously open future.

The fortunes of Emory C. Ferguson, like those of James Glover, tumbled in the ebb and flow of economic pessimism or confidence. There was a happy rise after the bad times of the early 1870s, and by 1877 he had done well enough to allow himself a wharf and a lumber mill. But that year the lumber market fell again into a deep slump. Ferguson had loans to repay, however, and he was forced to continue milling and selling at whatever price he could get. To cut expenses as the market continued to fall, he hired Chinese laborers who would work for half of what his white friends demanded, and this practice afflicted the tiny village of Snohomish with a series of ugly racial incidents. Finally several citizens exploded a dynamite charge on the steps of a laundry, and the Chinese made their sad exodus to Seattle, from which in turn they would be driven toward San Francisco in a few years by mobs. But even with cheap labor, Ferguson could not meet his obligations, and it seemed to him for a season that his essential securities were threatened: men left Snohomish, many of them owing him money, left to go back to the cities, or to the farms, or to join the army, then fighting the Nez Percé. A flood washed out the grain crops of the river delta, and the farmers there were destitute. Ferguson lost his mill. When diphtheria and smallpox struck through the region, most of the Indians died, and some white families lost all of their children.

These were grim years, yet the railroads were really coming—the Northern Pacific to Portland in 1883, then the mainline to Tacoma in 1887. The vital development, however, was the Great Northern. When it was clear that James Jerome Hill's mainline would integrate the territory by crossing boldly from Spokane to a terminus somewhere on Puget Sound, railroad ties began to sell very well indeed. The lumber market went up and up, the men returned, some with wives and families. Soon Snohomish had a newspaper, a literary society, a bank, a church, and Ferguson looked eagerly for his big moment.

Thereafter, it seemed, almost everything depended upon the moods and the calculations of James Jerome Hill. The great man himself appeared around Puget Sound in 1892 with his demands for rights-of-way and lands for depots. The people of the new commonwealth were warmly generous in these matters, none more eagerly so than E. C. Ferguson. It was soon obvious, however, that Ferguson had lost again, that Jim Hill's plans were big for Everett and Seattle but small for Snohomish. Ferguson was always the simple developer, not the speculator. He could never duplicate or imitate the manipulations of the sophisticated men who came West following Jim Hill, and we see his limitations vividly in an example that reveals two epochs: when his friend Ezra Hatch died in 1890, Ferguson represented the widow in the sale of the homestead which was the sum total of her estate. (She was an illiterate Indian woman Hatch had bought in 1873 for ten dollars when he had decided to have companionship in the forest which he would not sell to Pope and Talbot.) Ferguson sold the land to Henry Hewitt, an Everett speculator, for four thousand dollars. Hewitt in turn sold it quickly to F. D. Norton, his brother-in-law, who sold it to the Everett Land Company, of which Hewitt was president, for one hundred and twenty-eight thousand dollars. In 1893, just before the panic and just as Hill's mainline came down the river to Everett, the land company sold it to other speculators, piece by piece, for half a million dollars.

By then he was no longer the "king," but surely the "father" of Snohomish. Ferguson served as mayor across the bleak years of the 1890s, always keeping his eyes open for the final opportunity. In the early 1900s he made an almost implausible investment in gold mining, rising to the rumor that there were commercial deposits just east of his home in the Cascade Mountains. It was another loss which he survived with equanimity. When he died in 1911—at the age of seventy-nine—all the schools and businesses in his town closed for his funeral.

When he learned that the Northern Pacific would terminate at Commencement Bay, Elwood Evans moved his law office to the railhead where he found a practice as a senior attorney with the land company then selling lots in the new city of Tacoma. There for an inspired moment in 1873, the directors of the Northern Pacific had wanted a distinguished design for their terminal city, and they had retained the nation's foremost landscape architect, Frederick Law Olmsted. Olmsted's plan was one of gracious innovation: an absence of straight lines and right angles, a system of streets and avenues which followed the natural contours of the rising hills and bluffs, a location of residential areas high over the water and with full views of the bay, an elegant linkage of spacious parks and generous promenades. Though a few people thought that this design would make Tacoma one of the world's beautiful cities, the directors of the railroad and the land developers were utterly confused by Olmsted's concept of space and harmony; they wanted to get on with the urgent business of blocking lots so they could sell them. After only a brief consideration, then, they released Olmsted, abandoned his plan, and instead adopted the dull and conventional grid system that is fixed in most American cities.

There is no indication that the system did not please Evans, who for the rest of his life knew the success which as a pioneer he had always anticipated. As a land attorney he became prosperous, even wealthy. As a community leader he served as a member of the first state legislature and as a sort of well-dressed and aging volunteer in a lingering dispute with the Indians. He supervised the passage of laws with which the land company in ·Tacoma could strip the Puyallup Indians of their reservation lands in what became the industrial heart of the city. Through the 1890s this work brought him full increments of prestige and comfort, and it allowed him the leisure to pursue his historical writings in *The History of the Pacific Northwest,* a two-volume subscription history that had become his major work. In the extravagant language of a trial lawyer confident that he has already won the jury, Evans thus continued to glorify his compatriots of the 1850s. The handsome volumes were designed, he said, to illustrate "the complete justification of every effort put forward" by the territorial pioneers, and they were guaranteed to please those who had paid to have their biographies included. Such historical and biographical work still left Evans time to organize the first bar association for the state as well as its historical society.

If the industrialized Pacific Northwest symbolized for many people a vital dimension of the national consciousness, it was because the opportunities there for eminence like that attained by Elwood Evans seemed for a while open to all Americans. It seemed so to Horace Roscoe Cayton, who was born to a mother whose name he never knew and to a father who as a former slave had passed through the anguish of Reconstruction in Mississippi to become a farmer, proudly independent and determined that his boy obtain an education and leave the wreckage of the slave world behind him forever. Moved by these anxieties, the young Cayton became an intense student at Alcorn College, where he met the daughter of Hiram R. Revels, the first black United States senator. They were married in 1890.

The Caytons lived for a while among other black families in Seattle near the center of the city on land once owned by William Grose, a black cook who had come early, had done well in real estate, and had encouraged other blacks—fewer than five hundred before 1900—to take advantage of his own good fortune. Cayton worked as a news reporter, and during the Klondike boom of 1897 his wife rented chairs on their front porch to weary travelers who could find no other place to rest. Saving his and his wife's money, Cayton also invested in real estate, and he soon became the owner and editor of the weekly *Republican,* which in his hands attained a wide readership and a clear political, but not racial, identity. He was able before long to buy an imposing two-story home on Capitol Hill, which in that period was a fashionably new residential neighborhood for people wealthy enough to move beyond the city's business and industrial districts. There with an ambitious wife, who was more sophisticated, better educated, and better informed about contemporary affairs than most women in the state, and with bright and interesting children, Cayton for a while prospered in the lifestyle for which his own father had so urgently prepared him. There was a livery stable for the horses and the carriage, a Japanese house servant (kept firmly in his place in a class-conscious household), music lessons for the children, Shakespeare for all the family, political activity in the Republican party, acknowledged leadership in the black community, such as it was, and a solid reputation as a citizen of the most rigidly Victorian rectitude. In the presence of others, even their own children, he and his wife consistently referred to each other as "Mr. Cayton" and "Mrs. Cayton."

While Seattle grew from a town of forty-two thousand people in 1890 to a metropolis of nearly a quarter of a million by 1910, Cayton felt both the tensions and the strengths of its development. The tensions would have been considerable for any city of such rapid growth and of such markedly industrial character, but when Seattle became the portal to the Klondike, it became internationally notorious as a fleshpot of extraordinary proportions. And even after the gold had come and gone, the city continued to reach out for the kind of loose money that gamblers, prostitutes, and saloonkeepers could pull into a city's economy. When they selected their mayor in 1898 and again in 1900, voters chose Thomas Humes, a man whose sympathies reflected those of the businessmen who prospered when the fleshpots prospered. By 1901, the more lurid districts of Humes's open town fastened upon the city a violence, criminality, drunkenness, and competitive prostitution which projected a counterculture blatantly in defiance of the Victorian rectitude on Capitol Hill.

It was, indeed, to escape this counterculture that middle-class families like the Caytons had moved to Capitol Hill or to the other new residential neighborhoods designed deliberately to exclude the "industrials." This dimension of urban geography was even more apparent when the Seattle Park Board retained J. C. Olmsted (the stepson of the great landscape architect) to plan boulevards and parks for the city, a plan which in its beautiful execution became a major achievement in American urban design. For a time, as in Tacoma, serious people believed that Seattle might become one of the world's gracious cities, for the natural setting, adorned with the bourgeois elegance of the Olmsted plan, suggested that this was surely possible. Yet it was also a class-conscious plan, leaving the "streetcar parks" available to "industrials" while locating the "boulevard parks" where they could be used only by those who could afford the luxury of private transportation. It was a further assurance to the polite people of Capitol Hill that they might isolate themselves from the moral odors of the Skid Road—a section of the city near the waterfront, identified by an old logging term (where the logs had been skidded down a muddy road to their destiny), which had, in fifty years, become almost a moral metaphor.

But the competitive saloons and brothels and gambling dens nurtured a growth of their own that soon threatened every district of the city, and even the most wealthy could not forever escape the corruption and violence which were becoming predictable patterns in municipal life. Though one prominent newspaper editor, Alden Blethen of the *Seattle Times,* defended an "open town" policy which would relegate bawdy houses "to such portions of the town as would not disturb honest people," the editor of the *Post-Intelligencer* came to fear that the city was rapidly being dominated by "all that is low and vile," that it was being humiliated by a "tyranny of the criminal

WASHINGTON

A photographer's essay by Bob Peterson

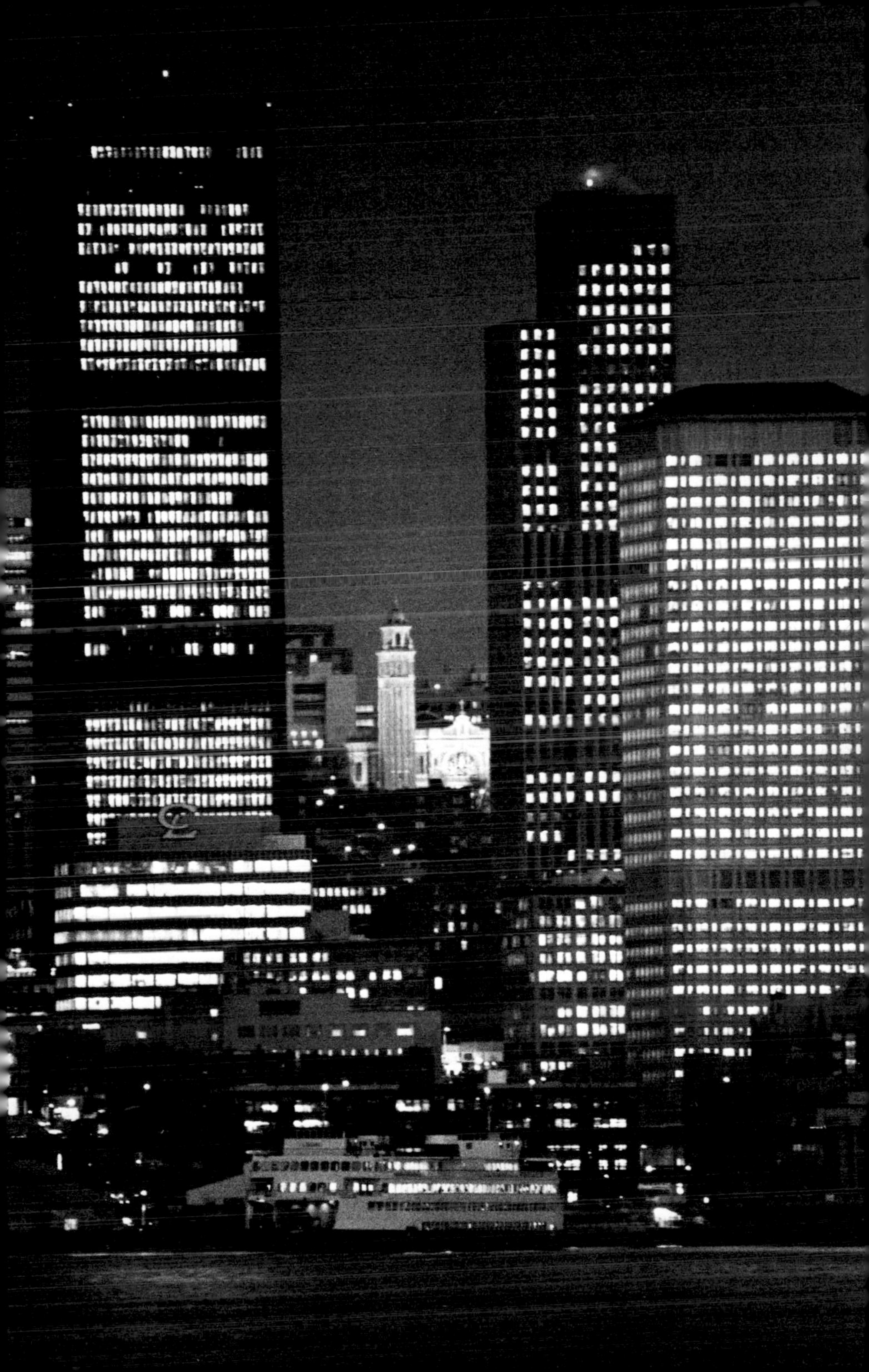

Photographs in Sequence

Freighter on Puget Sound, Mount Olympus in background.
Capitol Hill, Seattle.
Night skyline, Seattle.
Grand Coulee Dam.
Tramway over Spokane Falls.
Yakima Indians at the Yakima River.
Old Skid Road, Seattle.
Storm clouds over salmon fishers off Westport.
Salmon catch, Westport.
Ocean-going salmon boats.
Farming in Eastern Washington.
Wheatfield near Wilbur.
Grand Central Park, Seattle.
Apples in the rain, Wenatchee.
Bird over the San Juan Islands.

classes." [3] What most disturbed such men was the realization that officials not only "tolerated" illicit activities—"gambling and the social evil"—but that under Mayor Humes they positively encouraged them by taking payoffs from those who sought official favor. It was soon clear enough that Humes's chief of police, William L. Meredith, presided over what was really a criminal conspiracy, if not a criminal tyranny.

Cayton was among the most grievously offended, for not only did the Skid Road threaten his middle-class values, it attracted the poor and unemployed blacks—many of them outcasts from the coal mines south and east of Seattle—who in desperation might take whatever jobs the fleshpots could offer. In March of 1901, the *Republican* took note that Chief Meredith proposed "to run quack doctors out of business." This, Cayton suggested editorially, was a good idea which might become an even better one if while running off the quacks, the chief would "likewise run grafting policemen out of business, then perhaps the city of Seattle would be rid of Meredith himself." [4]

The chief, who had never been notably sensitive to civil liberties, ordered his men to arrest Cayton, to jail him, and to hold him until he could produce a cash bail. When on a Saturday night they came to Cayton's Capitol Hill home, one of them rudely threatened to beat him because he was not ready to leave immediately. If Cayton's editorial had not fully revealed his own character, his response to the threat surely did: "Take your muddy feet off my chair and your hat off your head," he said to the policeman, "and act like a gentleman." Cayton was in a cell for six hours before his friends could arrange for his release, and the next day there burst across the city and the state what the *Post-Intelligencer* quite properly called "a storm of indignation."

A fascinating detail of the newsstories which followed the arrest is that only rarely was Cayton referred to as "the colored editor." He was "Mr. Cayton" or "the editor of the *Republican*," then defended vigorously by eminent citizens—bankers,

3. *Seattle Post-Intelligencer*, March 26, 1901.
4. *Seattle Republican*, March 22, 1901.

ministers, businessmen, and editors. Amid the cries of "outrage" and "indecency" and "diabolical action" which were printed in most newspapers in the state, Cayton became a sort of middle-class hero—the champion, said the *Post-Intelligencer,* of the "business and professional men, mechanics and laborers" who were deeply apprehensive that the new society had so soon witnessed the "pollution of free government by persistent commerce with crime." [5]

Thus middle-class citizens who had turned stiffly away from a sordid reality were suddenly determined to attack it, and the first battle seemed to be joined around the case of H. R. Cayton. During the days of formal arraignment, the courtroom was crowded daily with Seattle's community leaders. As the testimony unfolded, newspapers printed almost every word of the bitter exchanges between prosecutors and defense attorneys. To demonstrate for the public record that Cayton's use of the word "grafting" had not been in fact libelous, his lawyers promised to subpoena gamblers, pimps, madames, and saloonkeepers as witnesses. Newspaper reporters looked forward to the most dramatic trial in the history of the city.

But the city experienced an even more lurid drama before the trial could begin. Dejected, humiliated, and finally sullenly irrational, Chief Meredith one day took a shotgun to the streets and sought out Seattle's most prominent gambler, John Considine, with whom he had quarreled about payoffs and protection. In the gunfight that took place in a downtown drugstore, Meredith was himself killed. From that day on, the issue of the "open" or the "closed" town was a significant dimension of municipal political life.

Horace Cayton was, of course, not convicted of any crime, and fame allowed him even more successfully to escape the tinge of embarrassment that lingered from the circumstances of his birth. He stood aloof from the black community of Seattle as it grew to some three thousand in 1910. He encouraged his own children to avoid the common semiliterate and often undisciplined blacks they saw on the streets around them—those still

5. *Seattle Post-Intelligencer,* March 26, 1901.

drifting in from the coal mines, or from the Midwest, or from the South, especially those who took what jobs they could find as menial laborers in the restricted district. The older he became, the more he detested the South and this yield of refugees whose lack of ambition, responsibility, and self-assertiveness (as he saw it) reflected upon him and his children. If they came to the Pacific Northwest, he felt, let them come as he had done, strong enough to win their dignity, courageous enough to demand their rights, intelligent enough to find a proper place in the polite society. Increasingly drawn to the writings of W. E. B. Du Bois, who was then urging blacks to do just what Cayton wanted, he was increasingly offended by the speeches of Booker T. Washington, who was still urging blacks to patience, acceptance, and endurance without protest. When Booker T. Washington came to Seattle to speak at the exposition in 1909, Cayton was his gracious host. Yet before the visit ended, Cayton again felt that he must assert himself, and he sat with the old and famous leader through a long night of sometimes piercing argument. At the end, Washington stood up testily to say, "You speak of the insanity in the South with regard to the Negro. I sincerely hope, Mr. Cayton, that insanity does not overcome you here in the relative freedom of the Northwest." [6]

Cayton seemed thereafter determined to demonstrate that freedom. He became an ardent admirer of Theodore Roosevelt—Cayton's son said that his father dressed like TR, even to the pince-nez and the bushy mustache—and he urged his readers to move away from old-guard Republican politics and toward the Progressive crusade. In this assertion he finally realized that even in Seattle there was a line he should not cross: when a political argument in 1912 exploded in a fist fight, he struck a white man, and he knew the enervating humiliation of hiding with his family in the darkness of the basement in their home.

After this incident, Cayton became, like Du Bois, morosely saddened by the plight of blacks everywhere in American life. His *Republican* printed more and more race-conscious news,

---

6. Horace R. Cayton, *Long Old Road* (Seattle: University of Washington Press, paperback edition, 1963), p. 20.

and circulation among his many subscribers in the white community began to fall away. Then at the worst possible moment—in 1917, when Seattle was seething with hysterical patriotism and when editorial prudence lay in praising the righteousness of the nation—Cayton gave prominence in his columns to a particularly barbaric southern lynching. The impression spread that Cayton had attacked or challenged the nobility of American character, and he was visited by federal agents. The circulation of his newspaper among white people collapsed, and within three months he had to close down the *Republican*.

First the horses had to go, then the carriage, then the servant, and then the fine house on Capitol Hill. He moved his family to an older neighborhood where, among recent Italian immigrants, his children felt their first real pangs of racist discrimination. But even this neighborhood was soon too expensive for them, and Cayton moved back where he had started, to the "Central Area," again among the blacks he detested, working as a janitor while his wife did housework for white families. Neither of them could conceal the bitterness that developed in their fall from middle-class grace, and it was soon a hostility which cut deeply into the cohesion of the family. The children rebelled—against discrimination, against family disintegration, against the humiliation of the family flight from the polite and secure world. Horace, Jr., dropped out of high school and was soon in trouble with the police. To his father's infinite sorrow, he was jailed for armed robbery. But this boy, after wandering as a laborer as far as Alaska, was graduated from the University of Washington and became a prestigious professor of sociology at the University of Chicago. He did not, however, rejoin the family. When he visited his father in the 1920s, there was, indeed, no family to join. He found then in Seattle that few people remembered the senior Horace Roscoe Cayton, or the *Republican*. He found further that only one restaurant would serve blacks. He saw his father as "an old, defeated, and unloved man."

Of the hundreds of stately and even distinguished residences in Spokane, the Hutton home was among the most grand, and

the Reverend Francis Short stood on the broad, carpeted stair-
way where his voice could be heard in the rooms above, and
throughout the main floor, and outside on the lawn where a part
of the crowd stood in reverential silence. It was October 8,
1915, an autumn day, bright and cool, precisely right for this
intimate yet public occasion. The minister had seldom faced a
group of such unusual disparities: a United States senator and
the elite of the city's wealthy classes standing next to labor
leaders, a group of black faces next to lavishly jeweled club
women, investors from the leading banks, miners from the
Coeur d'Alenes. And seldom had he seen such an elaborately
colorful and opulent array of flowers. There was a bank of
orchids from the Hercules Mining Company, a wreath from the
Clemmer Theater, a great spray from the chamber of commerce.
Among hundreds of individual tributes, many from men prominent in the political life of the city and state, there were wreaths
shaped like hearts and harps and broken columns, baskets from
organizations like the Spokane Democratic Club, the Afro-
American Women's Charity Club, the Mining Men's Club, the
Central Labor Council, the East Spokane Grange, and the Old
National Bank. Amid this almost overwhelming mass of floral
splendor, the Reverend Short began.

*Mrs. May Arkwright Hutton was born in the State of Ohio 55
years ago; she was the daughter of Mr. and Mrs. Isaac
Arkwright, folks of heroic mold and kindly manner. In the year
of 1887 she became the wife of L. W. Hutton, whose lot and life
she shared with fidelity until God's Angel of Mercy relieved her
of her physical suffering three days ago. Her spirit has taken its
flight from its earthly tenement. . . .*[7]

The earliest tenement had in fact been the grim and bleak
mining country near Youngstown, Ohio, and her father was
maybe everything but heroic: a sort of impoverished and itiner-
ant fraud, an unordained revivalist, an unlicensed herb doctor, a
generally uninvited guest and irrepressible orator. He took the

---

7. All quotations from the eulogy to May Arkwright Hutton are from Francis
Burgette Short, *In Memoriam: Mrs. May Arkwright Hutton* (Spokane: Smith & Co., Funeral Directors, 1915).

newborn Mary, as the child was first called, to his own aged and blind father because he, Arkwright, had preaching and orating and visiting to do which precluded his rearing his own daughter. He later legally married another woman and raised a family, of which Mary was never a part. We have, indeed, no firm record of Mary's birth, and we know only that she was brought up to be the guide and cook for a blind man whose friends were old and poor coal miners, and that she was ignored and disdained by the families of her grandfather's other children, at least until she revisited her birthplace in 1905. She then had bags of money to leave around if she wanted to, and she did leave them around everywhere with the pointed implication that they represented a relationship between wealth and respectability that she wanted to make very clear in Youngstown.

Her life [said the Rev. Short] *was abundant in the spirit of the real pioneer. . . . Hers was indeed the western spirit that resists difficulties, spurns dishonor. . . . That which she believed, she most fervently believed, and was always willing to pay the price for her belief.*

In an open and then brazen defiance of convention at the age of eighteen she lived with a miner named Frank Day. Then at twenty-two she was with Gilbert Munn, also a miner. Their lives were, for the times, scandalous, for she roomed and boarded others, cooking for them and making their beds, all the while dressing in a style regarded by polite society as outrageously revealing. And her shocking manners were coupled with a quick wit, a lively intelligence, an endless and vividly earthy vein of humor, an unbending sense of independence. She left Frank Day when it pleased her, and she abandoned Munn when he attempted to direct her ways. When in 1883 she heard that gold had been discovered in the Coeur d'Alenes, she determined to leave the grime and dirt of Ohio and seek the open West. She would either become a miner herself or cook for miners—it didn't matter. Going out on the Northern Pacific, she found her way to Jim Wardner's saloon at Eagle City and took over the chow counter, which her cooking soon made famous.

She was then still Mary Arkwright, though later it was

"Mame." In 1885 she had a restaurant and a cow and a stove of her own at what had become Wardner Junction. It was an exciting place to take meals—racy language and fresh-baked bread, roast pig with applesauce and proletarian radicalism, bear steak and blueberry pie with pervasively profane critiques of "the bosses." At about this time D. C. Corbin of Spokane—a partner of James Glover in several ventures—built a railroad into the region which soon became the Coeur d'Alene branch of the Northern Pacific. The first locomotive was driven by Levi Hutton—everyone called him "Al"—a quiet and utterly independent young man who had grown up in an orphanage and who, though sober and disciplined, had few tastes for polite society or its conventions. Ten weeks after he took his first meal with Mame, or May, he had married her in a short and utterly sober ceremony.

Mrs. Hutton was a home-maker . . . kindly supreme, both in theory and practice . . . But even this beautiful home life was not what really made her the most loved woman in this community. What was it? She was another one of God's own good Samaritans who found many a poor soul in a bruised body along the wayside, where it had been left by modern robbers to die.

To May it seemed perfectly clear who the modern robbers were—the absentee owners of the mines, the distant and unresponsive corporations, the anonymous but ruthless bands of financiers who conspired together to break the labor union, which was the only hope the miners had for a decent life. While May's friends labored ten hours a day underground, the boards of directors and their managerial hirelings met in plush offices in Spokane or Chicago or San Francisco, where their exclusive concern was profits—always profits, never health or hope or safety or middle-class decency for wage earners, always profits which could be filched away from the man who blasted and shoveled the ore. In the spring of 1899, when workers were being fired if they could be identified as union members, some of May's friends decided that the only way to make humanitarians out of robbers was with dynamite. As the word spread through the ranks of the Western Federation of Miners, a thousand men with guns boarded Al Hutton's train and directed him to take them to the Bunker Hill and Sullivan mine at Wardner, where they killed a man, burned the offices and the manager's residence, and with their three thousand pounds of explosives demolished almost everything in sight.

When the governor of Idaho declared the northern counties in insurrection, federal troops came in to arrest some seven hundred of the alleged "soldiers of discontent" who had been at "The Battle of Bunker Hill." These "soldiers" included Al Hutton, and while he sat quietly behind barbed wire, May—who had been penning lines of verse for years—wrote a book about it all, which she called *The Coeur d'Alenes, Or A Tale Of The Modern Inquisition In Idaho,* dedicated "TO MY HUS-BAND."[8] It was a historical novel, an extravagantly sentimental plot woven around the remarkable theme that the manager of the mine had himself set off the explosion in a wicked attempt to bring discredit upon the labor union. Leaders of the Western Federation of Miners were delighted, and they sold seven thousand copies of the book even before it had been printed. Meanwhile, Al went free because he claimed that he had been forced to steal the train, and most of the soldiers of discontent came home because no jury could be convened in northern Idaho which would convict them. May was then for a time a literary light on the industrial frontier, a dazzling and unpredictable blend of domesticity, militancy, energy, and intelligence. Before she left Idaho she ran for the legislature and missed by a mere eighty votes. Denied a seat in Boise, she stayed home in their modest house in Wallace, where her house guests were the criminal lawyer Clarence Darrow, the poet Ella Wheeler Wilcox, and the equal suffrage leader Carrie Chapman Catt, and others like them.

I feel like you feel, that her going from us is a sad, sad misfortune to this community. Who is going to take her place in the sweet and helpful ministrations to the needy ones among us? Who is going to feel, as she felt, that those who have wealth are

8. May Arkwright Hutton, *The Coeur d'Alenes: Or A Tale Of The Modern Inquisition In Idaho* (Wallace, Id.: M. A. Hutton, 1900).

under the holy obligation of using it for the purpose of blessing others rather than for the purpose of trying to satisfy themselves . . . ?

It came like a deus ex machina of an extraordinary drama in which one would have anticipated only toil, repression, tedium, and tragedy—the drama of railroads, robber barons, and the murderous determination of plain people to bring some dignity to lives shaped by the realities of underground dust and sweat and explosions. Yet her story shows us that life was not always that grim. The Hercules partnership began in 1896 when a man who knew very little about mining went broke and was desperate to sell his dubious claim. The talk that year around May's table was much about the free coinage of silver, and any mining property which seemed to have a silver promise at all was not to be dismissed lightly. It seemed a not unreasonable risk, when the Huttons took it, to buy a one-sixth share for $500. It was also a happy weekend hobby. With the other partners, the Huttons picked blueberries and sold them to buy tools, dug casually by candlelight when they felt like digging, or picnicked when they didn't. By 1901 they were a good 1,600 feet into the side of the mountain. Then on June 13, 1901, a partner carried out a gunny sack full of the richest ore ever seen in the Coeur d'Alenes—thirty percent of it pure silver. Of the other gunny sacks that came out that year, the Huttons received $750. But then it was soon $500,000, and within three years they had to admit that they were indeed millionaires.

With considerable misgivings, May and Al began to reshape their lives. The money was for spending, so in 1907 they left the mines and moved the short distance west to Spokane. Soon in a lavish apartment in the new Hutton Building, they tried on the various symbolic garments of upper-class affluence: a cook, a house servant, a chauffeur, a limousine. Neither May nor Al was ever comfortable with the servants, but May delighted in every material acquisition—books, paintings, furniture, clothes, chinaware, silver. One year she loaded the limousine with roses, and in her most astonishing hat and dress, drove in the Rose Festival Parade in Portland. But the more steady work of spending was in the Spokane Children's Home, which became

Al's adopted orphanage, and the Crittenton Home for Unwed Mothers, which May adopted and where she spent much of her time talking with the girls and corresponding with lonely ranchers in her efforts to identify steady and sober men for her girls to marry. Then there were the great food baskets for the poor, Thanksgiving feasts and Christmas gifts, and the Democratic party, and the Women's Club, and the Calvary Baptist Church, whose grateful members—all of them black—thoughtfully elected the white Al Hutton to full fellowship.

In 1908 May wrote to a friend to say that "You should see my Al. He is a banker now. Last night they organized the Scandinavian American Bank of Spokane. . . . When I told him to hurry up and make the toast this morning, he said I am a banker now and bankers do not make toast, but give them. Well I informed him that we would not have any airs. . . ." And, usually, there were no fancy airs. When they later moved to the large and even ostentatious house where they would live until May's death, the cook and the manservant regularly served to a table for three—May, Al, and the chauffeur.

It was during these years that simply being rich was never enough for May's energies, and we should try to get a glimpse of the woman as others then saw her. Benjamin H. Kizer, the Spokane lawyer, remembered her as a short woman, weighing more than three hundred pounds, a woman of impetuous and often explosive enthusiasm. In any audience, Kizer wrote, she always sat alone and was always obvious—in "her corpulence, her strongly marked, rugged features, and her outrageous taste in clothing. . . ." Yet, curiously, she never hesitated to address a new face. "Mrs. Hutton," said Kizer, "never knew a stranger. . . ." She shaped a role for herself as a friend of plain people, and she played it with confidence. Her conversation was "racy . . . full of impulsiveness, impudence, and ingenuity" in which most people took pleasure. It seemed quite natural that in her new home state she should become a willful rebel, eagerly available for social criticism.[9]

9. Benjamin H. Kizer, "May Arkwright Hutton," *Pacific Northwest Quarterly* 57 (April 1966): 49–56.

Should women work outside the home, or should they be homemakers? Let them be homemakers—if that is, in fact, what they want to be—but homemaking is work which deserves a decent wage. Should the state ban the saloons? She didn't care, but she would not herself rent any of her property to be used for a saloon. What about prostitution? It was an ugly commerce, a hell of a way to make a living—but if the girls must register with the police, then damn it, let their customers also register. Prison reform? We must learn the techniques of rehabilitation. Should municipal governments own public utilities? You're damed right they should. What about the direct primary, the initiative, the referendum? The country has been damned near ruined by special interests that have corrupted democratic principles; the country needs *more* democracy, and this means that we should indeed have the direct primary, initiative, and referendum. And it would have a more *sensible* democracy if the men of this state would abandon their damned, petty, idiotic prejudices against women. Should women then be allowed to vote, hold office, and sit on juries? There was no adequate response of one syllable here, for this was the sacred cause.

Mrs. Hutton's life filled a most conspicuous place both far and near. She could oppose without malice. She could argue without bitterness. She could take defeat without humiliation. . . .

She had voted, of course, in Idaho, and she had lobbied in Boise in the 1890s with Abigail Scott Duniway to help win for women. She was determined to do the same in Olympia. A woman suffrage amendment to the state constitution would require first the approval of the legislature, and then of the people, and May regarded this as an irresistible challenge. When she joined the statewide movement to win the amendment, she became the vice-president of the Washington Equal Suffrage Association so quickly and so aggressively that the more conservative leaders of the organization were openly distressed. These women—Emma Smith DeVoe and Cora Smith Eaton—were less than charmed by May's flamboyance, less than pleased by her ambitions, and they restrained her as firmly as they could without drawing public attention to their concerns. May, on her part, soon came to see them as the class-conscious and quaintly sophisticated wives of professional and business men in Seattle, penny-pinching and snobbish, who wanted only her money, and in a pique she determined to blaze her own way by organizing the Spokane Equal Suffrage Association. In 1909 she led her own personal lobby to Olympia.

Because she had very little experience in these matters and was not particularly eager to learn from Mrs. DeVoe or Dr. Eaton, May Hutton's work there was probably less effective than the fact that she was in the city and that no one could ignore her. She chose to talk more with the wives of the legislators than with the legislative committees, which she left to the skill of the Seattle leaders. But on one occasion, she wrote, she did enjoy assembling the jewels and the clothing to equip "our most charming member" for "the conquest" of one notably resistant committee chairman. This letter suggests nothing more, really, than that wholesome charm might "conquer" political persuasion, but DeVoe and Eaton feared far wider insinuations. They did, nevertheless, contain their disgust, and in the interest of victory worked stiffly with the Hutton forces. Together, the two groups easily won the legislative votes to move the amendment before the electorate on the ballot of 1910.

Emma DeVoe and Cora Eaton then planned a quiet and sedate campaign, one which would stress the intelligence and dignity of women, and they were again painfully perturbed when May Hutton went out to speak to labor union meetings, where her Idaho stories and earthy humor were always good for laughs as well as votes, and to parade around the state in open automobiles with kites and banners reading "VOTES FOR WOMEN." While May was in her glory, Eaton and DeVoe apparently became convinced that during her Idaho years May had been either a prostitute or a madame, maybe both, and their alarm about the implications of this to the movement was so great that they marshaled all of their power among Puget Sound members to drive May Hutton out of the Washington Equal Suffrage Association. May received a curt note from Dr. Eaton informing her that she was no longer eligible for membership "because of your habitual use of profane and obscene language and of your record in Idaho as shown by pictures and other evidence placed in my hands by persons who are familiar with your former life and reputation." We may wish that the Washington State Library, which has a copy of this note, had also the pictures, but it does not, and we do not know what May said to Al about the substance of this coercion. She considered a legal battle, but then reconsidered, she said, because she didn't want to divert attention from the suffrage issue or entertain the state with a sorry show of bickering women. She simply organized the Washington Political Equality League, directing its campaign from Spokane. It was an easy victory in 1910, and May was thereafter linked wherever she went with the cause of liberating women.

No, Mrs. Hutton is not dead. Like her Lord, she went about doing good, and like him, she cannot die. There is no death for those who live to serve. . . .

In 1912 she went as a delegate to the Democratic National Convention, hoping for William Jennings Bryan but willing to accept Woodrow Wilson, amusing news reporters by calling herself "fat" and "rich" and appearing in "astonishing" attire. Wherever she saw a dining room posted "For Men Only," she would, like some primary force, break through the doors. But she was then both very heavy and heavily tired, becoming in her fifties more coarse, more abrupt, more maudlin, more strident. She wrote poems and songs for world peace, "for the sorrow of Mothers who have born sons for the slaughter." But Bright's disease and a failing heart were taking a relentless toll, reducing her to a frail 147 pounds, a weak and whispering matron of reform and charity.

The Lord gave, and the Lord hath taken away. . . . One Spirit less on Earth. One Spirit more in Heaven . . . earth to earth, ashes to ashes, dust to dust. . . .

Al mourned quietly, lived plainly, and kept his own counsel. With unyielding determination he spent his money on the orphanage they had called the Hutton Settlement—two million dollars from their savings, another million left in trust, every penny that the government and May's relatives could not get away from him. "In my shroud," he said, "there will be no pockets."

The remarkably easy victory for woman suffrage in the state was an event, which, according to leaders of the national movement, "astounded the nation" and inspired the burst of action in other states which in a decade led directly to the revision of the federal Constitution. It was, of course, the votes of men in Washington which made this victory possible, and none took more satisfaction in it than George Cotterill, who had not only campaigned for years in the movement but had actually written the state amendment.

In Montclair, New Jersey, he was graduated from high school first in his class. He hoped to study law, for he knew even then that he might become a brilliant public speaker. But his father was a gardener, and there were eight children in the family— they had migrated from Oxford, England, when George was seven years old, in 1872—and going to college was out of the question. He went instead to Tacoma, walking away from the railroad station with twenty-five cents in his pockets and the names of a few family friends. To keep himself fed and sheltered while he explored his new opportunities, he worked as a bookkeeper and even as a house servant, and he soon found his open door—a job as a transit man on a survey crew with the Northern Pacific, which gave him the rigorous physical life he wanted as well as the chance to learn civil engineering outside the formal classroom. His short body filled out with broad and stout muscles, and he learned very quickly. His knowledge of topography was soon so keen that he could do surveying and engineering for the coal mines, then for R. H. Thomson, who made Cotterill his assistant when he became Seattle's city engineer in 1892.

Cotterill had by then married Cora Gormley, recently from Wisconsin, and they had settled comfortably in the city where they would live out their lives and raise their two adopted children. They would, indeed, become a family of great depth, for Cotterill brought both his mother and his father to live with them, and Cora had many close relatives, and the large house was usually alive with endless talk and congested with brothers and sisters, aunts and uncles, nieces and nephews, friends and neighbors. Because the Cotterills believed that the community itself was also a home which should respond to their aspirations, the talk was mostly about state and city politics, reform and woman suffrage, organizations and meetings and morality, and Cotterill was active as a Mason, a Shriner, a Good Templar, a member of the chamber of commerce, the Pacific Northwest Society of Engineers, and the Methodist church. He was, all the while, proving to be an unusually competent engineer, and Thomson gave him major responsibilities in the design and construction of the city water system, the sewer system, the ship canal, the commercial waterfront, and the bicycle paths which later became the city's boulevards and which saved a splendid portion of the lakefront from commercial development. He also laid out the Laurelhurst and Mount Baker districts, portions of the city which, from his inventive drawingboard, became neighborhoods where the streets could meander permissibly around the natural contours of the hillsides and lakefront, escaping the conventional grid patterns and attaining a measure of real character and distinction.

He and Thomson were then engineering the transition of Seattle from a muddy village into an urban permanence, tunneling for the railroads, channeling for the ships, even regrading the hills for modern commercial traffic, opening the city to the north and south and east. It was the work they most wanted to do, and it brought them rich emotional satisfactions. Their goal, however, included much more than meandering streets and topographical revisions, and during this happy period George Cotterill came more and more to represent people who wanted a creative integration of urban opportunities and necessities with the best of rural simplicities—efficient systems for water and sanitation; good schools and adequate transportation, available as a public service, not as a private exploitation; pleasant homes on safe streets in neighborhoods with parks and paths and churches, and interesting, changing vistas. They wanted, moreover, lives secure in a freedom from the moral pollution they could remember from older, less self-conscious cities.

For a while the vision was glorious because it was possible, perhaps even inevitable. Before automobiles began to reshape urban geography, most sections of the city were relatively classless neighborhoods of wage earners, capitalists, and professionals, and there were—apart from the Skid Road environment—few real slums. There were indeed saloons and saloon-centered areas, but most of them did not take the turn toward a sordid competition in prostitution, gambling, and narcotics until the turn of the century. From that time on, however, George Cotterill would learn that his social vision would have to be won again and again, and then aggressively protected against those who were in the city to exploit the urban environment—especially the private utility monopolies and the brewers and distillers whom Cotterill came to see as the enemy, "the interests." Cotterill came easily to the conviction that those who wanted healthy and beautiful cities must cheerfully leave their drawingboards to crusade against graft and corruption. When in the late 1890s he had to defend his plan for a municipally owned water system, he moved easily into the focus of public attention. He was soon appearing regularly as a dramatic and persuasive campaigner for woman's suffrage, for the public ownership of natural monopolies, and for laws to restrict the encroachment of prostitution and saloons. Like so many others, he was inspired by William Jennings Bryan—with whom he later corresponded—to develop his considerable talents for public rhetoric, and he remained Bryanesque throughout his career—forceful, lyrical, romantic, muscular, and usually almost interminable. Moreover, he was, according to a friend, a man endowed with a gifted memory, with "a goodly allowance of wholesome British stubbornness," and with "excessive self-assurance." [10] He was, then, superbly equipped for public service.

10. Austin E. Griffiths, "Great Faith: Autobiography of an English Immigrant Boy in America, 1863–1950" (typed mss., University of Washington Library), p. 209.

After 1900, Cotterill's private practice in civil engineering, with his speciality of municipal landscaping, was bringing him handsome commissions in Portland, Calgary, and Edmonton, among other cities, and these commissions kept him pleasantly affluent, increasingly free to articulate an ideal of "public service without compensation"—a service which should be in the cause of "moral and civic progress." He came to speak out repeatedly, even to personify the anxieties of those who—like the editor Horace Cayton—felt that the urban environment was the best hope they would ever have in the twentieth century for the good life. As defender of "the people" against "the interests," he moved casually through several political identities and found himself equally at ease among Populists, Democrats, Socialists, Silver Republicans, the Workingmen's League, the Commercial Club, the Non-Partisan League, for he never doubted that all decent people wanted essentially the same securities. Thus when he attacked the Stone and Webster Corporation of Boston, which wanted to add Seattle to its inventory of private utility monopolies, or when he attacked the "open town" of prostitution and gambling, which was the unseemly legacy of the Klondike Gold Rush, it seemed clear to him that in matters of municipal reform the Socialists, Democrats, Populists, Republicans—anyone who had a home and a family—all had a vital interest.

Like so many American reformers, George Cotterill soon learned that cities often lacked the powers to do what decent people wanted, and that to reform a city they must first reform a state. Thus he was in the state senate as a Democrat representing north Seattle, a leader of the "insurgent" legislators—Democrat and Republican—who were determined after 1906 to strip away the political power bases from the "Old Guard." These insurgents were vocal and ambitious men who, like citizens everywhere in the state, were reacting to the feeling that their new society was tilting crazily toward corruption and that only vigorous and outspoken action could right it. Farmers and businessmen, for example, were finding their hopes consistently frustrated by a fact that a railroad monopoly could strip them of the margin of profits they had hoped would be the financial basis of their new lives. And they found that the monopoly could defy regulation through its iron control of the state's political life. Political conventions were openly dominated by the railroads, and these conventions then presented voters with only railroad candidates, who then organized a railroad legislature to block political reform. Thus in 1901 powerfully conservative forces had combined under railroad direction to block the regulation of rail rates, to stop a proposed system of direct primary elections, and—in what was called the "Ankeny Arrangement"—to present the wealthy Walla Walla banker Levi P. Ankeny with a seat in the United States Senate. (This "arrangement," according to the most credible sources, cost Ankeny $49,000.) To attack such villainy—to regrade, as it were, the bases of political power that stood in the way of "moral and civic progress"—the reformers needed new machines, and it was then that Cotterill became one of the superintendents, or walking-bosses, of reform, advising, instructing, directing his colleagues in the use of the tools of the system he had seen so effectively demonstrated in Oregon.

These tools included direct primary elections to take nominations away from corrupted political party conventions, and recall elections to dump corrupted officials—changes in state law which Cotterill helped reformers achieve during the session of 1907. Then there was the woman suffrage amendment, which Cotterill wrote and eased through the legislature in 1909 for Mrs. DeVoe and Mrs. Hutton. In his mind all along, however, the major tool was one which would allow reformers to sweep around the institutional sources of corruption—the legislative communities, rules, party loyalties, lobbying, special interest pressures—to flank the system of representative democracy itself and place significant matters directly before the people. What he wanted was the signal achievement in the Oregon System, the sort of moral slide rule upon which one could align the standards of social decency with the dynamics of pure democracy—the new machinery of initiative and referendum. The experience of his generation make it obvious, he felt, that "the best remedy for the evils of democracy is more democracy, purer democracy." To achieve "true government by the people," he said, the state constitution must "give to the people the power of direct legislation."

That this "true government" might be called "romantic democracy" by those who distrusted its theory would not have alarmed George Cotterill, for he was much less the intellectual than the activist, much less the critical reader of philosophy or history than the speaker for all occasions. He was, however, fully aware that the theory would have appalled most of the philosophers who wrote the American Constitution. Among the hundreds of friends—like William S. U'Ren, the "father of the Oregon System"—who might have shaped Cotterill's thinking, the most influential was probably J. Allen Smith, the slow-moving but popular professor of political science at the University of Washington. Smith had what his colleagues saw as a "sad and ironic" face, and a reputation for radicalism, and when hired by the Populist regents in 1897, he had brought to Seattle a heavily self-imposed duty to stir his students to a social conscience. He spoke with great earnestness in his course called "The Trust Problem," and he was a thorny critic of privately owned utility corporations. He was also inclined to view anything he disliked as a vile conspiracy against sacred freedoms, and his analysis of American progress and poverty (*The Spirit of American Government*, published in 1907) seemed to expose the national constitution as a design to frustrate reform and true democracy. Professor Smith had in a sense preached in favor of a new American Revolution—one to occur through the ballot box and to appear as "Initiative and Referendum" and make possible the kind of people's government which the eighteenth-century constitution had circumvented.

Smith's work with Cotterill was especially close because of a young political activist and journalist who admired them both and whose name need not confuse the relationship—Joseph E. Smith. After being graduated from the Washington Agricultural College (later named the State College of Washington) in 1896, Joe Smith had also followed William Jennings Bryan toward the politics of the people. Indeed, he committed the "Cross of Gold" speech to memory, and he entered immediately into the reform activities and anti-vice crusades of several newspapers.

In 1897, when a vividly muckraking story about a county judge had brought him contempt-of-court charges, Joe Smith had escaped arrest by joining the National Guard, then bound for the Spanish-American War. He sent vivid dispatches to Seattle newspapers from the battlefields of the Philippines, where he was wounded, and he returned to the state in 1899 as a skilled writer who was also a public hero. He was then an admirer of Theodore Roosevelt, and when the "Trust Buster" began his attacks upon "the malefactors of great wealth," Joe Smith was already the state's foremost political muckraker and "progressive."

As he raked through Seattle and Spokane, he found the deepest evidence of wrongdoing around the manipulation of city franchises for water, electricity, and streetcar service. He was happy then to join Cotterill and J. Allen Smith in the reform movement which seemed to them the most immediately urgent—the municipal ownership of utility monopolies. Joe Smith's correspondence from this period is a warm and delightful record of the pleasure which reformers could feel when they brought intelligence and energy to the emotions of a crusade and were sometimes amazed by their quick achievements. The letters reveal Smith and Cotterill organizing the Direct Legislation Committee—Smith as a volunteer executive-secretary, managing the petitions, pamphlets, and mailings, Cotterill speaking often and eagerly—the purpose of which was to amend the city charter to allow initiatives, the first of which, they hoped, would advance the cause of municipal ownership. The purity of their motives inspired a minister, the Reverend J. M. Wilson, to preach a sermon on "The Moral Value of Municipal Ownership of Street Railways," which he saw as the Christian way to avoid graft and corruption. After the victory, Joe Smith's final report to the committee notes the collection and expenditure of exactly $42.25. They had brought initiative and referendum to the city in a triumphant example of "public service without compensation," one which led directly to Seattle's street railway system.

As a journalist, Joe Smith was intrigued by the work of the insurgents in Olympia. He, Cotterill, and the professor then gave much of their time to amending the state constitution so that the people might legislate directly with the initiative and the referendum. They organized the Direct Legislation League of Washington, which came together easily with the support of the State Grange, the State Federation of Labor, dozens of civic organizations, and thousands of individuals, including Republicans, Democrats, and Socialists. Cotterill was so impressed with the beauty of nonpartisan reform that he came to believe all right-minded people would soon fuse into a single reform league to fight monopoly and vice he was perhaps the last serious politician to dream that sectional, religious, and class fragmentations might so easily and so neatly be welded. Some years later he even worked up an initiative measure which would have abolished partisan labels from all state elections, but it ran to thirteen thousand words and never gained much support because it presented the appearance more of a sermon than of a law a confusion that was a common Cotterill weakness.

The state campaign for direct legislation moved smoothly on the proposition that in initiative and referendum there was something for everyone who had ever resented the intransigence or the deviousness of a lawmaker. Some saw direct legislation as the route toward municipal honesty and efficiency; some saw it as a necessary restraint on the growing political power of urban politicians; others saw it as the device which could abolish the saloons and prostitution, protect labor in industry, win the eight-hour day. And, surely, some saw it as an ultimate service to the people which would abolish the legislature entirely. Joe Smith's goal was to range over the state getting legislative candidates to pledge themselves for initiative and referendum, then to give broad publicity to the league's endorsements in both the primary and the general elections. These endorsements were effective in bringing more insurgents to Olympia, and direct legislation passed into the constitution without difficulty in 1912. As reformers cheered that democracy had finally come to the state, Joe Smith and the *Star* led a successful recall against Seattle's Hiram Gill and his vice-and-monopoly-ridden administration. And in 1912, Smith was pleased to help George Cotterill win election as the new mayor.

George Cotterill's adventures as a moral reformer at the vortex of urban evils—his term as mayor, 1912–1914—is so delightfully told in Murray Morgan's *Skid Road* that it should be read in that book, not this one. It is sufficient here to indicate what was predictable: that he spoke vigorously and at length (and thus made himself something of a municipal bore); that he advanced the cause of municipal ownership (and thus made himself the defender of Seattle City Light, the municipal electric power system which was soon a model for the nation); that he revoked saloon licenses whenever he had an excuse (and thus as the state's leading prohibitionist prepared the city to vote dry); that he tried to close down the *Seattle Times* when its editorials stimulated violence against labor union radicals (and thus made himself appear to be a tyrant); that he ordered city policemen, whether they liked it or not, to begin an intense campaign against prostitution (and thus made himself appear ridiculous).

Most of his friends would not have thought his insensitivity to civil liberties was in any way remarkable. George Cotterill represented the hundreds of thousands of people who felt real distress about the individual freedoms which frontier morality had so casually sanctioned, the people who were raising their moral vision beyond the period of frontier industrialization. In the turmoil of change, social priorities were those of the search for order, and what he and they wanted was indeed to impose restrictions upon the individual's freedom to exploit, debauch, and corrupt. The steps toward the good life were political steps, for there were ideals of public and private morality to be validated, principles of public and private ownership to be determined, issues of industrial health and safety to be resolved, environmental considerations to be weighed and measured. The good life demanded that politics be purified, that the exploited be protected, that wickedness be confronted.

4

Ordeals of Transition

*T*HE good life had, of course, many more dimensions than we have been able to see from our focus upon Glover, Ferguson, Evans, Cayton, and Cotterill. For example, the life of Wesley Jones could reveal to us much about business and farming and politics—he was the lawyer and congressman from Yakima who got federal money for irrigation projects, who protected Seattle's grip on Alaskan commerce, and who became the first United States senator in the state to be elected by a direct vote of the people. The career of Judge Thomas Burke, Jim Hill's man in Seattle and in several other cities, could show us the intricate steps through which Hill actually built his empire. We could study John Gellatly, who came to Wenatchee in 1900, who did well in apples and real estate, and who became mayor of that city because he felt there could be no good life so long as Wenatchee families were threatened by the sordid conditions of Wenatchee saloons. And Ernest Marsh of Everett for a while hoped that the new industrial order was not incompatible with middle-class securities. As leader of the Shingle Weavers' Union he urged wage earners and their families to find an escape from the boom-or-bust cycles of the lumber and shingle mills in a creative combination of farming and seasonal employment.

An ideal of the good life could also inspire a burning utopian vision. In 1897, Ed Pelton helped a group of socialist pilgrims found Equality Colony in the Skagit Valley, where on rich farmland and wooded hillsides they hoped for economic and social and political democracy so pure and so dramatic that a working model of a socialist state would emerge from the new state of Washington. And we could consider the triumphs and the troubles of Jay Fox, the Chicago anarchist who in 1910 crossed the water from Tacoma to dock at the colony known simply as "Home." He edited the *Agitator,* the anarchist newspaper there, and he early became entangled in a dispute about nude bathing in Joe's Bay, a sometimes bitter conflict between the factions he called "the nudes and the prudes." His editorials were inclined to favor the nudes and to show a sarcastic disrespect for a local justice court which favored the prudes, and for a few months in 1912 Jay Fox, a willing and amicable martyr in the cause of intellectual freedom, sat in the Pierce County Jail.

These and a hundred more examples can illuminate a series of hopes and desires, a history, as it were, of aspirations and ideals. Of all histories, this is perhaps the most mercurial, but it does raise again for us the ultimate bicentennial question. In shaping their good life, were these people actually advancing the rights of life, liberty, and the pursuit of happiness? At this point our answer must be that indeed they were—that in bringing stability to a disorderly society they were unusually sensitive to the expectations of opportunity and of equality which distinguish the most noble democratic traditions and which would have pleased Thomas Jefferson.

Their achievements, however, were often fragile and tentative. In 1910, across an idle afternoon in the small town of Prosser, an early homesteader named William Guernsey recounted his memories of "the good old days" when he, his friends, and his neighbors in the farm country "seemed as one family, sharing our joys and sorrows." But what, his young friends wanted to know, had happened to the good times? It was, he said, "a difficult thing to explain," but the big change, he believed, occurred "when money became the yardstick for measuring men and women." [1] This nostalgia—and this disap-

1. Pearl M. Mahoney, *Prosser, The Home Town* (Prosser, Wash.; 1950), p. 56.

pointment—was something more than a feeling which old men warmed and embellished: it signaled an uneasy transition from confidence to distrust, from enthusiasm to anxiety. For what was in fact ending was the brief period opened by the railroads when growth, development, and progress seemed to be healthy, natural, benevolent, and probably divinely guided. By 1910, the limits of such an easy optimism were almost distressingly apparent in the pace and the process by which frontier industrialization was destroying the natural environment, stripping away the very resources upon which such growth and development and progress depended. The timber cuts across the hills and the mountains, everyone knew, had already left their grotesque scars—enormous stumps and roots, many of them weighing several tons, most of them twisted with vines and debris over hundreds of square miles of debauched and abandoned wasteland that was quite beyond the abilities of individuals or of local governments to reclaim. The plowing of grasslands, which always promised a splendid yield of wheat, nevertheless removed the rich grasses which had for centuries held together the magnificent topsoil. On parts of the Columbia Plateau where the annual rainfall was inadequate for sustained dryfarming, the soil blew with the winds, and this land too became wasted. Along the Columbia, huge fish wheels could scoop fifty thousand salmon a day from the river. On Puget Sound, a single set of purse seines could net a thousand fish, and there were in the state still six hundred licensed fish traps. The depletion of fishery resources was as conspicuous as it was unremedied.

These maladies had broad public implications. In squandering natural wealth, the new industrial system was in many instances distorting the traditional patterns for funding social obligations assumed by most civilized communities, and even by 1912 the vital question of how the people would direct their government to dispose of its resources had not been clearly analyzed or answered. These resources, granted in 1889 by a generous Congress along with statehood, were indeed considerable: 2.5 million acres of land reserved for public schools; 100,000 acres for teacher training in normal schools; another 100,000 acres for public buildings and a state capitol; a full seventy-two square miles for a state university; and 200,000 acres for prisons, reformatories, and welfare institutions. Such an endowment could be managed or dissipated as the state constitution and the state legislatures might provide.

With the comforting assumption that this wealth was their share of the American heritage, the first state lawmakers provided that the lands could be sold within a period of twenty years and at a minimum price of ten dollars an acre—an income, they supposed, which might pay almost all the state's expenses and allow them an almost Jeffersonian freedom from taxation. Their assumptions also had encouraged them to shape a tax structure based on real and personal properties, and this meant, of course, that necessary state revenues which might not be forthcoming from the sale of state lands would have to come from levies against a man's acreage, house, tools, or animals. But such extraction—given their expectations of the demands for state lands—would, they had further assumed, never be really painful for citizens in a growing state. Moreover, there seemed to be no reasonable alternative, for they thought it very important that personal and corporate incomes be exempt from taxation so that such capital could flow freely toward the "development" of the state's total resources, a process from which all citizens would surely take advantage.

Their plan, by constitution and by law, emerged then as an attractive scheme for progress. It was soon clear, however, that the commissioner of public lands, an elected official, was usually more than eager to demonstrate how effectively he could hold down the level of personal taxation by his vigorous disposal of the landed inheritance. In 1908, for example, only a loud public outcry by the *Spokane Spokesman-Review* prevented the sale at ten dollars an acre of land in the Okanogan valley belonging to the State College of Washington—land easily worth more than three times that price. And there was soon impressive evidence that the commissioner had allowed casual herds of opportunists—like the "dummy entrymen" of homestead corruptions—to enter claims, obtain underevaluated state lands, then sell the titles to large timber corporations. Yet for years the state legislature made no specified tax millage levies for higher education, or highways, or capitol buildings, or reclamation, and in 1915 Governor Lister vetoed an appropriation for the completion of the state Temple of Justice on the capitol grounds because, he wrote, the state could not afford the expense.

Furthermore, the period of rapid development had fastened upon most people of the region some typically American but inordinately optimistic assumptions about industrialism and the inevitability of growth—assumptions which were locked into the almost sacred slogans of the chamber-of-commerce society and almost impossible to revise or abandon. The conviction seemed everywhere that the measure of social health was growth and growth alone—rather than, say, stability, or harmony, or a quality of life expressed in some other, perhaps nonmaterial achievements. After the recovery in 1897, most people cheerfully dismissed whatever misgivings there were lingering from the panic and depression. There seemed to be every reason for faith in a glorious future, and after the bonanza Klondike traffic and commerce there seemed to be reason again to suppose that development and progress would surely go on forever. From about a half million people in 1900, the population rose to over a million in 1910. After 1912, however, such rapid growth would not again open opportunities for that generation. Railroad construction halted, and clearly the era of colonization had ended. The census of 1920 showed an increase of another eighteen percent, but this was largely urban growth after 1916 stimulated by the Great War. During the following decade the growth rate was about fifteen percent, which was largely a natural and internal growth, not the immigration that had formerly given the state its vigor and excitement.

The realization that growth—and all that it gloriously implied—had practically ceased would not come easily to a culture rooted in a strident boosterism. This was particularly so east of the mountains, where areas which could sustain wheat were fairly well identified and where the good land was, quite simply, already taken. Some land on the margin of semiaridity had been claimed or purchased but never cultivated; some cultivated lands had been abandoned. By 1912, people in dozens of towns were brimming with confidence in anticipation of a growth they would never see. To the confusion and bitterness of their founding fathers, some small towns then became skeleton villages, and even established cities knew a loss of pride and energy. Walla Walla, a city of twenty thousand in 1910, had its supply outlets and storage facilities, its manufacturing of farm machinery and flour, a symphony orchestra, a fine college, tree-lined streets, and an enviable maturity—but it lost twenty percent of its population in the next decade. Spokane, which had grown so spectacularly to more than one hundred thousand by 1912, gained only thirty-five people between that year and 1920.

In the state's highly specialized economy west of the mountains, there was by 1912 a pervasive unrest which indicated a sickness not always obvious to those who suffered from it. The timber-products industry employed two-thirds of the wage earners of the entire state, yet except for a few small manufacturers in finished items like residential porch posts or staircasings—for local use, mostly—the industry after twenty restless years was still the raw lumber industry of very little healthy diversity. In fact, because it added so little value to the timber which rolled so profusely from the forests, the industry of logging and milling lumber could hardly be regarded as manufacturing at all. The refinement of raw lumber, and the value added to it, occurred usually in Chicago, St. Paul, or New York, and the state's timber economy was thus an export economy, which—unless American cities were to burn with some regularity—had no reliable future.

The terrible fires of San Francisco had been the great bonanza, luring hundreds of marginal operators into the industry after 1906, but inevitably the market slowed, the smaller mills cut prices, the larger mills dismissed their crews, and the commerce for a while collapsed. Lumber was stockpiling everywhere, and it was alarmingly apparent then that twentieth-century American builders were turning away from timber products and constructing more and more with steel, glass, and composition roofing, and that the Northwest mills had covered storage lots with more lumber and shingles than the country could absorb. It was an ironic fact that within a decade after the opening of the Pacific Northwest, the productive capacity of its primary industry was far in excess of the nation's or even the world's demands for its products.

The most common experience of businessmen in the lumber industry was ruinous competition, then failure, not success. Such experience can begin to illuminate the social attitudes of at least some of the major timber industrialists, who, when the railroads made it possible for them to invest in the region, had come quite deliberately to capitalize, extract, export, count their money, then get out. Their intentions were often to keep profits at an absolute maximum, regardless of the social consequences, to build their grand houses on the hills, send their children to private schools, bank a few more million, then retire to Santa Barbara or La Jolla. They were, accordingly, men who were often ruthless in their efforts to suppress organized labor, or reduce taxes, or to prevent social issues from erupting in any way that might cost them money.

Given this set of mind, it is easy to understand why many timber industrialists came to feel after 1907 that they were being threatened from every quarter. State legislators and tax assessors were sometimes unyielding in their beliefs that to tax uncut trees was good for "development"—that it would prod industrialists into cutting and milling and expanding employment. Timberland owners suffered tax increases of as much as three hundred percent in some counties between 1907 and 1910, and as the cost of holding timber rose, so did the cost of credit and fire protection, while the market price of lumber and shingles did not. Businessmen in timber were encouraged to cut and run as quickly as they could. And curiously, in contrast to almost all other American manufacturing, the productivity of the individual worker in the timber industry did not rise at all. In fact it fell, and this leaves us a stark vision of capitalists eager to ensure their own safe retirement with low maintenance budgets and unchecked disrepair of dangerously dated and unreliable machinery operated by sullen men.

And we can see now that the lumber industrialists—outside the Weyerhaeuser compound, at least—were often neither creative nor even very perceptive in their practices. In a falling market, they did little to advertise their products or to make them in any way more attractive. They spent little money to diversify, even less on research to find new uses for their raw materials. Nor did they cultivate public sympathy or do anything to counter the popular notion that the "timber baron" was a sort of prehistoric individualist given to spasms of unbridled greed and thoughtless exploitation. Their logging practices were then called "cut-and-run," which meant that they reduced virgin forests to acreages of dismal stumps, then abandoned the logged-off land rather than pay the county taxes. And because they so feared a rise of log prices, they stubbornly resisted the conservation movement which Theodore Roosevelt had adopted and raised to the level of a public crusade.

In a bad year like 1914, the cost of milling exceeded the market value of lumber. Smaller operators disappeared. Of the 1,143 mills operating in the state in 1909, only 389 remained in 1915. And as lumber and shingle prices fell, so of course did employment and wages, and a mood of genuine despair settled again across the region. This changed quickly as war brought its crazy prosperity, but when the war markets were gone, the mood returned as suddenly as it had lifted. This may, in the long run, be seen as economic "stabilization," but to the people who suffered with it through the shorter run of decades, it was the dizzy rhythm of social dislocation.

Around 1912 a new and disturbing sense of animosity and suspicion frequently rose up from the grange halls, the labor temples, and the offices of the state legislature. A Palouse farmer might feel strongly that he wanted nothing to do with the disorder of Spokane or Seattle. The loggers of the Olympics and the millhands of Everett might feel something in common with other wage earners, but they might suppose that farmers in the wheat country could never understand their dreams or common destinies. And we can see now that from the very beginning— because the Cascade Mountains had been a natural and nearly absolute barrier between two quite different societies—the territory and then the state had lacked much sense of integration.

For years all the interior traffic went up and down the Columbia, making Portland far more important in the daily lives of farmers and merchants served by the river than the cities of Olympia or Seattle. And when the railroads did finally open the passes to cross-state traffic, the inland towns and counties—their chambers of commerce, their fraternal and economic organizations, their legislative delegations—sometimes fought obstinately with the western cities for legal or financial favor or legislative advantage. Many farmers in the interior had opposed even the state constitution, so strongly did they feel that the almost foreign and surely alien lawyers and businessmen of Puget Sound were thrusting a tidewater statehood upon them. Their fears, many felt, were justified within a decade as more and more people moved toward the lumber mills and the polyglot, industrial and often corrupt life of the urban environment In 1909, the Spokane Chamber of Commerce, in an expression of serious hostility supported by many eastern areas, formally proposed the creation of a new state, to be called Whitman, whose western boundary would be the Columbia River. But because of opposition from central Washington cities like Ellensburg, Wenatchee, and Yakima, the plan never found favor with the legislature.

Thus in the crooked channels of twentieth-century progress, the year 1912 is a sort of navigational aid, a historical buoy marking a passage toward inescapable reefs and shoals. At this marker in the history of the state of Washington, we are looking back upon a period of prosperity and optimism and smoothly muted tensions; and we are looking forward into a time of rising sectional hostilities and social dislocations when people could no longer expect the easy swells of a growing population and an expanding economy to solve almost every serious problem. Because these problems had been central to the political experience of many states, at least since the 1870s, it is worthwhile to reflect for a moment upon the patterns of political response already historical, and, one might suppose, available to the people of Washington. In some states, the railroads and the heavily capitalized extractive industries combined successfully to suppress protest and to bend regional politics to their own advantage, at least until their distortions became matters of national concern. In Washington, however, the spirit of protest would not be so easily crushed; most of the people were newcomers, self-conscious of themselves as members of a new state and very much aware of the possibilities of bending the new society so that it might avoid the corporate dictatorships they had known in the states they had so recently abandoned. Some other states had burdened the solution of their crises upon a single individual, a man like Tom Watson of Georgia, whose private anxieties often complemented public anxieties and who could personify deep public emotions, the kind of mercurial demagogue who might rise to great personal power by fighting the vested interests in one season and accommodating them in another. But the people of Washington were never quite so depressed, never quite so frightened by racial or ethnic minorities as to be so vulnerable to such opportunists.

They were never so desperate that they were willing to forgo the kind of loosely independent political amateurism they had already begun. In some states strong political machines could impose a kind of rigid political discipline upon city governments and legislatures which allowed the bosses to accommodate only enough reform to serve their varied and vested interests. Such attempts were clear in Seattle, Spokane, or Olympia, but not for long: the state was too new, the cities too flexible, too unpredictable in their energies, and they lacked the kind of helpless immigrant population which in other instances gave bosses their base. And, finally, some states welcomed the rise of reformers who were distinguished by their political abilities, their convictions, their confidence, and their intelligence—men like Robert La Follette in Wisconsin, Hiram Johnson in California, or Woodrow Wilson in New Jersey—leaders of brilliance and personal charm who could unite moderate and generally well-to-do citizens in an active concern about the obvious social, economic, and political realities of their generation.

The leader who emerged in Washington lacked both the political strength and the reform passion that distinguished other reform governors. His election in 1912 represented, in fact, many of the state's instabilities, the first of which was that

Washington had since the turn of the century led the nation in the percentage of Republican votes returned in general elections, but in 1912 it led the nation in its ratio of Socialist votes—almost thirteen percent. Republicans that year were scattered, and Washington voters gave their presidential electoral votes to the supporters of Theodore Roosevelt, then of the Progressive party, which had repudiated the mainline Republicans who stayed with President William Howard Taft. The Progressives, however, even with their remarkable strength, were not organized to take the state government. Their candidate for governor was an unfortunate county sheriff of no particular distinction whose personal life broke open in scandal during the campaign when his wife left him and accused him of physical cruelty. And among Democrats, what appeared then to be an easy victory was very nearly a disaster: their winner in the primaries was a supreme court justice whose nomination was soon declared unconstitutional. Thus only three weeks before the general election, the Democratic nomination was handed to Ernest Lister, who had polled only 7,600 votes in the primaries, in contrast to the 69,000 votes given to the leading Republican. Yet Ernest Lister won the general election.

Born in England in 1870, Lister had lived in Tacoma since his immigration at the age of fourteen. His father had been a skillful iron molder who eventually owned his own foundry, and this asset provided a comfortable inheritance, which before 1890 Ernest and his brother had converted into the Lister Manufacturing Company. Lister married in 1893, fathered two children, and secured himself permanently among Tacoma's social establishment as a Mason, an Elk, a Methodist, a director of the Scandinavian American Bank. He golfed, played bridge, and was among the most enthusiastic owners of the new automobiles. He had since his youth worked in the temperance movement, and had since his early maturity been a political activist and city councilman, a close friend of the Populist-Democrat John R. Rogers and a campaign manager for him when Rogers won the governorship in 1896. With Rogers's victory, Lister served for one term as the business manager for the state's welfare institutions. It was clear in all of this that he was a young man of obvious energy and ability who had joined the wrong party. His political godfather, John Rogers, had been the candidate of protest, a bright hope for action and ideals, and he had carried the Populists to an impressive legislative majority in 1896. But he could never use his ideals to organize the protest before the depression ended, and his party had no power after his death in 1901.

Lister's popularity, such as it was in 1912—he was not supported by any newspaper and was the only Democrat elected to state office—rested on his solidly middle-class tastes and associations. He had recently spent five months touring Europe with his charming and handsome family. His wife, Alma, was an educated young woman whose interests ranged from photography to Chinese paintings and who responded warmly to the demands of a public and political life. His daughter Florence, seventeen years old in 1912, was close to both of her parents and took great pride in her father's election. The son, John, named after Governor Rogers, was a vocal nine-year-old whose loyalty to his father delighted reporters in Olympia. In the course of twenty years in Tacoma politics, Lister had supported woman's suffrage, direct legislation, and antisaloon legislation, and his actions had attracted the attention of many reform-minded citizens. In his hurried three-week campaign for election in 1912, however, he sought out dissident Republican as well as Progressive votes, addressing himself most forcefully to "Mr. Homeowner, Mr. Storekeeper, Mr. Taxpayer" with promises of a "marked reduction in public expenditures." This was indeed the theme of his first inaugural: "You gentlemen," he told the legislature, "are sent here by your constituents to get your share of the pie. I am sent here by all of the people to see that not too much is distributed." [2]

The statement was a graceless but accurate simplification which concealed the man who as a young friend of John Rogers had at length brooded over a considerably more profound approach to political thought. Rogers himself had been a most unusual influence—intellectual as well as political, an author of books and pamphlets, a philosopher-governor who, more eloquently than most, articulated the agrarian roots of the Populist revolt of the 1890s. Like Thomas Jefferson before him, Rogers supposed that people close to the soil were, by virtue of their toil with nature, both physically and morally superior to people who worked at machines in factories or at account books in offices. He believed that in America the ownership of land should be an inalienable right, and on this matter he was most specific: a man should have a homestead, and with it a freedom from taxation on any part of the land necessary to support himself and his family. In this sort of guaranteed annual income— possible, he thought, in a new state with a landed endowment— Rogers saw the emergence of an agrarian commonwealth which in the twentieth century could be the model for the nation. And if the people could likewise secure the right to free public education and civil liberties, he believed, they could surely resist the kind of special privilege which seemed then implicit in the personal and corporate fortunes made possible by the new industrial order. When Rogers had said in 1897 that the problem before the American people was "an orderly and peaceful return to the true Americanism of the fathers," he had seen his own election as an instrument for the restoration of agrarian ideals to a people wandering leaderless toward an urban and industrial Gomorrah. Thus Rogers's young friend Ernest Lister—proud of his background as an immigrant who had found opportunity in the promised land, proud of being called the "citizen governor," proud that he too might enrich the tradition of domesticating a frontier wilderness—thought of much more than simply "sharing the pie." "The greatest need of our time," Lister said in 1913, was "the creation of a high rural civilization." [3]

He was then prepared to meet this need with a program of comprehensive legislation. He asked the legislature to authorize and sponsor rural cooperatives, rural credit systems, and resident county agricultural experts who would assist farmers at the

---

3. Ernest Lister, Miscellaneous Clippings File, Gov. Ernest Lister Papers, Washington State Archives, Olympia.

expense of the state government. He pledged his energies to reclamation projects, especially the irrigation of more lands.
Among his more far-reaching proposals was a plan for the clearing of logged-off lands by county governments, through the
bonding authority of local improvement districts, which could
then make such reclaimed land easily available to people who
would farm it. This was in fact among his favorite schemes, for
he was convinced that the population would continue to grow
and that farming, not logging or industry, would attract the kind
of people he wanted for the new generation. In some of his
speeches there is evidence that Lister regarded logging itself as
a form of inexpensive and terminal reclamation, for it efficiently
ridded the land of trees and prepared it for the noble agrarians.
When as governor he spoke to national audiences, as he did at
governors' conventions, it was usually to criticize federal policies regarding conservation and national forests and to recite the
achievements of his state in terms of the wheat and hops, apples
and pears, vegetables and berries the people of Washington each
year harvested. And among Lister's papers in the state archives
in Olympia is a meticulous log he kept of his daily and sometimes hourly commitments. All of them were totaled in such a
way as to demonstrate clearly that the governor spent more of his
time—speaking, writing, conferring, and traveling—on matters
which were essentially related to agriculture than to any other
state concern.

The point of all this—sadly, it now seems—is that when the
growth stopped, as it had done in 1893 and again in 1912,
Rogers, and then Lister, raised an older and surely outworn
vision. The realities of 1912 were that city governments, then
struggling with private electricity and transportation companies,
were pleading vainly for the rights of municipal ownership and
for a greater measure of home rule; that there were more wage
earners in the state than farmers, and that there was almost everywhere a need for schools, colleges, employment offices, industrial accident insurance policies, and pension plans; that
most of the logged-off land was really not good for farming and
that the people would not bond themselves to finance Lister's
reclamation scheme; and that unemployment in the cities was

approaching the ignition point of demonstration and disorder. There was a major teamster strike in 1913, maybe the most serious the cities had suffered, though it accomplished little for the teamsters. And in 1914 the State Federation of Labor tried to quiet unrest across the entire timber industry by convincing most of the membership to support an initiative measure the federation had prepared for the ballot in November and which, if passed by the voters, would have imposed the eight-hour day throughout the state. Industrialists and most newspapers fought the measure with the argument that an eight-hour shift would force mills to close down, causing more unemployment. The initiative failed at the polls. Union men everywhere were thereafter inclined to jeer at political action as a cruel pipe dream, and the younger men were urging "direct action"—the slowdown, the boycott, the strike. Radicals angrily shouted down the moderates in 1915 when—amid the constantly rising costs of living—wages were reduced by twenty percent. Thousands of workers then walked off their jobs, at least a few of them calling for a general strike of all wage earners. Millowners in Everett and in Raymond responded by locking out the union men and opening their mills to strikebreakers, housing them in company barracks, and protecting them with barbed wire, searchlights, and armed guards.

The state was then surely a miserable place for an agrarian governor. After a bad winter in 1915–1916, lumber and shingle prices rose sharply with wartime demand, but millowners absolutely refused to discuss a return to the wage scale of 1914. There followed then a summer of picket-line violence. In November, Lister had to call out units of the National Guard after a free-speech demonstration culminated in the infamous "Everett Massacre"—hundreds of "deputies" organized by the millowners there fired across the deck of a boat loaded with members of the Industrial Workers of the World, causing the deaths of at least a dozen men on the boat or on the dock.

While he was learning about labor problems, Lister was signaling that in many matters of social and political reform his administration might be thoroughly "progressive." He had been an early advocate of equal suffrage, encouraging the movement in other states whenever he could. He favored an eight-hour day for women in industry, and a law prohibiting child labor, and a commission to administer a state-funded program of industrial accident insurance. He had enthusiastically supported the movement which achieved the initiative and the referendum. When the antisaloon initiative passed with a clear majority in 1914, Lister did not hesitate to give it his full support and to become the "dry" governor. He also signed the "red light abatement" law, which allowed county governments to condemn properties used for organized prostitution. There is in this record enough to suggest that Ernest Lister was alienating himself from the conservative leaders of his own weak party and seeking an alliance with liberals and reformers of whatever label—Democrat, Republican, Progressive. He wanted very much to win re-election in 1916, and he hoped—like George Cotterill—for a re-alignment of political loyalties around the principles of liberalism or conservatism. And there is much to suggest his growing awareness that the realities of an industrial society were frequently inconsistent with his earlier agrarian dreams—that the state had undergone a momentous revision in the way people could work or play or relate to each other and in the ways that great power might, for good or evil, be acquired and used.

A few days after the Everett tragedy in November 1916, Ernest Lister won his re-election and gave some shape to his desired liberal coalition. State politics would never again be quite what it had been before Lister, for he had by then deliberately cut himself away from the leaders of his own party and built a narrow margin of victory on the votes of people from all parties who were, like himself, deeply concerned with the quality of life in a state whose destiny seemed to be slipping away from them. Though still an economy-minded administrator—and he won votes on this as well—he had for most purposes abandoned the dream of an agrarian commonwealth and presented himself as a friend of the urban middle class and of organized labor. This was never more conspicuous than in 1916 when he successfully urged the defeat through referendum of the antipicketing ordinance that he had as governor himself signed into law. At a Seattle political rally, he shared a platform with George Cotterill, the Democrat who had done most to fight private monopolies in that city and who had been regarded by some editors as a "red flag" mayor; with James Duncan, generally regarded as among the most radical of the state's labor leaders; and with Anna Louise Strong, a young member of the school board whose reforming activism had already distinguished her in the local antiwar movement. Approaching the legislature in 1917, Lister began to work successfully with liberal Republicans toward improvements in industrial accident insurance, toward city control of public utilities, and toward the kind of urban-industrial harmony he then believed possible. Following an interview with Woodrow Wilson early in 1917, Lister told the legislature in Wilsonian tones that "We are approaching vast changes in our economic, social and political structure. . . . The nation as a whole is being reborn with a new and higher social conscience, with a keener appreciation of the duties and obligations between fellow men."

A misfortune of Ernest Lister's career, and of his state, was that events during the next two years prevented him from any significant leadership toward that rebirth, if indeed it were ever possible. When the nation went to war in 1917, the federal government thrust new priorities upon almost every agency of state government—as it did on almost every dimension of American life. With a methodical and very unsentimental discipline, the National Council of Defense organized the home front, coordinating industries and resources across the country and dictating almost every aspect of production and distribution. Under this authority the Washington State Council of Defense, with the power to set aside any state law, took charge of the principal economic activities of the state, especially the production of wheat and lumber and ships, which were so vital to the nation. In effect, the state was virtually under the control of the council and its chairman, Henry Suzzallo, the president of the University of Washington whose appointment Lister fully endorsed.

For a glowing moment, it seemed that everyone was eager to dedicate energies, even life itself to the cause of the great crusade which, as Wilson expressed it, was simply and finally the cause of democracy and freedom. But by the summer of 1917, when the economic depression had disappeared in a great cloud of industrial smoke, it was obvious to many labor leaders, industrialists, social reformers, and patriots that the sudden prosperity and the mood of dedication had lifted both material and spiritual visions toward postponed ideals and achievements. The Great War seemed to justify the kind of moral commitment necessary, for example, to the final victory of the prohibition movement. The legislature was suddenly inspired with a determination to dry up not only the saloons, which had been closed by initiative, but the drugstores, the mail-order houses, the railway express agencies, and the "bone-dry" movement quickly outpaced the older antisaloon crusade. And moral reformers quickly convinced the federal government to protect its soldiers at Camp Lewis by doing what no city administration in Seattle or Tacoma had yet done thoroughly—cleansing the cities of their ubiquitous prostitution. Municipal reformers believed that patriotism and national efficiency surely justified the conversion of public transportation systems and electric utilities from private to public monopolies. Labor leaders were determined that the "new and higher social conscience" should include decent wages and the eight-hour day.

It was the bold movement toward this last goal which was by far the most costly in terms of the kind of cohesion and social confidence which Lister had supposed the war could make possible. Even while the prices for timber products soared the industrialists opposed negotiations over wages or working conditions, refusing in any way to consider labor's proposals. And union leaders were themselves determined that the industrialists would not use the war to enrich themselves at the expense of labor, even furiously determined that the war should yield at least some of the progress which had been frustrated for a generation. Ominously, then, the mills became quiet. The AFL unions, supported eagerly by the Industrial Workers of the World, called a strike which paralyzed the entire timber products industry.

What followed was a massive deterioration of the new social conscience. The millowners seemed so irrationally rigid that even some conservative officials lost all patience with them. Lister announced that "peace . . . cannot come to the industrial life of the State of Washington until the principle of the eight-hour day is established," and he indicated strongly that this was a principle with which he was in "full accord." [4] As shipyard workers refused to work lumber produced by mills on ten-hour shifts, United States Senator Miles Poindexter, a Republican, prepared a bill to mandate an eight-hour day in the lumber mills. Senator Wesley Jones, also Republican, wanted to prohibit the interstate shipment of ten-hour lumber. But even when the secretary of war pleaded with the lumbermen, they would not retreat. Then in the early fall the workers themselves, desperate for wages and then angry both with their own leadership and with state and federal officials who had been unable to settle the strike, moved back into the mills to produce the lumber but with their own subtle and sullen version of the eight-hour shift. The radicals were preaching a form of devastating but nonviolent guerrilla warfare called "taking the strike to the job." By slowing down the work, by feigning incompetence or ineptitude, they demonstrated that they could stretch eight hours of work across a ten-hour day, and, if they chose to do so, easily destroy the efficiency of any mill. Federal and state officials were appalled at estimates that as many as seventy-five percent of the workers had left the AFL Timberworkers' Union and joined the radical IWW.

But at this point, the state council, as did most citizens, equated such industrial sabotage with the most grievous perfidy—murderous treason designed to help the Kaiser—and both the state and the national governments moved quickly against it. Using the Espionage Act, federal officials sent IWW leaders and Socialists to jail. The state council assisted the army in organizing a uniquely official union, the Loyal Legion of Loggers and Lumbermen, which was open to men who would take a no-strike oath and pledge their loyalty and patriotism. Workers in the woods and the mills were thereafter largely under the di-

4. State of Washington, Bureau of Labor, Eleventh Biennial Report, 1917–1918, p. 67.

rection of an army colonel. And having thus assured the industrialists of an obedient labor force, the state council then demanded an obedient industry: it decreed the eight-hour day and thereafter enforced it. When a group of lumbermen threatened him at a climactic moment, implying that they could remove him from his university presidency, Henry Suzzallo was so outraged at their iron-headed intransigence that he ordered them "to get to hell" out of this if they wanted to stay in business at all, for he would not, he said, allow "their greed to masquerade as patriotism to the hurt of the people of the state." [5]

It was then an ugly and menacing industrial peace, charged with the kind of suspicions and hatreds which at best generate bigotries and at worst encourage a police state. While their leaders went to jail on charges they felt to be unconstitutional (advocating opposition to the war effort), some IWW members raised sinister threats of reprisals which accelerated rumors of intended violence. These deeply disturbed both Governor Lister and Henry Suzzallo. Lister soon informed the secretary of war that neither state nor local authorities could adequately protect the railroads, power plants, irrigation dams, and warehouses essential to war production, and he requested the assistance of federal troops. By 1918, armed soldiers seemed to be everywhere, guarding tunnels, powerlines, crops, and bridges, and watching restlessly in the towns and in the labor camps for spies and saboteurs.

When members of the IWW left the harvest and snowbound logging camps that winter, many people came to believe that they intended to terrorize the cities. In the hysteria which followed, vigilante groups like the Minute Men (organized by Spanish War veterans) and the American Protective League (volunteer informers for the Department of Justice) were guided by local officials to detain, question, and even arrest any person whose loyalty might be under suspicion. Like the secret police in Germany, such groups assigned agents in each city neighborhood to report statements or behavior which might suggest

5. Unpublished and undated notes of Stevens Papers, University of Washington Library, Seattle.

anything less than full-hearted patriotism. Some of the results were that teachers of the German language were fired, the study of German was dropped from the public schools, labor leaders were constantly spied upon and harassed, and hundreds of innocent men and women were detained, some of them for months, while federal agents determined whether to jail or to deport them. When a United States attorney, Clarence L. Reames, came out as a special investigator of the state's problems for the Department of Justice, he found near-chaos: "Every public officer," he wrote, "federal, state, and municipal, including the members of the Fire Department, and all volunteer organizations exercised the privilege of unceremoniously arresting citizens, aliens, and alien enemies and throwing them unceremoniously into jail, where they were booked for investigation. . . ." Reames reported more trouble with officials and "official" conservatives than with those radicals accused of sedition.[6]

And here, surely, if history is to be a humanistic dialogue as well as narrative, something more than reference to the antiwar radicals is in order. The origins of the doctrines of the Socialists or the Industrial Workers of the World need not concern us, but the circumstances which nourished them were indigenous and endemic to regional industrial life. Since the 1890s, many wage earners from the mines of the Coeur d'Alenes to the logging camps and lumber mills of the Cascades and Olympics had been converted to certain principles of industrial reality: the iron law of wages was the law of the region; wage slavery was inevitable; and the only effective action was direct action.

In competitive mining, logging, or milling, the iron law indeed seemed inexorable, for if one competitor lowered wages, then other competitors, unless they were willing to lose their competitive positions, must surely follow. As wages thus degenerated to a subsistence level, the environment of work itself deteriorated toward circumstances almost fiendishly grotesque. Cave-ins trapped miners, logs crushed young men in the woods, exploding steam engines killed whole crews, knife-edged saws took fingers, or arms, or life itself from over half the men who operated them. In many mine and mill towns, industrial accidents were the primary cause of death. This wage slavery (as many came to see it) was not always distinct from the cotton slavery of the older America. ("Son," a Wobbly named Red told Horace Cayton's younger son, "you got to realize that your people, and my people, have been the victims of a hundred and fifty years of slavery. . . . There's wage slavery, too, and we've got to join together. . . .") [7] And given the cut-throat nature of the competition, given the inexorable profit motive and mandate, capitalists could not be sweetly reasoned toward humanitarianism. They would respond only to threats aimed directly at their profits or at their very existence. This, then, was the substance of the brotherhood and the mystique of inevitable conflict: "The working class and the employing class have nothing in common," ran the IWW slogan, and "there can be no peace" while working people are enslaved by competition and condemned to deprivation. The working class—this was a favorite oration—has the historic mission of abolishing the rotten system, which included its slave religion, its middle-class aspirations. "Work and pray, live on hay, you'll get pie in the sky—that's a lie."

This mystique of historic destiny was the bond of fellowship and courage: to defy Christianity and capitalism, to suffer beatings and jailings and even martyrdom, to sweat in a mill by day and preach on the street by night. And to oppose a world war—a capitalist, imperialist war in which the workingman had nothing to gain and everything to lose—this was an evangelism of noble minds. Thus we have one historic image of the IWW: romantic, idealistic, pledged almost sacredly to physical and spiritual transcendence.

Yet these qualities were often integrated with a lifestyle con-

---

7. Horace R. Cayton, *Long Old Road* (Seattle: University of Washington Press, paperback edition, 1970), p. 107.

spicuously impulsive and indelibly marked by the environment which by its very deprivations did indeed encourage anger, brutality, and instant gratification. After William O. Douglas had worked with Wobblies in the wheatfields, he concluded that most of them led lives which were "empty and filled with despair." Some might at any moment be equally disposed to sing a song, preach a street sermon, go to jail, walk off the job, drink and brawl in a whorehouse, to cut the powerlines to a mill—if perhaps the owner seemed reluctant to install safety devices—or to mail threats of terror to a bullying foreman. Others, if dedicated and often martyred, were also rudely boisterous: young men, most of them under twenty-five, often impishly inclined to be daringly outspoken and belligerent, impudently opposed to politeness, courtesy, or compromise. More were inclined to demonstration and protest than to intellectual critique, and they could never coherently address themselves to the immediate problem, which was not humanitarian bosses or the lack of them so much as it was too many mills producing too much lumber for there to be any health in any part of the system.

Thus what they proposed that the brotherhood do about "the system" was never clear. They rejected democratic political action. Capitalists, they said, will use their newspapers and money to manipulate the ballot box, which was closed to many workers anyway because of their nomadic mobility. It was equally clear that they never had enough votes to attract the political alliances necessary in a democratic society. They had forsaken negotiation because the bosses would never recognize them, never grant them integrity, never regard them as anything but a red line in the books of the profit system. So they developed "direct action," which was a phrase of deliberate and cunning ambiguity, loaded with overtones designed as much to create confusion as to inspire fear or terror. What did "sabotage" really mean to the IWW's "Wobblies"? Did they really believe in the destruction of private property to achieve their ends? Their own answers were always predictable: we are all leaders; one man's preaching is not necessarily another man's practice; but only a fool would destroy the means of earning wages; sabotage was the slowdown, the frustration of the profit system, "the conscientious withdrawal of efficiency," "a poor day's work for a poor day's pay." There is no clear evidence that these responses were not sincere, for stories of dynamite in the mill, sand in the gearbox, spikes in the logs, fire in the granary, lead the historian only to the kind of crooked rumor and clouded memory which he can never trust. But this is not to say that in a moment of impulsive fury, a man or a group of men might not decide that a certain millowner was an enemy of the working class and did not deserve to have a mill at all.

Their ultimate disservice to the reform movement was that they made no effective effort to frustrate the equation in the popular mind of labor protest with physical violence, and this ambiguous indifference led to the even easier equation of labor protest with disloyalty and treason. Thus the middle-class mind, in the new and unstable society, might easily see the Wobbly as the wicked and conspiring foreigner—and many of them were of foreign birth—as the impetuous and delinquent youth of no firm values, as the abusive nihilist, the rogue of wanton criminality. This feeling did not rise simply because Christian ministers and industrialists gave it image in the American West. It had been rising in the American mind at least since the insurrectionary and bloody violence against railroads in Pittsburgh, Chicago, Saint Louis, and San Francisco in the 1870s, the Haymarket Square bombing in 1886, the mining wars of the Coeur d'Alenes in 1899, and the murder of William McKinley. The course of American history since the Civil War had fashioned a fearful role for the IWW and their more radical Socialist friends, a role they played at least in part because they did often associate revolution with gloriously romantic rebellion and because they never made clear what "direct action" in a time of labor strike or world war might really mean. Their glib allusions to force and violence made certain that violence would be inflicted upon them.

Shortly after the American declaration of war in 1917, Ernest Lister's sensitivity to civil liberty and to labor problems caused him to put his veto on a bill designed to crush the IWW. This was a proposed law against what was then called "criminal syndicalism," a crime which was to include the advocacy of violent social or economic change. As a practical police matter, the law would have allowed the prosecution of men and women even for the possession of an IWW card, newspaper, or pamphlet. Such people were soon being jailed anyway, and Lister's courage was but a flicker of restraint in a state where the government had no control over its own resources, where criticism and protest were quickly associated with treachery or treason, and where pseudopatriotism easily became a vicious weapon in industrial conflict.

One might have supposed that the wholesale violation of civil liberty would have ended with the armistice, but it did not. The most urgent matter before the legislature as it met in 1919 seemed to be the criminal syndicalism law, which lawmakers quickly passed over the governor's veto. Many citizens were then alarmed that some labor leaders had expressed open admiration for the Russian Revolution, and the hysteria became then not simply anti-Wobbly, but, in a pervasive way, anti-radical, anti-red. In February, postwar labor unrest in Seattle led to a shipyard strike, which almost every local union in the city chose to support with its sympathy. This swirling of frustrations suddenly became the Seattle General Strike, the first major incident of this character in the American experience. Sixty thousand workers left their jobs, and an almost incredible silence fell over their factories, mills, public transportation, schools, stores—everything but absolutely essential food and medical services. When the streets were deserted, it was said that no one knew where it would end. Some people could easily see a Communist beginning in Seattle, or an IWW insurrection, or at least something planned by Russian agents, and under the circumstances it was easy for Mayor Ole Hanson and others around him to believe that they were watching the first major event of an American Bolshevist revolution.

But there was no violence, no mass protest, no martyr, hardly any rhetoric other than a muttering of frustration. When it was clear to the strikers that after four days their leaders would lead them only to protest, and that protest had only limited advantages, they drifted back to their jobs. What they had accomplished was, in a sense, nothing at all. But they had given the nation a frightful demonstration of what workers could do when they lost all patience and when they feared that they might slip again into prewar deprivations.

These were, as we noted earlier, wretched times for a governor who had thought that he might lead a society of small farmers. Ernest Lister was, however, tireless in his efforts to understand what was happening in his state. Even before the war, he had traveled almost every week, and he actually spent no more than half his time in Olympia, where he usually worked each Sunday. He sometimes delivered as many as twelve speeches during a day, and one evening at an Olympia hotel, within the course of one hour he addressed four banquets. The war had of course severely taxed his strength and added to him an immeasurable burden of worry and anxiety, a burden which overcame him toward the end of the special legislative session in June 1918, when he collapsed of fatigue and entered a hospital. Even then, however, because he sensed the critical mood of his state and society, he refused to give up his office to his lieutenant governor, Louis Hart, whose abilities and attitudes Lister could not respect. (Hart, a Tacoma Republican, had been booed by a Republican audience when, in 1918, he had referred to a proposal to allow the expansion of Seattle City Light—which he saw as a socialist conspiracy—as un-American and pro-German.) Lister thus continued to work through the season of the Armistice. But he suffered a heart attack when he returned to his office to meet the legislature in January 1919. Then fully aware that his energies were gone, he asked his attorney-general, W. V. Tanner, to act for him. Tanner felt himself unequal to the task, but he agreed to form a legislative liaison if he could depend upon the assistance of Henry Suzzallo, the university president who, still chairing the state council, thus became even more the acting governor. During the Seattle General Strike, Suzzallo refused to send the National Guard to the city, as Mayor Hanson had requested, and instead relied upon federal troops from Camp Lewis to protect property. The call for troops was not, as we have seen, ever necessary. When the strike ended and it seemed for a while clear that the state faced no immediate crises, the governor did turn his office over to Louis Hart.

Ernest Lister then disappeared from public view. Though he was not yet fifty years old, his health was utterly broken, his private and public consciousness abruptly closed. He rested in the care of his physician and his family while he sank quietly into a coma on June 14, 1919, which was the last day of his rich and expansive life.

During his last years, Lister had been unable to assuage the conflict between capital and labor, but he had at least prevented the excesses which would have followed his signing the criminal syndicalism law, or his taking seriously the many urgent reports from around the state that James Duncan, the Seattle labor leader, was a "Bolshevik," or that workers in several industries were actually planning domestic violence, or the American Bolshevist revolution was scheduled to begin in Seattle. But Lister was too soon gone, and if in the general strike we have the penultimate scene in the drama of the Progressive movement, the final scene was one of unrelieved madness and tragedy.

While celebrating the first anniversary of Armistice Day in 1919, members of the American Legion paraded through the streets of Centralia along a route which, according to Wobblies in the city, indicated that the war veterans intended to bring their patriotic ceremonies to a climax by attacking the hall then rented by the IWW. But instead of fleeing, nine Wobblies foolishly armed themselves, and in a terrible moment of confused motives—it is impossible to say with certainty who really were the aggressors—they opened fire with rifles and pistols. Suddenly three Legionnaires were dead on the street, another was dying, and several others were wounded. The Wobblies themselves were quickly captured, and across a terrible night one went mad while another was dragged from the jail and hanged from a railroad trestle. There followed an open season on Wobblies as vigilantes combed the woods in bloodshot passions—passions which would soon burst across the region and the nation.

At the height of the regional "red scare," the editor of the

Seattle Business Chronicle urged "real Americans" to "put to death" all Wobblies and union men of whatever label who had criticized American participation in the war.[8] When the *Seattle Union Record* suggested that Wobblies had a right to defend themselves, U.S. Department of Justice officials seized the press, closed it, and arrested and detained the staff on charges of sedition. Following the Centralia Riot, in an atmosphere choked with prejudgments, seven of the Wobblies were quickly convicted of murder, and though the jury recommended leniency, the judge sentenced them to long prison terms. No charges were ever brought against vigilantes or against Legionnaires.

In all of this, Governor Hart was a passive spectator, himself totally opposed to the IWW and quite incapable of raising a voice of reason. His personal inadequacies were then considerable, and he actually desired no prominent role in the postwar world. Afflicted with diabetes, he was often overcome with indifference. He was seldom physically capable of sustained work and often fell asleep at his desk toward the middle of the day. Yet he had a sense of responsibility to the future of the state and to the moderate wing of the Republican party, especially to men like Mark Reed, a wealthy lumberman who as a party leader had protected Hart's political career and who as a legislative floor leader had made the reforms of the Lister administration possible. Thus when Hart sought and won election in 1920, it was only because Mark Reed himself would not do so, and it was clear to everyone in Olympia thereafter that during the next few years the center of power would not be the governor.

Long before the transcontinentals moved West, Thomas M. Reed had left Kentucky for California, where he tried a hand at the diggings before he married and then moved to Olympia. He taught school, edited a newspaper, then organized a company of volunteers—the government refused them because of the ex-

---

8. The editorial appeared as an ad in the *Seattle Post-Intelligencer,* Nov. 18, 1919, and is quoted in Harvey O'Connor, *Revolution In Seattle* (New York: Monthly Review Press, 1964), pp. 183–184.

pense of getting them East—which he offered to President Lincoln in 1861. Thereafter, Reed worked with the surveyor-general of the territory, sat in the legislature, served as a delegate to the constitutional convention in 1889, then became the state's first auditor. He was among those few who had come early, but had not come as extractors. He had built a home and a modestly comfortable life, and he intended to stay.

Of his five children, two survived the diseases of infancy. The second son, Mark Edward Reed, was born in Olympia in 1866. Guided by wise and sensitive parents, the boy grew in a community that gave him orderly measures of excitement, education, and stability. He was riding logging trains with his father at the age of ten. He walked the forest trails in the rain, and he followed the driftwood on many beaches. He worked in a dry goods store and a printing office and attended the University of Washington. After the 1893 panic, he failed in a logging venture, then helped his father in the auditing office, and worked as a secretary to the state land commission.

When Mark Reed then sought his full independence in 1897, he was a young man of unusual promise. Literate, articulate, and skilled in the quantification of land areas and values, he knew the state as few men did, especially its woods and the mechanical interior of the governmental bureaucracies which managed land and taxes. He was also tall and personable, genial, thoughtful, and even-tempered. And though he did not appear to be driven by any consuming vision or private ambition, he learned very fast, and he did almost everything very well. Thus when he went out into the woods to direct a logging camp for one of the most able and farsighted entrepreneurs of the older generation, Sol G. Simpson, their meeting was a happy and significant convergence of energy, experience, and intelligence.

Simpson had come from Quebec and started logging in the 1880s, before the big mills did any logging for themselves and when there was a constant market at the Port Blakely Mill. He soon learned that he was working the lean end of a period when loggers could simply cut near the beaches and skid their timbers into tidewater, and Simpson's sharp eye for what was practical and efficient gave him a mastery of the new technology: tractors and rails and locomotives to replace the skid roads, steam-powered "donkey" engines with steel cables to move the timber. As he expanded his company to five camps and three hundred men, he demonstrated his ability to enter almost any business and make a great amount of money. The Simpson enterprises, as Mark Reed worked through them, included merchandising, shipping, banking, and, except for Weyerhaeuser, the most extensive timber holdings and logging operations in the state.

Simpson trained Mark Reed, promoted him, directed him through the books and practices of his various companies and toward a marriage with his daughter, Irene, in 1902. Between that year and the older man's death in 1906, Reed's sure hand accelerated the movement his father-in-law had begun in the innovative use of rail lines and electrical machinery, the extension of holdings into other logging companies, timberlands, banks, and merchandising. With the death of Simpson's older partner, A. H. Anderson, Reed became president of the extended family enterprises, managing and directing both the Simpson and the Anderson properties, and, increasingly, the growth of his own personal wealth. It was said then that he controlled more private capital than any other individual in the Pacific Northwest. It has been said since, of course, that when a man somehow acquires capital, there is no easier way to make big money than in the extraction of natural resources. This may have been true in the early 1900s, for surely investments in simple machinery, labor, and raw materials required intellectuality of no high order. Reed, however, had insights into complex linkages and interrelationships which escaped most of his fellow capitalists, and he manipulated these to the astonishment of men who hoped to equal him.

At the base of his wealth were the thousands of acres of standing timberlands which Simpson had accumulated and which Reed steadily expanded. Because these holdings were so extensive, we should like to know precisely how Simpson and Reed acquired them, and to say that they bought them is merely to beg a question which the records of history cannot answer with satisfying precision. We do know that as land titles on the new frontier passed from the state and federal governments toward the Weyerhaeusers, Simpsons, and Reeds, the passage was often blurred and confusing, often clouded by heavy tracings of fraud or swindle. This is not to say that the larger companies initiated frauds or swindles, which were usually the devices of lesser men. But these companies could not have accumulated their lands without the help of lesser men and their devices. In the early 1900s the penetration of federal forest reserves, for example, came frequently through the corruption of registrars and receivers—men of federal patronage—who could be persuaded to open for homesteading such lands as they might define as "agricultural." The "settlers" were sometimes simply timber pirates—as had been the case since the time when Emory C. Ferguson had first learned to herd "entrymen." One "homesteader" in the Puget Sound forests cultivated one-twentieth of an acre on a hillside to validate a claim which included over twelve million board feet of prime timber. He sold it to a logging company, which sold it to another, and through similar practices two-thirds of the region's timberlands passed through homesteading to timber holdings. The acquisition of state-held lands, as we have seen, was usually a matter of mendacious squatters or speculators convincing the state land commissioner to release acreages at the minimum price of ten dollars an acre. In any event, the growth of Reed's holdings was in no way uncommon, except that in an age when most loggers still seemed to believe that the forested lands were infinite, he was more eager to buy than others.

What was most uncommon, however, was the use to which he put these lands. Sol Simpson had taught Reed to retain the logged-off land, a practice which appeared at the time to be one of quixotic idiocy. Almost all loggers still worked in the "cut-and-run" tradition of stripping off the timber, then through calculated delinquency relieving themselves of the cutover acreages by forfeiting them to county governments, which had to take them when loggers refused to pay their taxes. On the face of it, that practice made economic sense: the land was worthless because the huge stumps were almost impossible to clear away or burn and because the soil beneath them was usually sandy and rocky, poor in the kind of fertility required for wheat and vegetables or any cash crop; yet the taxes were eternal. But Simpson, like the Weyerhaeusers, would have no part in it, and before Mark Reed had ever met a forestry scientist or heard of a tree farm, he insisted that the old man had passed on to him a sense of stewardship which was much more than short-term economic prudence. It was, in his broad view, a just and proper relationship which included the exploiter and the land and the society. To men who marveled at his folly, Reed's response was to say that in this state where land was the basis for governmental revenue, the quality of state services was a responsibility which those who used the land should not avoid. Thus while Reed expanded his holdings, he retained the lands which were even then slowly reseeding and might in the future be scientifically cultivated.

In Mark Reed's social and political comportment as well as in his forestry practices we see this enlightened self-interest as inseparable from community interest, for in dominating his mills and mill towns he demonstrated a sense for subtle harmonies not often shared by others who worked in the world of unpredictable markets, uncontrolled prices, rapidly changing technology, and ruthless competition. Reed often recalled that during his first night in a logging camp he lay awake for hours, unable to sleep because of the sour straw and filthy boards which were his bed. As he thought about it, he said, he promised himself that he would work to build camps that gave men a sense of dignity and decency. He was then among the first of the industrialists to take an enduring concern with the notorious conditions which had often poisoned relationships between management and labor—the lice-infested bunks, the foul air, the grubby food, the criminal indifference to safety precautions and sanitation, the arbitrary firings and discriminations, the long hours at wages which denied men any hope for middle-class security.

As Reed assumed more and more authority, he worked a quiet revolution. By 1920, his camps were models of technical efficiency, to be sure, but also models of middle-class cleanliness and comfort: painted and scrubbed bunkhouses, fresh sheets and blankets, hot water, electricity, clean kitchens, warm and friendly dining halls, recreational facilities, attractive reading rooms stocked with recent books and newspapers. Reed had been an early supporter of the Workmen's Compensation Act, which after 1911 required the state to carry industrial accident insurance. He usually paid better wages than most of the loggers and millers, and, in an innovation not generally appreciated by his competitors, he provided life insurance for all his men.

Thus a Reed-Simpson employee knew that unless he proved the contrary he would be treated not as a commodity, or a liability, or an indolent lout whose natural laziness and incompetence would threaten the company, but as a person of dignity, integrity, and discipline. This humane treatment of course allowed Reed to choose among persons of dignity and integrity and discipline, and though he never approved of labor unions, he had very few troubles with organized labor. While unrest and violence plagued the industry after 1913, Reed escaped entirely the Wobbly hysteria which developed among many less secure owners of mills and camps. In 1917, when the Timberworkers' Union and the IWW demanded better wages and working conditions and the eight-hour day, Reed was among state leaders who urged the industry to accept these reforms. He was among those who, with the assistance of the federal government, finally imposed the eight-hour day upon the often furiously outraged capitalists. Throughout this period his most diligent and skilled workers stayed with him, and this was another advantage that astonished his competitors, some of whom regarded Reed's industries as "socialism."

After the war, industrialists were both fascinated and envious as they watched Reed's movements toward independence from the mills to which he had always sold his logs. Near his home at Shelton he built a complexly interrelated manufacturing center, which became the economic base of a new city. As his own engineers worked out a system of rail lines which could approach hemlock at high elevations, he persuaded the Northern Pacific to establish yards and connecting lines in Shelton. With new electric machinery to process the hemlock, he built the Reed Mill, and alongside it a new electric shingle mill. Through banking interests that reached into San Francisco to the Zellerbachs, he persuaded them to use the waste hemlock, and they built the Rainier Pulp Mill adjacent to the Reed Mill. And finally, he convinced an old Simpson friend, Henry McCleary, to build a sawmill there and help in the construction of an electric power plant which would burn waste from all the mills and serve them as well as the city.

Thus, indeed, did Shelton become a city, shaped substantially by the character and the personality of one man. Determined to integrate his life with the industrial environment he was creating, Reed had lived in Shelton since his marriage, since it had been no more than a muddy tideflat and a clearing for a few frame houses. As late as 1912, a person could buy logged-off land there for less than a dollar an acre. But under Reed's direction—he became mayor in 1911—the city paved its streets, acquired permanent buildings and a water supply, and built a model hospital. The Simpson and Anderson widows donated the town hall and the library, while Reed himself in large measure financed many of the other facilities. With his new industrial complex he gave the city its high school, which he named for his wife, and where he was happy to send his sons as they prepared to enter the University of Washington. Shelton was his home, and he hoped never to leave it before his death.

This is not to imply that Reed's career was one entirely of lofty magnanimity or of unguarded benevolence. Though he could often afford a larger view of these matters than most other timber capitalists, there was never a time when he was indifferent to the costs of production. Taxes, especially, moved him to exercises of personal power which few capitalists could equal. He could apply pressures upon county tax assessors which were both ruthless and relentless—even to the extreme of marshaling votes against them, and the people of Mason County often voted as Reed advised them. When at the urging of Governor Lister, Reed entered the legislature in 1915, it was, to be sure, with a sense of the obligation which wealth conferred upon him, but it was also as a businessman exploring public life for ways to reduce the taxes on his own properties. The costs of government were rising sharply and painfully—two hundred seventy-five percent between 1910 and 1920. Seventy percent of this had to come from levies against real property, and timberland taxes rose accordingly. Reed hoped to reduce these costs as well as to adjust in some way the structure of the tax burden, and in this he usually represented his own industry as its leading spokesman. He often planned his political strategies with the Weyerhaeusers, and though he was at critical times the "conscience" Republican upon whom Governor Lister depended, he was at other times the thoroughly conservative, special-interest politician.

It was during this period that Mark Reed effectively opposed salary raises for state officials and state employees. It was Reed who directed the enactment of anti-alien land laws in 1921 and 1923 which made it very difficult for Orientals to hold real property and caused almost eighty percent of the Japanese farmers to leave the state. He opposed the public power movement. He proposed a sales tax, and a utilities tax, and he supported higher tuitions for the state colleges and the university. In 1921, Reed pushed into state law a poll tax of five dollars, declaring that he believed "every person over 21 years of age receiving the protection of our laws should contribute something towards the cost of government." But in response to loud protests from every corner of the state, especially from organized labor—when union wages in some industries were fifty cents an hour—Reed reconsidered the matter and then in 1923 led the repeal of his own measure.

Labor newspaper editors were sometimes inclined to see Reed's legislative leadership as simply a technique for unloading a tax burden from the Simpson-Reed interests onto the wage earners, but they respected the fact that he had brought through the legislature the higher industrial accident benefits that the state federation of labor wanted. And they were aware that for two decades he was the most prominent of the "conscience" Republicans who hoped to encourage both conservation and industry by taking the tax burden off timbered lands and placing it instead upon cut timber. If Reed could have thus shifted the tax base away from land and towards income—which he wanted very much to do—he might have created order from disorder and brought the tax system sanely into the twentieth century. But in this he was consistently frustrated by legislators from the farming counties who wanted the timbered lands, and those they regarded as the timber barons, to bear an even heavier burden of state expenses.

Though he failed in this matter, Mark Reed always maintained a rapport with other legislators which softened the conventional hostilities of sectional and partisan politics. Everyone knew what he stood for. He wanted to cut expenses, but he supported a highway program, and workmen's compensation, and good schools, and the university. During Louis Hart's elected term, Mark Reed was known everywhere as the speaker of the house, as the leading industrialist, as the real power in Olympia, as the most widely respected man in the state. He was urged from all quarters by newspapers, politicians, and businessmen to run for governor, and the office would surely have been his had he chosen to take it. But he refused, as he had in 1920 and would again in 1928, maintaining that too many people were dependent upon him and that his business interests were too complex and too demanding to be entrusted to anyone else. This was to say that his sons were not yet old enough to assume his responsibilities, and that his ultimate loyalty was to the Simpson and Anderson families, as well as to his own, and to the people of Shelton. It was an honest excuse, but after 1924 his refusal meant years of political turmoil and disharmony, for it allowed what Reed himself later regarded as a political disaster—the governorship of Roland H. Hartley.

Among the many friends James Hill invited to Washington was David M. Clough of Minnesota, who had made a fortune in timber a decade before he took Hill's private rail car West in 1900. He liked what he saw at Everett: cheap land on waterfront, a fine rail connection, fine timber almost within a stone's throw of his proposed mill. Summoning relatives and friends to join him, he organized the Clough-Hartley Company, whose great assembly of steam-powered saws and conveyances could soon produce a million red cedar shingles in a ten-hour shift—more than any other shingle mill in the world. Like the

Weyerhaeusers, the Cloughs and their associates found their place in the baronial design, for it was with good reason that Hill was called the "Empire Builder."

The design soon included Roland H. Hartley, born in 1864 in New Brunswick, where his father had been an impoverished rock farmer and an occasional preacher. He was twelve years old when with his brothers he migrated to the United States. Except for one year in business school, Hartley was diligently and tirelessly at work: hotel clerk, cook, farm laborer, logger, then bookkeeper, manager, executive. At the age of twenty-one he joined the Clough lumber firm in Minneapolis, and he soon worked his way into the confidences of the extended family of nephews, cousins, and friends over whom David M. Clough presided. Hartley married Clough's daughter Nina, and he served as private secretary to his father-in-law while the older man was governor of Minnesota in the 1890s.

When Hartley settled in Everett with his wife and two sons, he was fascinated by the woods and by the technology of logging and milling. He rolled the logs, cruised the timber, operated the machines, exulting in the work and in the proof that he could sustain a pace that exhausted larger and younger men. In a few years he knew the woods and the mills, and he knew when to be firm, when to be ruthless—and how to avoid ruthlessness in an industry where cut-throat competition was an almost daily assurance that only the fittest would survive. Then in 1906, at precisely the moment when he had tested his insights and skills, the fires of San Francisco created a market which for a glorious year offered an insatiable demand for the Clough-Hartley products. While lumber and shingle prices doubled, the mill barons experienced the first extended period of baronial profit. Hartley built a five-bedroom colonial, a home with spacious lawns and servant quarters overlooking Port Gardner Bay. He ordered a new automobile, vacationed in Santa Barbara, and prepared his sons for Yale. Always gregarious, he had moved smoothly into fraternal and civic affairs, becoming a Mason, an Eagle, an Elk, a member of country clubs, private clubs, and chambers of commerce. He was a man who could quickly warm an audience, and in turn be warmed by it, a man who thoroughly enjoyed public speaking, especially when he could extemporaneously expound about the evils of labor unions or the righteousness of the business-way-of-doing-things. He also enjoyed argument, even belligerency, for he was not only articulate, but outspoken and flamboyant. Thus while the other capitalists waited impatiently for another really first-rate municipal conflagration, or hoped that the Panama Canal would open unknown markets, Hartley turned his energies quite naturally toward the state's political life.

In 1909 he became mayor of Everett. His pleasure in office expanded with personal acclaim, and his friends were surely as dedicated as his enemies. The latter naturally grew in number as his career lengthened and broadened, and their growth was in great part because he was a man of frozen prejudgments and adamant principles. At a time when the Socialists were winning a number of significant municipal elections in the state, he was determined to stamp out socialism. At a time when some citizens wanted to build a great state university, Hartley opposed the very idea of publicly-financed higher education. At a time when some people hoped for an attractive state capitol building, Hartley set himself to reduce taxes. When he retired from the mayor's office in 1911, he was articulating these principles at every opportunity. It was clear that he was bound for Olympia.

After a straightforward conservative's campaign for the governorship in 1924, he won his victory. Hartley had never modified his strong opinion that the state itself should withdraw from any intrusion in the affairs of rugged individualists. In his inaugural address, he labeled as "bolshevists" and "pusillanimous blatherskites" all those who supported child labor laws; he condemned as "disproportionate and alarming" the costs of the state's educational system. "We are drifting," the new governor said, "into a dangerous and insidious paternalism, submerging the self-reliance of the citizen." He pledged himself to safeguard "the majority's pocketbook" from the "clamor" of certain "minorities" who were always demanding "more government and increased appropriations." His administrative program, as it emerged in the strikingly convoluted language of this and other speeches, was to be one of protecting the "common people" from the "interests." [9]

Hartley never lacked the courage of his convictions, and he thereafter never hesitated to identify these "interests." They were the logging companies, which were buying state timber lands at prices that denied the state its rightful revenues and placing on the "common people" an unconscionable burden of taxation. They were the advocates of higher appropriations for schools—not only for the public schools but for colleges and the university—taking a man's hard-earned taxes to give some other man's lazy son an expensive and frivolous education. They were the highway lobbyists with their demands "for hardsur-faced joy-roads," and the supporters of reclamation projects, state libraries, state park systems. And Hartley never concealed his deep personal hostilities: "the interests" included the leader of the legislative majority, Mark Reed, leaders of the Parent-Teacher Association, the president of the University of Washington, leaders of the state federation of labor, and members of the state land commission. In a remarkably short time, he had quarrelled publicly and bitterly with virtually every state elected official, most persistently with the secretary of state, the state treasurer, and the superintendent of public instruction, making it clear that he resented their constitutional powers and that he intended if he could to seize their power bases and make them his own. This is not to say that Hartley in any way approached the stature of Huey Long—who was far more intelligent, far more willing to soak the rich, far more skillful in arousing the poor, and as a leader of public opinion far more compelling. Nor is it to say that he approached a clearly fascist role, though he was surely inclined toward suppressing labor and civil liberty, linking the power of the state to the power of industrialists, and trumpeting a mystique of race and nationalism. Few industrialists hated labor more than did Hartley, and few elected officials were less sensitive to intellectual freedoms. What Hartley actually tried to do was to revive and to distort the rancid ideals

9. Washington State *Senate Journal* (Olympia: State Printer, 1975), p. 56.

of the sort of stumpfarmer commonwealth which Lister had earlier abandoned.

The term "stumpfarmer" has not always been disparaging. Even in Lister's time, as it became evident that growth for some was not always affluence for others, the stump farm had provided substance for the refugee tradition. By 1902, for example, a number of families had settled in the valley of the Lewis River, people who had names like Nousiainen, Tillanen, and Tiisari. Some were from Pielavesi, Finland, others from Finland by way of the mines in Montana and Wyoming. In the shadows of the Cascades they found the necessities of the stumpfarmer, found them indeed in abundance—cheap logged-off land, transportation for carrying cash crops to a city, and some seasonal employment. They worked in the logging operations near the town of Woodland, and they were a vigorous and intelligent people, eager to advance as they found varying success in raising dairy herds, beef cattle, or chickens. They built their churches and saunas and barns, some of them remarkably distinguished in design and craftsmanship, and they built their socialist halls, for many of them were refugees from troubles associated with the Western Federation of Miners and the Industrial Workers of the World. Their sons and daughters usually inherited a large measure of ambition and passed from disciplined schools on to urban employment.

But at that time, and ever since, the stump farm had also drawn people who for less positive reasons built shacks on muddy acreages where they could take fish and game illegally, raise chickens and potatoes and cabbages, and find an easy security in circumstances of rural squalor. They were inclined not toward churches or socialist halls or co-operative houses, but, like the mountain men or the "oyster-boys" who settled in the 1850s at Willapa Harbor, toward being left alone and uninhibited with their semiliterate children, glorifying their individualism and demanding freedom from any social obligations, especially taxes. Their social attitudes were in fact traditional for the American frontier, and across the industrialized frontier they attracted many people who had never burned a stump—families on marginal wheatlands or orchards who resented the enduring agricultural poverty of the 1920s, many urban wage earners whose share of the extracted wealth following the collapse of wartime wages was so miserable that their very survival sometimes depended upon their escaping taxes. We are, then, using the term "stumpfarmer" generically and perhaps invidiously to refer to people who, for whatever reasons, would cheer any effort to reduce or to abolish the kind of taxation upon which a rising level of state services depended. Hartley's achievement was to speak for these people and to bring them together, in leagues of tax-hating voters, with the state's least public-spirited industrialists.

His method was usually to seek public support with highly visible and dramatic attacks upon the "interests." A Hartley campaign around the state was a sort of stumpfarmers' sideshow—a barbershop quartet to bring people to the stump; the display of a 75-pound brass cuspidor captured from the capitol to demonstrate the heartless extravagance of liberal legislators; a black satchel, never opened, alleged to contain enough evidence of high-level corruption to jail all of his opponents. But in Olympia the show was for the newspapers. When it was obvious to him in 1925 that the Republican majority would oppose his drastic slashing of state appropriations, Hartley appeared before the full legislature to attack the state land commission, accusing its members of conducting timberland sales behind a wall of secrecy which masked their frequent underpricing of these lands and their steady dissipation of state wealth. (This was indeed what the commission had for years been doing—and Hartley himself had earlier taken advantage of it.) The accusation was itself stunning, but Hartley went on to indicate that the man who had for years directed such conspiracy and corruption and benefited from it most was the leader of the legislative majority, Mark Reed from Shelton. This brought a roar of outrage from the floor, and as Hartley left the chambers he was treated with open contempt. A resolution condemning his abuse of executive privilege for purposes of personal vilification passed quickly through both houses the next day, and Hartley became the first governor to be so censured. But thereafter his announcements about almost any topic had a directly personal focus which gave them the widest possible public discussion.

Hartley was also happy to keep his prejudices on a full range of public problems vividly within the public view. For example, in the spring of 1925 he was invited, at no expense to the state, to appoint a delegate to a child welfare conference in New York. At first he ignored the opportunity, but when Sophie Irene Loeb, president of the Child Welfare Committee of America, wired Hartley's secretary, urging that the governor have someone represent the state, Hartley finally returned a telegram. "Child Welfare!" he wrote. "What is the matter with our children today? In my opinion, they are being made to pay the penalty for an overabundance of altruistic twaddle. . . . Too many mothers and fathers are giving their time to saving their neighbor's children. . . . What we need is to get back to the simplicity of the old fashioned truly American family circle and to stop a lot of this uplift gush, this indiscriminate spending of money on so-called charity and welfare work." He was delighted when excerpts from this message were printed in the *New York Times,* and he took occasion to send the full text of what he called his "performance" to Nicholas Murray Butler, then president of Columbia University and a Republican much admired by Hartley, explaining to Dr. Butler that in Olympia he was trying to "put into operation some old fashioned ideas" and welcomed the attacks of "lame ducks, political tramps, and ne'er-do-wells . . . disgruntled politicians, grafters, greedy promoters, uplift agitators, and all other hounds of Hell." [10]

In this he was no doubt sincere. It is possible to conclude that in all of his cantankerous disputations Roland Hartley was simply doing what conservative governors usually attempt to do—centralize authority, reduce expenses, and prohibit governmental agencies from using their power to broaden their own bureaucratic interests. It is quite reasonable to suppose that in his public life and private life Roland Hartley was "performing" as most conservative people would have liked to perform during the 1920s, resisting wherever they could the inexorable advance of a lifestyle then radically changing the character of

10. Hartley to Loeb, May 4, 1925, and Hartley to Butler, Oct. 17, 1925. Nicholas Murray Butler Papers, Butler Library, Columbia University.

American civilization: the pervasive influence of automobiles, telephones, movies, and advertising upon the opportunities for individuality and for individual indulgences; the liberation of women from agrarian sex roles; the loosening of family tyrannies; the realization that in a new urban society more comprehensive social services were essential to human dignity. It is, moreover, clear that this performance was quite effective. It brought him the power to present the character of his administration in an electrifying climax when he determined to humble an old enemy, the University of Washington.

Henry Suzzallo, the university president and former wartime administrator, had come from Columbia University to Seattle, where he intended to build a great center of higher education. With Hartley's election, however, he knew that the state government he had once directed was in motion against him. In 1925 Hartley had not only called for the end of fixed tax millages for higher education; he had requested that the university get no money at all that year from the state's general appropriations. Suzzallo felt that he then had to organize alumni pressure groups and to work openly with Mark Reed among legislators, assembling a majority friendly enough to the university to override a Hartley veto of the appropriations bill. When the override passed during the special session in 1926, Hartley was furious, and he linked the "loggers" with the university lobby as "interests" that were ruthlessly taking money from the people's pocket. In stumpfarmer rhetoric, he then attacked Suzzallo for his intellectualism, for his high salary ($18,000), for the "extravagant" library he was then building on the campus, and even for his Americanism. ("I was born in America and not in Italy," Hartley was reported to have said to newspaper reporters—when any reporter could easily verify that Suzzallo had been born in San Jose, California, and Hartley in Canada.) The governor then dismissed from the university board of regents those members who were not loyal to him, and in October 1926—after the primary elections indicated the new legislature would lack the anti-Hartley votes for impeachment—the board demanded Suzzallo's resignation. When he refused to offer it, the regents summarily dismissed him.

Almost immediately, a host of anti-Hartley forces—from

organized labor, the university, women's clubs, PTAs, reclamationists, liberal Republicans, Democrats—came together in anger and tried to recall him. Some six thousand people attended a protest meeting in Seattle, and while prominent university alumni used the radio to call for action, other meetings were taking place all across the state. In a matter of weeks the Hartley Recall Organization had a committee of more than two hundred organizers and the support of most daily newspapers. It seemed for a moment that the recall—a reform instrument yet to be used at the state level but one fashioned for precisely this kind of situation—might remove Hartley from Olympia.

But it would not be so simple. The recall device required the signatures of twenty-five percent of the voters (a number then close to one hundred thousand), and this was no easy undertaking in a state with few highways. And many of these voters, it was soon clear, were reluctant to use the device in this situation. The governor had committed no crime (the charges against him were a vaguely phrased "malfeasance"), and for this reason even Mark Reed was not active in the movement. Suzzallo himself was soon gone, and the issues surrounding him were so complex and so ambiguous that they were easily forgotten. Thus the required signatures were not forthcoming. And when the governor met the legislature in 1927, he was more compromising than anyone could have predicted, suggesting more money for highways and for the university than the legislature itself had dared to request. During the campaign of 1928, he took his usual demagogic flair against a field of weak opponents and again won election.

When other banks failed in 1929, Mark Reed's was never in danger. When prices dropped by fifty percent between 1929 and 1931 and the mills were everywhere closing, Reed's managers informed him that common economic self-interest dictated a shutdown. Reed's response, later recalled by one of these managers, was nearly perfect expression of his sense of stewardship: "These people," he said thoughtfully, "came in here, bought or built homes, and they mortgaged them. The banks hold the mortgages. The merchants are carrying these people on their current purchases; and the banks are carrying the merchants. A lot of these people have growing families; they have hospital and doctor bills and they are behind in their payments. The hospital is beginning to suffer. And remember, without payrolls we have no taxes to support the town or county. So, why don't you go home and think about that for a few days; then come back and talk to me again." [11]

The decisions a few days later were to cut the losses, not the costs, and to try to keep things running. But when in 1932 the storage yards were full and Reed himself had to admit that he could not even give away lumber, he did have to close the mills and camps. Even though he himself then feared that the depression might last five or six years, he held the community together by extending generous credit at the Lumbermen's Mercantile, his company store. The workers, he reasoned, had made it possible for him to accumulate a large reserve of cash, and now he should make it possible for them to continue living in Shelton. Later he devised a way to operate his mills as chipping mills— at no profit, but in such a way that the Rainier Mill could resume its pulp manufacture. When the town was working again, his bookkeeper brought him the many notes of credit from the store, and Reed ordered him to "wipe these off the books and forget about them . . . tell the people to go ahead and get back on their feet again." [12] They did, and when later in the decade unrest again exploded across the industry, the Reed plants were models of peace and efficiency.

In 1930, Mark Reed was emotionally shattered by the death of his son Sol, murdered by a demented logger who had been crippled in an industrial accident. After the funeral, Reed found it impossible to remain in Shelton, and in an unfathomed depth of grief, he moved to Seattle in 1931. But there he was soon drawn again into politics, and he became the state's most faithful apologist for Herbert Hoover, whom the people of the state soon decisively rejected. Reed had anticipated this, as well as

11. In C. H. Kreienbaum and Elwood R. Maunder, "Forest Management and Community Stability: The Simpson Experience," *Forest History* 12 (July 1968):11.

12. Kreienbaum and Maunder, p. 12.

the downfall of Hartley in 1932. As a Republican, Reed was usually loyal and devout—except for his opposition to Hartley—yet he was no fanatic. He soon accepted Franklin Roosevelt and the New Deal, and a new Democratic governor, and at Roosevelt's urging he took a major responsibility for writing NRA codes for the timber products industries shortly before his death in 1933. This was his last public service, rendered finally to the federal government when it was clear to him that from that time on, the problems of Shelton and of the state of Washington were then national problems which demanded national solutions.

5

Amid Hope and
Tribulation

*F*ROM the farms of Nebraska in the 1890s, a young man of ambition might work his way to the West Coast, then north to Dawson City and the Yukon, and Rufus Woods did so as railroad section hand, hotel clerk, surveyor, teacher, and riverboat steward. Though El Dorado was something less than he had imagined, Woods never considered the idea of failure: he would find the good life somewhere in the new towns and cities of the new states and among the new people. After his Klondike dreams, he returned to the family homestead, where he had been born in 1878, and with his twin brother, Ralph, he enrolled in law school. After graduation they both took rail tickets for Seattle, Ralph entering a law office there while Rufus continued to search for the open doors he had not yet found. With a borrowed twenty dollars he came finally in 1904 to Wenatchee, a town of some two thousand people who, he understood, were trying to make the most of their position on the Great Northern mainline, their fabulously productive orchards, their new irrigation canal, and among whom, he already knew, a college education—even literacy itself—would be in high demand.

He edited news in the office of the weekly *Republic,* but his impressive abilities and limitless enthusiasm quickly brought

145

him to businessmen who knew that the opportunities they themselves hoped to grasp were beyond the reach of a rural weekly.
With loans and promises, they made it possible for him to
become editor and publisher of the *Wenatchee Daily World,* and
from the moment he took his editor's chair, his editor's column,
and his editor's authority, Rufus Woods became the spokesman
for "development" in Wenatchee and Central Washington. His
principles, he announced, were that he would swear to no political loyalty (though he was transparently a progressive Republican), that he would favor good roads and the policies of the fruit
growers' association (though no one had ever thought he could
oppose them), that direct legislation was the route toward political liberty (though he had uneasy moments with initiatives sponsored by private power companies or saloons), and that decent
men supported the Women's Christian Temperance Union
(though he seldom used his columns to preach their program).
For his own role in the community, he said, there would be this
motto: "By thine own soul's law learn to live/And if men
thwart thee, have no heed. . . ." He thus took his position as
pontificator of righteousness, defender of the right, enlightener
of the truth, scourger of the false—a role which fit him perfectly
and gave him an identity which delighted him through four decades of momentous change.

Woods went again to Nebraska to marry Mary Greenslit, and
she came with him to settle in the town he already regarded as
uniquely his own. There were good and exciting years of
growth—the orchards prospered, the irrigation canal opened extensive new acreages, thousands of new people moved into the
valley, and Wenatchee matured toward an economic and political independence from either Seattle or Spokane. The *Daily
World* increased its circulation to about three thousand in 1912,
when Woods's voice was clearly the voice of literacy up and
down the valleys along the Big Bend country of the Columbia.
But then the farms were all taken, and there was no water for
future development, and there were perhaps too many businessmen. The years of 1913, 1914, 1915 were years of uncertainty,
insecurity, and soured expectations. The failing *Republic* resented Woods's success as much as his politics—his admiration

for progressives like Robert La Follette, Theodore Roosevelt, Hiram Johnson, and Washington State's own insurgent U. S. senator, Miles Poindexter—and it slandered Woods as a " 'crook, briber, cunning knave, brazen blackmailer, shrewd scoundrel, grinning clown.' " [1] Woods was for a moment stunned by the weight of such bitterness, then he was eager for a lawsuit, but he was deeply in debt, and Ralph advised that he take it all as an inevitable tradition in western journalism and forget it. While Rufus brooded—which was not often—Wilma and Walter, the first two children, were stricken with a disease which may have passed through the valley in cow's milk, and within days they both were dead. After the funeral, Rufus and Mary were gone from the town five weeks, driving together to the most remote roads and outposts in the high rough country of the Okanogan.

If learning to live in retreat by "thine own soul's law" revealed to them any ultimate options in the course of life or death, Woods held them close to himself as he revived his energies. Aside from the solace of rivers and forests, Woods's trip brought him contact with the dozen or so small settlements in adjacent counties that he could reach in his 1912 Ford touring car, and in each of them he met people eager to discuss schemes of development which would promote their towns, and, of course, the *Daily World*. Woods returned a confirmed salesman, and he traveled often thereafter, becoming better known in Central Washington than any other man, better acquainted with the people, their problems, their potentials, their aspirations. He was, more than any other person in the region, also more shrewdly inventive with the devices of development. He was soon urging everywhere that the federal government offer extensive lands of the Colville Indian Reservation for settlement—a land grab, or land swindle, which had been possible since the Dawes Act of 1887, but which the Interior Department had never fully facilitated. By advertising blatantly in some four hundred newspapers and magazines across the country that the

1. In Bruce Mitchell, *The Story of Rufus Woods and the Development of Central Washington* (Wenatchee: *The Wenatchee Daily World,* 1965), p. 4.

government's decision to release the lands was imminent—and that inquiries should be addressed to the *Wenatchee Daily World*—Woods practically forced the opening of half a million acres. In a vast confusion of expectations which reminded people of the "Sooner" days in Oklahoma, nearly ninety thousand people actually came West for the homestead drawings in 1916. About fifty-five hundred of these drew the right numbers and claimed their land, while the less fortunate got to see the Inland Empire, where they could consider settling near places like Wilbur, Colville, Omak, Republic, and Wenatchee—places where the land, if not free, was surely inexpensive, places where the future still seemed to be broad enough and wide enough for people of energy and ambition. Rufus Woods was himself delighted that in one bold move he had doubled the population of the area served by his newspaper and his city, which was growing vigorously while the rest of the state drifted in stagnation. Of the affairs of Central Washington, he was then the unchallenged master.

He was a working editor—writing the columns of opinion, editing the pages, drawing the ads, planning the promotions—for the soul's law required almost constant action. He had to *do* things, and what he did had to bring him public acclaim. For how else would the soul know of its own existence? Thus he worked and he spoke and he traveled, hail-fellow-well-met, hailing the blithe spirit, everyman's spokesman, everyman's friend. Even as a journalistic stylist Woods could not resist the flamboyant. His editorials would smash any subtleness with parenthetical exclamation marks (!), and he so often yielded to the temptations of capital letters that his paragraphs moved with the emphasis of a pulpit harangue. He would write about "how there was used a Gigantic Hoax—POLITICS—INTRIGUE—MISINFORMATION—THREATS—DECEIT—BIG MONEY—RIDICULE—INTIMIDATION . . . and HOW THEY FAILED!" And readers knew that in Wood's case the style was surely the man.[2]

---

2. Rufus Woods, *The 23-Years' Battle for Grand Coulee Dam* (Wenatchee: *The Wenatchee Daily World*, 1944), pp. 1–7.

Woods's consistent and fervent admiration of Theodore Roosevelt was at least in part because the president's physique and character and personality were remarkably close to his own. Woods was, in fact, at his best when attacking the malefactors, demanding the conservation of natural resources, hiking for days along the Cascade Crest Trail, chopping trees, driving automobiles, drumming out a booster speech, or defending Americanism. During the Great War there was no more superpatriot than Rufus Woods, lashing the slackers at draft time, the niggardly at bond-buying time, and at all times the hated opponents of the war. On one occasion he stormed an antiwar speaker's platform, demanding to be heard, and got himself a head wound from a blow with a chair. He was proud of it, and those who knew him best could never predictably distinguish in him the clever from the roguish from the impetuous. When he visited England in the 1930s, he could not restrain himself in Hyde Park, where with his high voice and sweeping T. Roosevelt gestures he lectured to the crowd about the health of America and the wisdom of FDR.

There was something curiously compulsive about his attraction to the limelight, and in 1937, at the age of 59, he left Wenatchee for several weeks to tour the country with the Cole Brothers Circus as a real clown. Had Wenatchee produced a Sinclair Lewis, Rufus Woods would certainly have suffered as the satirist's model for the ethos of boosterism, for the chamber-of-commerce mentality, for the growth-for-growth's sake philosophy, for the man of shallow principles and mercurial enthusiasm whose visions of the good life or of the good in humanity were narrowly defined by experiences in Wenatchee, Washington. Yet his visions were usually consistent. The man himself was usually above hypocrisy, his energy and intelligence capable of enduring achievements.

After the opening of land, as Woods saw it, the key to development was the irrigation of arid hillsides around Wenatchee and of millions of acres on the eastern plateau called the Columbia Basin. At one time he promoted a fantastic plan to pipe water from Lake Wenatchee, far up in the Cascades, the pipes to be held as high as one thousand feet by huge trestles until they reached the plateau. At another time he supported a plan to build two hundred miles of canal and tunnel from Lake Pend Oreille. He was in fact easily captivated by any scheme for the reclamation of these lands, which in the exhaustion of natural moistures by the early farmers had gone to weeds and dust. It was finally William Clapp, a lawyer in the dusty little basin town of Ephrata, who made Woods aware that the region's greatest asset might be the Columbia River itself, even if it seemed hopelessly beyond reach six hundred to one thousand feet below the plateau. Clapp observed simply that during a past ice age, thousands of years before, a great wedge of a glacier had dammed the river, and that conceivably modern machines could build such a dam in the twentieth century, and that the rising water could be drained or pumped by the hydroelectric power of the river itself so that it might again flow through ancient channels across the basin. It was a staggering concept—a slab of concrete a mile long and thirty-five acres at the base, the largest thing ever built by man, which, at first thought, was maybe incredible, maybe even impossible. But the United States had built the Panama Canal, and was winning a great world war, and Clapp saw no cause to think the idea unreasonable. His was the first proposal for a dam at Grand Coulee that people ever took seriously, and Woods wrote his most famous story, in July 1918, about a plan to turn the Columbia "back into its old bed in Grand Coulee, by the construction of a great dam, the reclamation of between one and two million acres . . . and the development of a water power approximating Niagara Falls." This was the beginning, and throughout the 1920s he continued to write that Wenatchee would, he was confident, soon be the center of "THE MOST UNIQUE, THE MOST INTERESTING, AND THE MOST REMARKABLE DEVELOPMENT OF BOTH IRRIGATION AND POWER IN THIS AGE OF INDUSTRIAL AND SCIENTIFIC MIRACLES." In the Pacific Northwest, he wrote, "will be developed probably the richest and most blessed region in the whole world." [3]

3. Woods, p. 12.

This was not, of course, an idea that caused Woods any unseemly sacrifice or that in any way did a disservice to the *Daily World*. The concept of a great dam was, in fact, one he hoped others would take up and plan for and carry forward, for he himself hardly knew what to do with it. Neither he nor William Clapp had any real knowledge of practical politics. They could write columns and make speeches, but these would not yield congressional appropriations, and for a while the plan floated around as an inflated proposition without an anchor. There were, however, groups of men who took it very seriously, and they quickly joined forces to sink it. They came, most significantly, from the Washington Power Company and the *Spokane Spokesman-Review,* and from these bases they enlisted in their favor the Spokane Chamber of Commerce, which in turn organized the Columbia Basin Irrigation League to promote the old idea of watering the land with Pend Oreille water. They opposed the high dam because, as a spokesman candidly wrote to Woods, such a dam would generate electric power which would inevitably compete " 'with existing power companies which have ample facilities to care for all of the needs of the Northwest for many years to come, if not for centuries ' " [4] Furthermore, though the spokesmen never clarified these points, the Washington Power Company was then tying together a neat power monopoly by buying out small utility companies all across the Inland Empire, and the "gravity plan" for Pend Oreille water included provisions for the state to build canals which during the winter months would dump excess water into the Spokane River and thus give the company's generators there a bonanza of premium wattage. This "Spokane Group" of "gravity planners" quickly produced a report endorsed by George W. Goethals, builder of the Panama Canal, which praised the design for gravity flow and dismissed the high dam as ridiculous.

This "Spokane Group" might indeed have had its way if the "Ephrata Group" of "pumpers" had not organized the Columbia River Development League, made Rufus Woods its presi-

4. In Mitchell, p. 12.

dent, and found an astute and indefatigable executive secretary in James O'Sullivan. Two years older than Woods, experienced in engineering and college teaching, he had practiced law and farming near Ephrata before working on construction projects in Michigan. O'Sullivan was a lean, tall, and thoughtful man, but he was also an aggressive intellectual who, when he encountered a disputed ideal, might offer to fight with his fists as well as his words. When he returned to the state in the 1920s he was far more knowledgeable politically than either Clapp or Woods, and the Ephrata plan intrigued him. He at once dedicated himself to the cause of the high dam. He would himself have liked to build it, and in a sense he did—refining the proposals with his expertise, explaining them to everyone, countering every criticism, refuting every misconception or deception, carrying the plan to Congress, marshaling the political pressures until they were relentless.

Since the 1930s there has been spirited discussion about who really was the "father of Grand Coulee Dam," and the point at issue has usually been whether or not Rufus Woods upstaged James O'Sullivan in accepting more than his share of the personal triumph. There is no question that Woods enjoyed his share—a radio dramatization of his life as a frontier editor, articles featuring him in national magazines—or that he took all he could get, or that this eager identity with the project often obscured the diligence of O'Sullivan through more than ten years of challenge and crisis. Though Woods did leave to O'Sullivan the daily problems—the committee meetings, the long conferences, the congressional lobbying, the burden of propaganda and counterpropaganda—this was O'Sullivan's job, and he did it very well. He probably could not have done it nearly so well without help from Rufus Woods. Actually, neither man was ungenerous. Woods referred to the "Dam University" at Ephrata where, he said, O'Sullivan and Clapp were the distinguished professors. And when O'Sullivan was asked to list a "Grand Coulee Hall of Fame," he named himself along with Woods and Clapp to the first-rank positions. He also included men such as John S. Butler, the army engineer whose study repudiated the Goethals report and was vital for congressional approval; Albert S. Goss, a brilliant lobbyist who was master of both state and national grange organizations; Sam B. Hill, the congressman who obtained the first federal money for the project; Clarence D. Martin, the governor after 1932, who supported every step; and United States Senator Clarence C. Dill, who in the congressional delegation was the most persistent, keeping the idea alive during the Republican 1920s and carrying the idea and the persuasion to Franklin Roosevelt in 1933, converting the president to Woods's vision of a federally developed river, of farms and jobs and abundant electricity in the promised land.

These men of course took great advantage from the public power movement which had risen in the state since the first achievements of publicly owned municipal power systems and which in the 1920s was gaining strength throughout the nation —often from the inspired leadership of James D. Ross of Seattle City Light. Yet advancing their vision required considerable political skills. Besides frustrating the devices of the Spokane opposition (who tried to pre-empt the high dam by obtaining a permit to construct a private power dam at Kettle Falls), O'Sullivan and Woods had to make delicate but critical alignments among the fragmented components of the old progressive alliance—the Grange, the public power spokesmen, organized labor, friendly Democrats and Republicans. In the beginning the Grange opposed the whole scheme as a needless reclamation which would generate unwanted farm surpluses—an argument O'Sullivan could not overcome until he convinced farmers that nonprofit electric power could provide them with the rural electrification which private power companies denied them. The idea of public power, however, would not come easily, and Woods himself at first opposed it because it looked to him like socialism. He resisted until O'Sullivan made it clear that the high dam must be integrated with the idea of cheap electricity, that they simply had to win over the farmers and then the urban wage earners and the entire range of middle-class citizens in the country and in Congress who would never accept the astronomical costs of the project (then seen as one hundred million dollars) unless they could explain that the sale of hydroelectricity could ultimately pay for everything. This matter came to a regional climax in 1930 as the politics of public power played out in a classic case study of direct legislation. Homer T. Bone of Tacoma, as a Socialist, then a Progressive, then a Republican, had for years supported public power and for years called for the state government to authorize public utility districts (PUDs). When the legislature refused to pass such a law, Bone wrote a PUD initiative measure which he and his many supporters persuaded the people to pass in 1930. It was a vital link in the whole scheme, for PUDs could then purchase electricity from federal dams, if there were ever to be any, and distribute it at nonprofit rates.

The victory in 1930 made it finally clear that the people of the state were ready for the high dams if the federal government would build them. Yet President Hoover stood adamantly opposed to the expense, and as late as 1932 Rufus Woods himself, after speaking with Hoover, turned part socialist and proposed that the people of Washington pass an initiative which would allow them to build the dam themselves and "become the greatest power state in the union, own our own power and sell it outside for what the traffic will bear." In Washington, D. C., he said, "WE ARE LICKED." [5]

What he felt then in the capital was a pervasive doubt not only about socialism but about the nation's need for such a project. The proposal was ridiculed as a plan to reclaim desert where there were but a few farmers, none of whom needed more land, and to generate the greatest block of hydroelectricity in the world where there were more jackrabbits than industries. There was no easy counterargument, and in one of the many cynical discussions then common in the city, Woods heard an unnamed engineer—a man who knew intimately the history of Hoover Dam—comment profoundly that "If you never build it, you'll never need it." [6] This then was the ultimate problem—to get it built so that they would need it— the problem for which the Great Depression became the ultimate solution. As Franklin

5. Woods, p. 54.
6. Woods, p. 54.

Roosevelt and his advisors looked out across a grim decade, and as they listened to Senator Dill and to O'Sullivan, they determined to make Grand Coulee a symbol of New Deal recovery and opportunity—jobs and payrolls for the unemployed, reclamation and homes for Dust Bowl refugees, cheap abundant power for the farms and the cities—the illumination of opportunity, the opening of a last frontier, the gift of the last promised land.

When the cold statistics of deprivation in the 1930s drop like stones into the well of history, the mood of the Great Depression comes to us in a mist of subliminal images: the rain dripping from tarpaper shacks, and morning vapors, like the essence of poverty itself, rising from the squalor of a hobo jungle or a Hooverville; the silence of children; the fearful shuffling of striking farm workers at a rural crossroad; the tension of brutality sweeping through a factory picket line about to erupt in burning automobiles, teargas, bleeding faces, and lead-pipe violence; the drift of gray fog over lines of sullen men and women.

Across the state in 1933, the number of people working for wages was only half of what it had been in 1926. In some westside towns, nearly everyone was out of work, for many mills and logging camps had closed down entirely. Where managers tried to maintain production schedules, the problems of wages, hours, and working conditions festered as envy, fear, and resentment, and the question of who should work, if any were to work, could fall heavily upon the delicate harmonies of any community. At Grays Harbor, Filipinos and "Hindus" came in as strikebreakers, and whites, stopping just short of riot, drove them from the county. Aroused by strike agitators, vigilante farmers gathered with pick handles near Selah and inflicted a bloody punishment upon a few last martyrs of the IWW. In King County, some seventeen thousand families were without means of support—and couldn't expect any. In the Skagit Valley, county commissioners tried to fund road work for men with families—at two dollars a day, four days a month. In Anacortes, the city government was trying to make six dollars a month available to its unemployed men. To the south and into the mountains, mayors of smaller towns organized committees to maintain storehouses for food they could beg from farmers and businessmen—and these storehouses were regularly raided. In Spokane, Benjamin Kizer lost more than one hundred thousand dollars in his private investments. Then in a solemn moment he reported to directors of the consortium of banks he represented that they could no longer support the city and county by buying the bonds these governments had been issuing for emergency relief. The city, he informed them, had no more credit, the county had passed its legal limit of bonded indebtedness, the work-relief projects had come to an end, and within a month, Kizer predicted, the cities of eastern Washington would see real starvation.

He was describing the ignoble collapse of an ideal virtually unchanged since the time of American Revolution: it was, simply, that assistance for those in need was first a family responsibility, then perhaps a matter for parish or community efforts through charity, and ultimately a municipal obligation—the poorhouse, the work farm, the work-relief measures which might be sponsored by city and county agencies. In Washington, as in most states, the state government had built a state school for the deaf and the blind (1888), a northern and an eastern hospital for the insane, and an institution for the feeble-minded (1905). But since 1854 the constitutions of the territory and the state had imposed upon the county commissioners the "entire and exclusive superintendance of the poor." For helpless or destitute individuals in 1932, there were across the state still twenty-four county almhouses struggling in the pitiable traditions of Elizabethan England, grotesque ghettos of the crippled, the orphaned, the epileptic, the mentally retarded, the infirm and aged. When it appeared in 1932 that people within and without the almhouses were facing starvation, county commissioners began regularly to petition Governor Hartley for a special session of the legislature to confront the crisis, but their petitions received no answer from Olympia. When a large group of unemployed men marched together to the Capitol to plead with the governor, he would not see them. And when President Hoover finally made at least a few construction loans available to the state governments, Hartley refused to sign the necessary applications.

To such iron-fisted intransigence, there were many angry and unco-ordinated responses. Some local chapters of the Unemployed Citizens' League in Seattle were taking their leadership from old Wobblies or young Communists, for the predictions of Karl Marx seemed nowhere more accurate than in the desolate manufacturing economy of Washington State and in the attitudes of Roland Hartley. Other radicals of the city found a warm refuge in the Parish House of the Pilgrim Congregational Church, where they painted the walls with strikingly symbolic murals—a starving family in a hovel "protected" by the national defense budget, a Christian missionary astride the horse of capitalism trampling over the helpless bodies of starving peasants. The state had maybe fifty thousand newly converted Technocrats, and nobody could estimate how many Communists—among them Horace Cayton's younger son, Revels Cayton—whose strong voices seemed chorded for political revolution. And an army was indeed at hand. The loose brigades of the transient and the homeless soon included more than ten thousand men who were drifting toward the larger cities. When a new legislature finally convened in 1933, it almost immediately took notice of the "hunger marches, discontent, social unrest and incipient insurrection" which justified drastic departures from deflated traditions. In deep apprehension, people in the state waited to hear Franklin Roosevelt and their new governor, Clarence D. Martin.

He had been born in Cheney in 1887, and his life had been shaped by the happy freedoms of a childhood among the lakes and pine forests and hills and by the great good fortune of the growth years in eastern Washington. His father had come early to mill grain and was quick to see why the directors of the Northern Pacific (one of them named B. P. Cheney) were colonizing there just sixteen miles southwest of Spokane: an ideal rail bed covered with scab rock and bull pine, easy routes to the Snake River and west to the Cascades, ground receding gradually to a northern plateau and a marvelous vista of the Palouse hills rolling west and south. In 1890, these hills were producing

forty bushels of beautiful wheat an acre, and Martin could buy
land for fifteen dollars an acre. The town itself rested in a park-
like plateau of ancient pine trees. It had a grain elevator, a state
normal school with seventy-five students, a bank that had never
foreclosed a mortgage, a spacious and attractive residential area
of thirteen hundred people, a business district advertised as free
from "demoralizing influences," and, shortly, the Martin Mill.
At the age of twenty, Clarence Martin helped his father redesign
and rebuild the mill, which after 1907 was the largest and most
prosperous of its kind in the state.

As manager, the young Martin extended generous advances
for crops, paid attractive prices, and himself experimented with
farming techniques which might stimulate greater productivity.
He soon had the farmers' full confidence and loyalty. He was
graduated from the university, but he met his future wife while
she was studying music in Cheney, where they built their home
and raised three sons. Martin moved naturally through positions
of trust and leadership as an Eagle, an Elk, a Moose, a Kiwanis,
a Methodist, then as city councilman and mayor. His leadership
secured for Cheney the municipal ownership of electricity—an
achievement then regarded by people like Rufus Woods as
shamefully socialistic—and then with his own money he paid
for the street lighting system. He was chairman of the state
Democratic party by 1928, and in 1932 he presented himself in
the primary nominations for governor. He faced serious opposition, but it came from two men who were both from the westside and both of an angry, liberal-radical persuasion in contrast
to Martin's eastside, farm-rooted, traditionally moderate position. Many people were surprised when the Puget Sound urban
vote split neatly, giving Martin the nomination and a certain
victory in November.

Though he himself had a deep feeling for local solutions to
local problems, Martin saw in the great Democratic landslide of
1932 a mandate to abandon the older definitions. He acted
promptly to extend the scope of state-level services, and he was
soon thoroughly committed to Franklin Roosevelt and to bringing to his state as much aid as he could from the programs
which emerged as the New Deal. The Washington State

Emergency Relief Administration in 1933 assisted more than three hundred thousand persons, about twenty percent of the state's population. Even so, Martin was fully aware that more relief was urgently necessary: the state would have to raise its debt limit, bond itself heavily, and use every resource available to find the matching money—two state dollars for one federal—then demanded by the federal government for work-relief funds; there had to be a system of pensions for those unable to work; and the state government would have to save the public schools, then on the verge of closing in many towns and cities.

The legislature co-operated splendidly. It raised the debt limit and it raised the bonds, ten million dollars worth, and these acts were in themselves signal triumphs over the stumpfarmer prejudices of the 1920s. But it was soon evident that the state had no resources—neither the fabulous treasures unlocked by the railroads nor the urban-industrial society built around them—which could respond to the emergencies of this depression. After Martin found enough federal money to organize the Washington State Department of Public Welfare, that agency in one way or another and at one time or another during 1934 helped a total of more than six hundred thousand persons, nearly half the state's population. These included many of the drifting homeless—assistance to eighty thousand single men and ten thousand families—but did not include the ten thousand young men Martin that year helped place in Civilian Conservation Corps (CCC) camps. But even federally funded work-relief projects could not provide enough jobs soon enough, and an expanded system of direct relief and pensions was essential. Martin went then begging to the federal government for money that required no matching, and he advised Harry Hopkins of the Federal Emergency Relief Administration that without such relief many people in the state would simply starve. By the end of the year the federal government, which had already begun the vast constructions at Bonneville and Grand Coulee, was paying for ninety-four percent of the costs of relief measures in the state.

Direct relief was never enough for a decent standard of living, yet in Washington, compared to other states, it was relatively high—$1.20 per person per week. And because of the governor's aggressive pursuit of federal funds, Washington was among the first of the states to pass an unemployment compensation law and to organize for social security pensions. These measures had a quick impact, and there were fewer desperate people in the state in 1935, fewer still in 1936, when the state government had removed the burdens of relief from the cities and counties and rescued the public school system. The rising level of state expenditures had also saved the system of higher education from the almost total neglect of the Hartley period. The governor's commissions had revised the state liquor laws, and, with a system of state stores, put the state into the liquor business, and they had taken the responsibility for operating most of the state's ferry systems.

This was a remarkable series of triumphs over the obstacles, both legal and emotional, to raising the kind of money required for this new definition of state-level obligations. Like most people then, Martin wanted to protect home owners from losing their homes because of tax delinquencies. This sentiment had become law as an initiative measure in 1932, which set forty mills as the upper limit on property taxation. Such a low limit would, of course, deny the state its necessary revenues, and to compensate for the loss Martin would have been happy to accept a graduated net income tax, which, as a companion initiative measure, also passed easily during the same general election. For a brief moment the people had moved to free themselves from the chains of the property tax, but the state supreme court soon determined that the "progressive" feature of the tax on incomes was inconsistent with the requirement that "all taxes shall be uniform upon the same class of property," and it declared the graduated net income tax unconstitutional. The legislature thus faced the necessity of raising matching funds along with the impossibility of raising them from property under a new and severe forty-mill limitation.

Though he did not care for the principle, Martin suggested that the only way the state could join the New Deal immediately would be to levy new taxes on sales and on businesses and occupations. These expedients were locked into the tax structure, and the state thereafter had to draw most of its revenues from the tax on money which people spent for food and clothing and on businesses that somehow managed to avoid bankruptcy. In 1937, which was a year of still deep depression, Martin asked the legislature to appropriate $165 million, a fourth of it for relief and pensions, and the lawmakers complied readily. The sum may not now seem impressive, but at the time it represented a peaceful revolution: as the largest appropriations bill in the history of the state, it signaled the conversion of a government which had so recently been stagnant with stumpfarmer inertia into one which was thoroughly liberal and New Deal.

Even so, Clarence Martin was certainly never free from major frustrations, the most serious of which was the sum total of animosities, antagonisms, rivalries, and downright perversities within the inflated ranks of his own political party. The Democrats, as we have noted, had not attained any real political power in the state before 1933. Of the 1,526 positions filled for the state House of Representatives between 1900 and 1930, all but 156 had been won by Republicans. But in 1933 the Democrats had almost total control, and as they contemplated the thousands of government jobs becoming available in the administration of relief, many of them were unseemly eager to have immediate shares of these political spoils. Yet Martin resisted. His election, he felt, had been possible only because Republicans—Rufus Woods among them—had trusted him, and to the outrage of old party loyalists, he insisted upon bipartisan appointments. There was no political "housecleaning" in 1933. Then Martin wanted—and this seemed incredible to party regulars—a corps of professionals in the welfare offices, not an army of political hacks. For a while it troubled him that many professionally trained social workers were good New Dealers but poor Democrats, but no matter—he refused the demands by major Democratic clubs that only "deserving Democrats" be appointed to such positions.

While party leaders kicked against this restraint, infuriating to many of them, it was soon clear to Martin that if he were to sustain any power at all it would be at least in part under conditions in which organized labor would play an important role. The unions had been long repressed, and they were then determined to have full advantage of the encouragement and legitimacy which New Deal Democrats had extended to them. When in 1934 the longshoremen called for recognition of their union and for collective bargaining, employers refused, and a major strike closed down most ports on the West Coast. While some cargoes rotted in the holds of ships and while industries dependent upon the cargo trade had to suspend operations, the business of Seattle, especially, was grievously afflicted. As longshoremen wrestled with private policemen and strikebreakers, violence became a daily occurrence. Finally the mayor of the city, trying himself to direct a break through the picket lines which sealed off the city dock, called for the launching of teargas, which the fickle winds of Elliott Bay swirled back toward the attack squad, and the mayor became a victim of his own strategy. But there was little humor in the conflict: the death of a striker brought a procession through the downtown streets of hundreds of hard-faced longshoremen in mourning behind a black coffin. Friends of the employers organized a vigilance committee to arrest "communists" and to rid Seattle of its "red reign of terror." Others called for the mobilization of the National Guard, but Martin refused. The strikers were, he believed, entirely within their rights, and their union should be recognized—and he thus appeared to be a New Deal friend of labor.

But in 1935 a strike of the International Timberworkers, supported by longshoremen, teamsters, and carpenters, closed mills all over the Pacific Northwest. Martin found then a much more complex situation. The timberworkers lacked the solidarity of longshoremen, and millworkers eager to hold what jobs they could resisted the union and often attempted to cross picket lines, where pickets were increasingly inclined to violence. To make matters worse, the union itself was shattered by infighting among its leaders, some of whom wanted an early settlement based upon union recognition, others of whom would keep the industry shut down until they had won significant improvements in wages, hours, and the conditions of work. Thus, if the conservative leadership signed a contract and opened a mill, insurgents might close it with their own "radical" union pickets, and among union men themselves there was much violence.

This confusion encouraged millowners to resist even the recognition that the Timberworkers' leaders wanted.

Martin's analysis was that the insurgents were not only threatening the labor movement itself by making it impossible for the timberworkers to honor their contracts; they were also aggravating the depression by preventing good union men who desperately needed their jobs from returning to work. He then mobilized the National Guard and sent units to Tacoma, where in July there were full-scale riots around the mills of that city and where for weeks the troops patrolled the streets in a posture close to martial law. The governor indicated that he wanted a strong union but would support the principle that a person had a "right to work" when he could find a job. He encouraged an uneasy peace across the industry in which the union won its recognition and the eight-hour day. The insurgents, however, then looked upon Martin as an open shop reactionary who had thrown his military power to the industrialists, and they were thereafter set against him.

By 1936 a sizeable body of radical opposition had formed against the governor—unionists, Socialists, old Wobblies, Communists, Technocrats, old time populist grangers—an articulate if not always coherent body of discontent held together in the conviction that the New Deal nationally and Martin's new deal in Olympia were far too conservative ever to cure the fatal illness of American capitalism. These groups in 1935 formed the Washington Commonwealth Federation, which, though vaguely related to the Cooperative Commonwealth Federation of British Columbia and to the American Commonwealth Federation organized that year in Chicago, stood on its own grievances, apart from other organizations or programs. The principal proposal of the WCF was similar to Upton Sinclair's famous idea of "production for use" to "End Poverty in California"—the proposal that, because of the failure of "production for profit," the state governments should take over idle land and factories and, in a large measure of state-level socialism, command the instruments of production. Just how this was to occur—specifically how it was to be financed and operated—was never quite clear, for WCF members could organize opposition much more effectively than they could organize the complex economic matters that might have advanced their often admirable humanitarianism. But their goals—employment and security and a commonwealth of citizens pledged to the welfare of all—were in a dark era brightly attractive, and membership continued to swell.

The movement produced two impressive spokesmen— Howard Costigan, a former Whitman college student who said that witnessing the Centralia riot in 1919 had made him a radical, and who had a wide radio audience for his views, and Burt Farquharson, a university professor of engineering who, as a sort of godfather to about forty young radical legislators, planned the first "production for use" moves in Olympia. Between 1933 and 1937 these moves included efforts to put the state in the business of retailing gasoline and electricity, to make milk a public utility, to stop the sales tax, and to develop a much more comprehensive system of public welfare than the one which Governor Martin imagined. These efforts failed because Costigan's influence never spread far beyond Seattle; because members of the Farquharson seminar could never marshal the votes of enough moderates or conservatives; and because they could never take the governorship.

But in 1936 they made their great try. In a period poignant with envy and enmity, it was not difficult to attack a mild-mannered, millionaire-businessman-governor who spoke like a banker and whose elegantly attired wife sang and played classical music for millionaire visitors to Olympia. He was a tall and rather awkward man whose sparse, rectangular mustache— then not much in fashion—and whose bright eyes under steel-rimmed glasses might have been caricatured as those of a heartless industrialist or of an impossibly snobbish professor. One might suppose that he had conspired to bring about the sales tax levied upon the purchases of food by poor people, that he had maliciously resisted pension programs which could provide decent standards of living for the aged and for impoverished families with dependent children. He was in fact, like most of the pre-depression Democrats, a relatively conservative man who did indeed believe the most pointed criticism of "production for use"—that it would discourage investments in the state by eastern capitalists.

And had the old convention system of nominating candidates still prevailed, the federation might well have been able to deny Martin the nomination. Members of the Farquharson seminar were not at all adverse to the tactics of calculated disruption—defiance of the rules, intimidation through demonstrations, bareknuckle fist fights to seize a microphone or even the chair itself. They had studied the soft underside of Robert's *Rules of Order* and were quite prepared to exploit it, and they did so in 1936 by turning the Democratic convention into a turmoil which yielded a "production for use" platform. This achievement made them all the more eager to seize the governorship.

That this did not occur was the result of a recent and unique revision of the state's system for primary elections. In 1935 the legislature had approved a measure (supported by the Grange and other groups who felt reason to fear the radicals and to support Governor Martin) called the "blanket" primary system, which put all participating parties on one large ballot, allowing voters to cross casually from one party to another. A voter in 1936 could, for example, vote in the Democratic gubernatorial primary, then cross over to vote among Republicans in the selection of nominees for lieutenant governor and attorney general; he might cast a vote among Democrats running for the house, then vote among Republicans running for the senate. With this wide-open opportunity in 1936, it seems clear that as many as fifty thousand voters who might otherwise have confined their selections to the Republican ballot were alert to the facts that no Republican could possibly win the governorship in November, that a vote in the Republican column would thus be a wasted vote, and that a prudent cross-over vote for Martin could stop the WCF candidate, John Stevenson. Martin won the nomination, 166,000 to 129,000. In November, he overwhelmed the Republican contender, former Governor Roland Hartley, 466,000 to 189,000.

This election shattered party loyalties and identifications in ways that would surely have pleased Ernest Lister and George Cotterill, who had worked years before for a nonpartisan politics. Primaries since 1936 have given state voters an extraordinary degree of independence, allowing conservatives, moderates, liberals, and radicals to find their candidates wherever they might be on the "blanket" ballot. That election also marked an end to any impressive radical or WCF power in the state, for in 1936 the group lost more than the governorship—its "production for use" initiative went down in defeat by a staggering margin, 370,000 "No" votes to only 97,000 "Yes," and state-level socialism was therafter never regarded as a serious possibility. The federation during the next few years was more and more open to Communist influence and torn by ideological infighting. Howard Costigan himself was excommunicated, and when the new leaders emerged they were men and women whose statements on American foreign policy, after the Stalin-Hitler Pact, so obviously reflected the Communist party line that the WCF soon lost all significant public support.

In November 1936, Clarence Martin was elated by the success of the New Deal nationally and of his own rather tidy new deal for the state of Washington. The radicals had been beaten back, and his own direction of the affairs of state seemed practically sovereign. The federal works along the Columbia River were becoming wonders of the new world of development, reclamation, and the public power movement. The state's school system had been saved, welfare seemed both professional and effective. By the end of that year he saw no urgent need for direct relief—the need which four years earlier had brought the state to the edge of insurrection.

But this elation soon choked in bitter disillusionment. Thousands of people were suddenly arriving from the Dust Bowl states—five thousand families were counted in January 1937—and when state agencies attempted to respond to their plight, their directors discovered that the federal money they anticipated was not forthcoming and that the state was sinking rapidly again into the quicksand of depression. It was soon evident that Roosevelt, Hopkins, and their advisers had supposed that the national economy was healthy enough to move again without the federal crutch, and that they had withdrawn much of the relief monies which had until then sustained employment. The crash that followed—the "Roosevelt Depression"—spread renewed panic across 1937.

The gloom measurably darkened when the major field of employment, the timber products industry in the Pacific Northwest, became the battleground for the worst jurisdictional dispute in American labor history. It began when the American Federation of Labor tried to recapture the contracts it had recently lost when thousands of woodworkers had joined the new industrial union—the International Woodworkers of America of the Committee for Industrial Organizations. The AFL ordered its carpenters to boycott any lumber from CIO mills. CIO longshoremen then refused to move lumber from AFL mills, and AFL teamsters began breaking through CIO picket lines. The crisis was one in which the industrialists had played no direct part, one curiously removed from the classic conflicts between capital and labor. The industry was paralyzed while unions fought unions, and soon most people were again out of work. There was bloody violence, or the threat of it, surrounding almost every dock, lumberyard, logging camp, and mill. The social landscape turned suddenly desolate, and by 1938 there were more people in the state receiving some form of public assistance than at any time since the Great Depression began.

This dispiriting reversal brought Clarence Martin to his own personal depression—a lost faith in a New Deal that seemed to him then to have been one of bungled planning and of tinkering expediency. He came to the conviction that organized labor was viciously irresponsible, and he expressed a grave doubt that public assistance could ever solve the nation's problems. Martin was, moreover, increasingly disturbed by a system which took tax money from honest farmers and diligent businessmen in eastern Washington and gave it to people living on public assistance in the chaotic, radical, labor-ridden urban turmoil of Seattle, Everett, and Tacoma. He became, in a word, more conservative than he had ever been before, and he did not hesitate to act.

When he cut back relief rolls by twenty-four thousand, there was great noise from the WCF and a series of minor riots in Seattle. When he tried in 1938 to cut the social security budget for the state from forty-three million dollars to thirty million dollars he was openly defied by the legislature. When he proposed drastic revisions in public assistance—while two hundred thousand people were still on relief rolls—he called it a "return to self-reliance and the re-establishment of family responsibility," and he was attacked as a cruel and heartless reactionary. When people understood that he intended to cut from public relief all those whose children were of legal age and were in any way capable of providing for their parents' assistance, Martin had charted his own political doom.

Yet he felt that he had been a responsible leader and that the liberals had no good reason to abandon him. He had, he believed, followed the New Deal to its dead end. In other matters vital to his friends, he had insisted that higher education be opened to the average graduates of the state's high schools, not just to the distinctly talented. His "open door" policy had brought about a conversion of normal schools into colleges with expanding curricula and broader proposes, and this development of colleges was itself a notable advance in state services. In 1937, he had signed a law which repealed the old statutes of criminal syndicalism and thus eliminated a major irritation to liberals. Then in a gesture pleasing to civil libertarians everywhere, he released from the state penitentiary Ray Becker, the last of the Centralia prisoners.

But the "responsible" support he expected when he sought a third term as governor was not substantial. Republicans in 1940 had their own lively primary contest and were eager to prepare Arthur Langlie, the young mayor of Seattle, for the governorship, and they did not cross over to support Martin. Democrats then rejected Martin and chose C. C. Dill, a former U.S. senator thoroughly identified with the New Deal and known to have been most instrumental in bringing to the state the projects at Bonneville and at Grand Coulee. Conservatives and moderates of both parties grouped in November to elect Langlie by a narrow margin.

During the 1940s Rufus Woods had other irons to heat, and he had himself written that "At sixty a man has committed enough mistakes to make him wise. . . . He should do better and live better than in any decade of his life." There were crusades to lead—against liquor, cigarettes, dirty books—and there were promotions to make, for he looked forward then to the full industrial development of his region. He could see the population increasing again by ten times, all of it because of cheap electricity, and he became a dependable spokesman for the public utility districts which he had once opposed, especially the Chelan County PUD, which at Rocky Reach Rapids above Wenatchee would soon build one of the last of the great dams. In the decade of his wisdom, Rufus Woods never tired of being photographed against the background of Grand Coulee, never tired of glorifying the achievement. It was the soul's law that one should see himself as a part of history, and Woods's vision was particularly ebullient: in the hour of his death in 1950, as his heart finally failed him, he called hospital attendants to his bedside to tell them again of the man-made marvels on the Columbia. He echoed then for the last time the awesomely self-conscious sense of destiny which had possessed him when, as he saw the dam completed, he told the graduating class of Grand Coulee High School that centuries hence, even ten thousand years after the first water rushed through the turbines or was pumped into the dry reservoir of the Grand Coulee, people would look at the dam and say "Here in 1942, indeed there once lived a great people."

6

New Voices in the
Promised Land

N regional history as in personal history, there are certain periods of acceleration or of dislocation, certain points of departure so abrupt or of beginnings so new that traditions crumble, certainties fade, and the established expectations of a way of life are never again the same. Within the scope of only two centuries in the Pacific Northwest, the invasion of Caucasians was surely one of these, shattering, as it did, the complex and subtle culture of native Americans. The coming of the railroads was another such social watershed: hundreds of thousands of people overwhelmed the disjointed and tentative colonial settlements and formed a new industrial ethos. Then the circumstances of World War II set in motion forces which would drastically change the necessities and hopes which had shaped the distinctive qualities of regional life for a generation.

The impact of this most recent change is at first vivid in the statistics of growth and economic expansion. During the war, many states in the nation actually lost population, and those which gained most were on the West Coast—California first, Washington second. The hydroelectric turbines at Bonneville and Grand Coulee were turning, and the manufacture of aluminum, plutonium, aircraft, and ships was creating entirely new urban centers. Aluminum plants were clustering around the

170

dams, and more than eighty shipyards were operating night and day, employing tens of thousands of men and women. In the quiet and remote town of Bremerton, for example, a minor shipyard developed suddenly into a major naval depot with some thirty thousand new workers and their families. In the Richland-Pasco-Kennewick area, a dusty farm district of maybe two thousand people in 1940, more than fifty-one thousand "defense workers" arrived in a few months to construct entirely new towns and mysteriously secret installations. The work force at the Boeing Airplane Company rose from four thousand to more than forty-five thousand in four years, and with a pace related to hot or cold wars, this growth continued across the 1950s. By 1960, the state's population of 2,853,214 was nearly twice the figure of twenty years before. The Puget Sound area, particularly, was then congested with new industrial plants and nearly a million people, more than half of whom had settled there since the depression, many of them bringing social or moral priorities not often consistent with distinctive regional traditions. And when the new aerospace industry alone was employing more workers than were employed in the traditional logging, milling, and manufacturing of the timber-products industry, it was clear that regional society was shifting toward a new economic base and that the cycles of supply and demand in the native extractive economy would have a diminishing influence upon regional securities and desperations.

The man who had perhaps the most intimate view of these changes and their implications was William M. Allen, who in September 1945 left the firm of Holman, Sprague, and Allen to become president of the Boeing Airplane Company. He was then forty-five years old, a graduate of Harvard Law School, an experienced and respected attorney who for twenty years had managed most of the company's legal affairs. During World War II he had drawn the first of the famous "cost-plus-fixed-fee" contracts so admired by American industries then building new plants for war production, and the "cost-plus" device allowed Boeing, like so many hundreds of others, to use federal monies for a fantastic expansion. Allen had indeed demonstrated a virtuosity with such expedients, but in his long service to the company he had never concerned himself with the engineering and manufacturing that were the most urgent matters at the moment of his ascendancy. The day before his appointment, the company had stopped its production of B-29s, then being assembled in Wichita, Kansas, and on the day he entered his office the army summarily terminated most Seattle production. Boeing was then, with the exception of a few airplanes still on the assembly lines, virtually out of business. In the course of only a few days, Allen had to cut back his Seattle work force from forty-five thousand to about fifteen thousand, and the future for those fifteen thousand was far from certain. His estimates were then that in the Puget Sound area each Boeing worker's pay check was vital to at least three "support-service" workers—teachers, grocers, salespersons—and Allen knew full well that his action would throw the economy of the entire region into severe dislocation.

It did just that, and many people began to relate prospects for their economic health to the character of a man who, until a few weeks before, had never made an executive decision. But to the curious, as to the anxious or the ambitious, Allen would offer insights which were remarkable only in their lack of substance. "Be confident," was his motto. "Bring to each task great enthusiasm, unlimited energy," he told men who were positively craving for some clue to the principles of life and comportment which had guided him toward pre-eminence. Presenting the image of a homespun, uncomplicated, and unsophisticated lawyer, he attributed success or failure to the expertise of "the organization" and to a common "exercise of judgment based on facts." This image was strengthened by Allen's steadfast Puritanism, for he was a man of deep family loyalties and of little leisure, a man who with conviction could tell a news reporter that leisure time served him only to "develop an appreciation of the joy that hard work offers." Though he might take an infrequent sip of scotch while he paused for a moment of cowboy music or dropped out for an infrequent afternoon of golf, he was a man totally dedicated to the "exercise of judgment," to the facts, the organization. In the next few years Allen would make great decisions, take great, even staggering risks, and even prove that in a quiet but relentless way he could be a merciless antagonist. Yet he frustrated business writers with a stubborn refusal to strike a heroic pose or to take any personal credit for his achievements. This enigma of an apparently colorless personality activating and coordinating momentous events was not at all unique in American business history, and it served Allen well, allowing him the assurance that public attention would focus upon international economic turbulence which buffeted the company rather than upon the really extraordinary resources of its new president.

The lines of these resources, however, were fairly clear. There were the basics of a strong and healthy body, a great reservoir of energy, a high, keen intelligence. In a small Montana town of fewer than one hundred souls, his father had been an able mining engineer, his mother a woman of deep religious faith. Insulated from music, art, and literature—and from depravity, anonymity and dissipation—his parents had almost total control of the years which brought him to embrace the work ethic. Thus the greening of an imperturbable knight of the Puritan order: the penetrating mind, the passion for the mastery of details and for absolute precision; the student who found the study of business law a persisting fascination; the youth unmoved by religious or aesthetic curiosities, taking a firm pride in decisions firmly made; the young man untroubled by social unrest; the adult who could say that he was "a Protestant and a Republican" and say it with ultimate authority so that all further questions were deflated. One could easily believe that Allen took his departmental reports to bed with him each evening, studying them until he fell asleep, but one could not imagine him setting aside a day to fly an airplane, or climb a mountain, or sit by a river in quiet introspection. One could imagine him campaigning against the union shop—as he did in the case of an initiative measure in 1958. But it would have been out of character for him to have his company finance scholarships or sponsor a Bach society, or to have his experts calculate the social impact of a major Boeing decision on schools, housing, transportation, taxes, or ecology.

Allen in fact had very little in common with the company's founder, the tall, dapper, exquisitely mustached playboy of the American West named William E. Boeing. After schooling in Switzerland and at Yale, Boeing had taken his inheritance from Minnesota to Seattle, where in 1903 he invested in timber. For the young man, the good life was almost immediately available. When he wanted to sail, he acquired not only a yacht but a shipyard that could maintain it. When he tired of card games at the University Club and found a new interest in airplanes, he of course bought several. As he learned to fly them, he hired a team of curious engineers and mechanics and pilots to join the crew at his shipyard and guide him in his new hobby. In 1916 he built his first seaplane and organized the Boeing Airplane Company.

The Great War stimulated Boeing to build a few machines the navy wanted for flight training, and from this experience he developed a "flying boat" for airmail service between Seattle and British Columbia. During the 1920s he had several contracts to assemble navy fighter planes, each of which, to the delight of people in the city, he enjoyed testing and modifying—and sometimes nearly sinking—around his dock on Lake Union. These activities, however, were not demanding, and Boeing had many obligations—he had yachts to sail, parties to attend, friends to entertain, traveling to take, investments to make, timber to sell, and affairs to supervise for the Association Against the Prohibition Amendment, an organization he supported generously after his home had been mischievously raided by Prohibition agents. He did, nevertheless, intend to build a business, and his small factory-shipyard even turned out occasional pieces of bedroom furniture, which, with the timber sales, covered the losses of the airplane company. All the while he was steadily investing in the most modern engineering equipment, personally supervising each phase of the constantly refined experimentation, and by the end of the decade he was, among the few airplane manufacturers in the country, the leading innovator. His major achievements were to produce an all-metal plane, and then in 1932 a twin-engine transport plane which made commercial air traffic possible. Even in the depth of the Depression, the company had brilliant prospects for profits and expansion, but William Boeing had still other obligations, and he sold most of his stock so that he could fulfill a personal ambition, which was to retire at the age of fifty-one. Under new direction in the 1930s, the company continued to assemble transports, employing several thousand people and providing Seattle with an interesting and moderately active economic diversification.

William Allen had watched most of it: the continuing development of commercial transports; the army contracts for a four-engine bomber, the B-17; then the production of the "Super Fortress," the B-29, which after 1944 became a major weapon in the war against Japan. He also watched while the war changed the Boeing Company from a modest local industry into a sprawling colossus totally dependent upon federal contracts which terminated abruptly in 1945, dropping the company into an unexplored economic wilderness. Allen, then, would be the explorer. During his first hour in office he moved toward decisions which twenty years later would cause *Fortune* magazine to name him as one of the first fifteen laureates chosen from two centuries of American history for its "Hall of Fame for Business Leadership."

The first of these decisions was that the company should endure. The Super Fortress project had brought together resources of scientific talent and equipment unequaled anywhere—2,700 engineers with laboratories, testing devices, and research-in-progress on missiles and jet aircraft, supervisors who had refined techniques of on-the-job training which could convert inexperienced workmen into highly skilled craftsmen. Allen was determined to hold these resources intact, and to do so he committed the company to the production of a transport plane called the "Stratocruiser," for which he had no known commercial market. This airplane lost the company millions of dollars, but for Allen it won valuable time—the time necessary to prepare for a great gamble that the Boeing Company could become the world's first major manufacturer of jet transports. He was still studying for this decision—and still operating at a loss—when in 1948 he faced what he regarded as his second really threatening crisis.

The labor contract then in effect still carried a work clause extended from wartime which required the company to retain or promote workers on the basis of seniority, rather than merit. Allen regarded this provision as antiquated and debilitating, a barrier to quality when quality was all the company had to offer. The issue broke open when after a period of frightful inflation in the cost of living, the Aero Mechanics Union demanded a new contract which would include an increase in wages as well as an extension of the seniority system. When the company refused both, about fifteen thousand workers—defying the work contract still legally in force—went out on strike.

For the labor union, the strike was a bad move. Allen insisted that in striking, the Aero Mechanics had not only illegally repudiated their contract; they had forfeited their exclusive rights to any future contract, and he was sustained in this view by the federal district court. He then refused to negotiate, breaking the strike by hiring men only at wages determined by him and on the basis of demonstrated merit, not seniority. It was a ruthless business, but in Allen's view absolutely necessary. After three months there were enough workers for production, but no union shop, few seniority privileges, and only a modest wage increase, though Allen did handsomely reward those supervisors who had supported him. Leaders of the Aero Mechanics Union (the AM) charged that Allen had actually agreed to an arrangement with Dave Beck's teamsters—then already reputed to be imperialistic, brutal, and corrupt—to break the AM with a classic "sweetheart deal." In any event, there is no doubt that when Beck chartered the Aeronautical Workers, Warehousemen and Helpers' Union Local 451 to recruit strikebreakers, the Boeing Company encouraged workers to join it. The devious Beck forces never won enough support to represent the Boeing work force legally, in arbitration, but while the two unions struggled, Allen manipulated the ordeal to assemble the elite crew of production workers which could carry the company into what he would call the "jet age."

The company was soon drawn into production rhythms which

after 1948 reflected cold war anxieties and called for building more military aircraft and missiles and advancing the design of "pure" jet bombers. When Allen knew that the largest bomber, the B-52, was in fact a signal triumph in the development of aerospace technology, he could see the coming revolution in air travel. He then organized the company's resources for the production of commercial jets—the turning point in transportation history which many writers regard as Allen's most critical decision. In the history of American capitalism it was beautifully timed, emerging as it did from a configuration of classically appropriate conditions: his labor problems had been solved; he had an adequate aggregate of capital and credit; he had the richest pool of aerospace talent ever assembled, and the new computer science was available to this team; he had the most advanced testing equipment and manufacturing plants -built largely by the government with his cost-plus contracts from the war. With twenty-four percent of the company's net worth (then sixteen million dollars) he ordered his team to produce what they would regard as the best commercial airplane in the world.

From a design in 1952, the production model of the Boeing 707 was ready in 1954. It was a dazzling object—four jet engines mounted on swept-back wings with a span of 130 feet, an incredibly symmetrical bird-like tube of silver metal 128 feet long that could rise like a rocket and cruise at twenty-five thousand feet with a speed of 600 miles per hour. When Allen allowed the first public flight demonstration of the 707 during the Seattle Seafair festivities in 1955, the test pilot, "Tex" Johnston, was so eager to convince the world that this was indeed the world's greatest airplane that he flew it confidently above a crowd of two hundred fifty thousand people and twice rolled it over at an altitude of five hundred feet. (Johnston subsequently learned that such rollovers were not consistent with Allen's stern view of a test pilot's responsibilities.)

The 707 brought the Boeing Company the reputation which made it not only the largest producer of commercial transports but also one of the largest military contractors. In the 1950s work was in progress on the 707, the 727, the Saturn V rockets, the Minuteman ICBMs; and employment at the many plants and laboratories and testing sites rose to about seventy-two thousand.

The cold war, however, inspired competitions for military contracts which made the economy of the entire region subject to forces which were utterly unpredictable. Boeing employment dropped to fifty-eight thousand in 1960 and to fifty thousand in 1964 during a period of significant regional economic distress. It was not until 1965 that the company's commercial contracts finally equaled the military contracts, and economists could suppose that someday the regional economy might be released from the grip of war fear and war preparation. Pushing constantly toward such a future, Allen then gathered a staff of twenty-two thousand, called the "elite of the elite," to design Boeing's entry into the competition for a federal contract to build a supersonic transport—and won, but then lost when Congress withheld funds and later turned away from its initial enthusiasm for the project. At the same time he was also approaching another climatic high-risk venture—the decision in 1966 to invest a full ninety-eight percent of the company's net worth (seven hundred and fifty million dollars) and build a mammoth jet transport, the 747. In 1968, Boeing employment soared to ninety-five thousand.

By then the Boeing Company dominated what was called the "Pugetopolis"—the area north and south of the "Boeing Basin" from Oregon to Canada. It was a region that seethed with disorderly growth and the myriad of social and political problems drifting in the wake of war-born prosperity to plague American urban civilization. These problems were of course not entirely new for the state of Washington, but their intensity after 1940 made them newly urgent. The industrial growth of the war years, which had meant salvation from the depression, had imposed upon the state a rash of urban afflictions that by the 1950s could be measured in environmental pollution, crowded housing, poor highways, understaffed schools and colleges, and the erosion of most of the state's vital services. And the war years had fixed several black ghettos upon the state, each of them potentially threatening to the uneasy but predictable racial harmony that had endured since the 1920s.

In August of 1940, the ashes of the elder Horace Cayton were scattered over silent waters in Puget Sound, a symbolic and harmonious immersion of the man in the water and land he had chosen. At the time of his death he was eighty-one years old, a sad but proud man, a man again of considerable prestige among the blacks in Seattle who had known two decades of social tranquility. Still numbering fewer than four thousand, most of them lived on land William Grose had claimed almost a century before, yet there were no brutally obvious racial demarcations in the urban geography. Whites, Chinese, Japanese, and maybe still a few Indians lived in the "Central Area," which, with a middle-class pride in its neatly-kept homes and sedate neighborhoods, had a warmer sense of community than most districts of the city.

But Seattle was nevertheless a thicket of pervasive if subtle discriminations. Though most black males had semiskilled jobs, none worked at the Boeing Company, where the Aero Mechanics Union adamantly refused to admit them. There were a number of black longshoremen, a few black teamsters, a few seamen—among them Cayton's radical son, Revels, who worked as an organizer. Most shops and unions had doors almost impossible for blacks to open. Downtown, the business offices were consistently white, so far off-limits that Cayton's daughter Madge, who had been graduated from the University of Washington, could find work only as a cashier in a black restaurant. Even with the fast pace of war prosperity, department stores were interested in "white applicants only," and the shadow of Jim Crow fell heavily across merchandising, transportation, education, and recreation. Following Cayton's early rebellion and his consequent fall from grace, most blacks had learned to accept or to avoid the predictable humiliations and to live thereafter with securities that were sustained by a deep but tender sense of prudence. They became both cautious and conservative, and, like Cayton himself, many were keenly class-conscious and self-conscious of the distinction between themselves and those who did the unskilled and menial work of the city—the janitors, bellhops, redcaps, and house servants, most of whom had always been not black but Oriental.

The war years broke rudely upon these securities. In February 1942, the Federal Employment Practices Commission opened jobs for blacks at Boeing, and even though the Aero Mechanics Union still refused to change its racial policy, the company began recruiting workers from southern states. Within two years, the black community in Seattle had grown from four thousand to around twelve thousand, and the city bulged with new people and new confusions. There was, for example, a serious shortage of housing for white workers, and for blacks this meant not only a problem but a predicament. The patterns of discrimination that were loose enough to allow whites and Orientals to live in the Central Area were not so loose as to permit blacks to leave it, and the older residents had no choice but to accommodate the new. Even as they did, the sudden presence of the migrants, white and black, and of black servicemen from training camps diffused the shadow of Jim Crow across the state with "whites only" signs from Bremerton to Tacoma to Walla Walla to Pasco.

A critical part of this social commotion for Seattle's black community was the lifestyle which the native-born quickly associated with the migrants, whom they often saw as disorderly, irresponsible, drunken, undisciplined, inclined toward public, rather than private, indulgences. There were soon tense episodes of racial and class abrasion on the city's buses and in the parks, movie houses, restaurants, and taverns, episodes so frightening to black leaders that they soon asked for help. Cayton's older son, Horace, was then widely known for his work in sociology and for his militant articles in *The New Republic* and *The Nation*. Among blacks he was respected as a "race leader" and as a "race man"—terms he had won for his role as a national critic of discriminations. To the church and fraternal groups who gathered to hear him in Seattle in 1943, his message was that the new black migrants would remain in the city after the war and that for the black community to know any stability at all it must assimilate the newcomers and work with them. He advised the leaders to act with tolerance, patience, understanding, and brotherhood, but he encouraged both the old and the new to unite in spreading a mood of rising expectations. To a remarkable degree, the black community accepted this message, for within a few months after Cayton's appearance in Seattle the local chapter of the NAACP increased its membership from 85 to 1,550.

This group moved forward after the race riot in Detroit that year, pleading to Mayor William F. Devin to act quickly and vigorously to avoid a similar terror. They reminded him that cases of bigotry attracted the energies of white radicals whose aggressive and antagonistic intervention usually made matters worse by propelling every racial scene on toward a rapid confrontation. This argument impressed Devin, and his response was to appoint in 1944 a Civic Unity Committee, the counterpart of such agencies in hundreds of cities being organized then with the urgent assignment of exploring moderate but constructive routes around racial violence. Devin's appointees were lawyers, judges, professors, physicians, clergymen—cautious and pre-eminently respectable—who began to study discrimination in housing, transportation, employment, and recreation. When they identified a situation of potential upheaval, they worked without publicity to mollify white or black intransigence— usually with informal and individual suggestions for progress and compromise in an atmosphere of "crisis patriotism." They were particularly effective in persuading newspapers to dampen stories of racial incidents. These methods served the city well during the war, and the committee came ultimately to represent all minorities and to becalm the unions, farmers, and patriotic organizations that would have resisted the return of the Japanese in 1945. In a quiet achievement, the committee opened housing for the first Japanese family ever to live in the University District in 1951.

After the war the Civic Unity Committee for a while sheltered the Washington State Board Against Discrimination in Employment, which was created in 1949 by a legislature and a governor who, in view of the flow of federal monies into the state, could agree at least that some action against bigotry was important. Though this was the first state agency ever concerned with discrimination, Arthur Langlie's appointments to the board were conservative and dignified men who distinguished themselves in their determination to avoid heat or controversy. It was not until after 1956—after the Supreme Court decision against segregation, when there were forty thousand blacks in Seattle alone, and when the tide of militancy was rising sharply across the nation—that Governor Albert Rosellini brought to the board a bold and aggressive young lawyer, Kenneth A. McDonald, under whose direction the agency began to dramatize the clearly predictable lines of bigotry that made the state more and more congruent with the nation. The National Urban League then had twenty-five volunteer and professional staff members in Seattle at work to discover and coordinate opportunities for blacks in education, employment, housing, welfare, and health. The Congress of Racial Equality soon had an even larger staff, preparing the Seattle business community to accept the profound social changes which would soon overtake it.

But there were defeats, some of them bitterly disappointing. In 1964, the voters of Seattle and Tacoma voted down proposed ordinances for "open housing" by overwhelming margins of two-to-one and three-to-one, and a CORE effort to boycott downtown retail houses opened only a few jobs for minorities. At that moment the executive director of Seattle's Urban League was telling citizens that they must somehow be cured of what he saw as a peculiar regional "syndrome"—the easy feeling among both the concerned and the indifferent that the Pacific Northwest was secure in its shallow traditions of racial tranquility and loose discrimination, the supposition that racial hatreds might ignite Detroit or Los Angeles, but that such eruptions "couldn't happen here" because the benign history of white-black relationships since the time of George Bush had left the state of Washington somehow different from the nation. This attitude was itself a bigotry, he believed, vicious in the depth of its deception and in its restraint upon significant action. He soon became the most inspired spokesman of those who hoped that before it was too late people in the state might be brought to understand that they enjoyed no special moral superiority in matters of racial relationships.

Born in Florida, Edwin T. Pratt had worked his way through a black college, then through the Graduate School of Social

Work in Atlanta. In 1956, he came to the Seattle office of the National Urban League, which before his directorship was a sort of sophisticated employment service for educated and skilled blacks hoping for direction across the barriers of discrimination. Pratt himself was representative—married, with two children, an Episcopalian, he lived in an upper middle-class neighborhood where there were far more whites than blacks, and he moved easily among the city's white professional and business classes. His work was at first in grantsmanship, acquiring money from the Ford Foundation, the Department of Labor, the National Urban League, and then from the federal Office of Economic Opportunity to subsidize job training, to organize instruction in racial sensitivity for public school teachers, to support a sort of real estate bureau to bring black buyers and white sellers together, and to publish research studies.

These studies were brilliantly illuminating. Pratt could show, for example, that the state did indeed have less of a quantitative problem than most states——that only about two percent of the population was black and that blacks were in fact less than half of the non-Caucasian minority. But Seattle and Tacoma were about seven percent black, and that figure was constantly growing. He could show that blacks in the urban areas knew less poverty, less housing density, and more actual integration than in Detroit or Los Angeles, but that in Seattle, Tacoma, and Pasco they nevertheless suffered from employment and educational discrimination that was real and painful, from gross inadequacies in public transportation and medical services, and that they harbored an expanding group of unemployed youth whose cynicism and lack of constructive activities was increasingly ominous. He could show that the status of blacks was indeed improving—the prosperity of the 1960s spilled over on most people—but that the economic and social distance between the races was actually growing. Most blacks did not have middle-class incomes, and as whites fled to the suburbs, de facto segregation was becoming the most conspicuous feature of Seattle's educational and social life.

What he saw, then, as he crossed back and forth through the city, was the rising cost of the status quo. He felt he could measure it in the increasing need for welfare pensions, in the incidence of crime and delinquency, in the dismaying performance on standard tests by blacks in the nearly segregated schools, in the inexorable waste of human potential. Seattle's Central District, he said, was "a virtual black ghetto of high-cost, sub-standard housing—a breeding ground for the social diseases of crime and family disintegration." Like Martin Luther King, Jr., Edwin Pratt felt that the nation was—in Pratt's words—"in a race with time to end the poverty and bigotry which distort our state and national life." There must come the day, he said, when Americans "will boast of an integrated neighborhood, school, business, and even church, with the same enthusiasm that so many of our forefathers boasted of the exclusiveness and segregation of these institutions in the past." As one of the most effective speakers in the region, he electrified hundreds of audiences with this theme and soon became the most eloquent and implacable enemy of Pacific Northwest complacency.

Though he went about his work with great skill and spoke with great authority, Edwin Pratt was sometimes a quiet, brooding, deeply thoughtful man, complex in his many motivations. Like many others, he may at times have thought that there were other, more pleasant lives he could lead than the one which events had thrust upon him. Yet after 1964 Pratt saw his mission—to speak across the racial gulf to Seattle whites and make them aware that their regional biases no longer had any validity, that they no longer had any regional insulation against what was clearly among the most portentous of national problems. His speeches emphasized what most whites in the state chose to ignore—the character of discrimination that one could actually measure in housing, jobs, schools, and social services. He pressed on to analyze racism in city and state employment, in unions, at the University of Washington, and there is no doubt that he prepared most of these institutions and agencies for their achievements in integration that marked the next decade, for their rising levels of moral sensitivity and social conscience.

He appeared before real estate salesmen, school administrators, college students, youth groups (both black and white), clergymen, social workers, businessmen, policemen. In demanding that people be aware of what they hoped to ignore—and thus refused to rectify—Pratt found passionate opponents as well as supporters. He came to know the hatred of black as well as white separatists, and he was moving the city toward a precarious polarization. Then when, for better or for worse, he focused his remarkable energies on de facto school segregation—and began to urge programs of shifting school boundaries and of voluntary "bussing" that would bring white and black children together—he did indeed polarize the city, and the weight of both white and black anxieties fell down upon him. There were riots in the summer of 1968—three nights in Seattle—not terrible ones, but real ones nevertheless. The race against time was going badly. Edwin Pratt was then surely a man with a cross to bear, and with each speech he made a fateful step toward an awesome destiny. It was then that he began to receive serious threats against his own life and against the safety of his family.

These were years of serial tragedy in American life, memories of which can yet cause us to cry out for mercy against the perversions of needless war, needless poverty, convulsive riots, casual murders, and premeditated assassinations. These misfortunes also marked the experience of Americans in the 1860s, and we grope to define the curse which amid great perversities causes assassins to arise whenever leaders arise who can shout a sense of purpose or a version of community across racial and social chasms. From the shot which killed Abraham Lincoln, we can follow the curse forward to the death of Martin Luther King, Jr. In the somber hours of the 1960s, no state escaped the traumas, for in an age of instant communications, there were no boundaries for mourning. One moment, however, spread an almost unbearable anguish across the face of Seattle—the evening of January 25, 1969, when Edwin Pratt was murdered in the presence of his family, in the doorway of his own home. He fell before two gunmen whose color and whose grievance have never been revealed. He was then only thirty-eight years old, and his death was a tragedy in a surfeit of tragedy which proved the truth he had all along been teaching—that the conscience of a state was then inseparable from the conscience of the nation.

7

Notes for a Tricentennial
Historian

*A*S it crosses the forty-ninth parallel, the Columbia River no longer shimmers with the clarity and speed which once caused men to stand back in fear and wonder. If it moves at all, it drifts sluggishly toward the Kettle, where there is no trace of *La Chauldiere,* the boiling cauldron of twisting currents and crashing white water. The ledges of Kettle Falls lie beneath the smooth surface of Franklin D. Roosevelt Lake, which covers the former channels and rapids above Grand Coulee, and which in the year of the bicentennial announces that the Columbia is for the most part no longer in fact a river. It is, rather, a series of lakes, each of them burying the rhythm and brilliance which from the Selkirk Mountains to the North Pacific Ocean has through all but the most recent years been central to the region's historic character.

The Spokane River, which once broke from a rocky canyon to churn the race of crystal-clear water, now carries "industrial" and "sanitary" wastes away from the city, which, for a few glowing years during the 1920s, the poet Vachel Lindsay had praised as representative of the purity and innocence of the great American West, a community of strength and virtue where true individuals might fulfill lives of sensitivity and purpose. His sentiment was so lyrical that he convinced even himself,

186

and he lived there in the Davenport Hotel, accepting the hospitality and the generosity of the city's liberal elite, marrying a
high school English teacher, and writing his boldly cadenced
song and verse. But his exaltations cooled, and in 1928 he returned to Springfield, Illinois, which he then thought to be more
poetically and more historically American.

Though he was never much of a social prophet, what Lindsay
in this instance did detect and leave behind him was a loss of
civic confidence which continued unabated through the Great
Depression. Rail traffic declined, new highways allowed smaller
towns to lure away banks and retail stores, and the years of contraction brought a steady erosion of Spokane's earlier energies.
The city missed even the mood of rising expectations which
came to other communities with Grand Coulee Dam and the
prosperity of World War II. Then while most other cities in the
state were growing again in the 1960s, Spokane lost more than
ten thousand people, and in the abandoned houses, even abandoned neighborhoods, the fact that Spokane no longer represented the spirit of the Inland Empire was painfully obvious.

But—we may reasonably ask—what material representation
can there be anywhere of the spirit of a region? Can a city or a
town, or even a poem or a song, ever project an aggregate of
energies, ambitions, strengths, fears, insights, or traditions? We
have noted that to the centennial *voyageur*, the Columbia River
was more than a symbol; it projected an inescapable definition of the terms of his existence. But to the twentieth-century
observer, the great wedge of concrete extinguishing the upper
Columbia seems to define both the personal and the social
circumstances of the region's people: in the Inland Empire,
Grand Coulee Dam is the inescapable presence of the bicentennial era. It is, from one perspective, a massive and awesome monument violating the centennial reality of a wild and beautiful river,
its salmon, its primeval landscape, the rush and flow of its penetrating rhythms. And a part of the reality is that there is no retreat from this violation. Yet from another perspective it is a
happy monument to technology, progress, and development, the
realization of a brilliant dream: great pumps splashing clear
water to spill across fertile lands, water to flow into bright new

towns, all of them neatly linear, clean, and prosperous. It is the dream of Rufus Woods and James O'Sullivan and of the migrant minstrel named Woody Guthrie, who sang in the 1930s that the river would be tamed and trained to change "darkness to dawn," to "run the great factories and water the land / Roll on, Columbia, Roll on!" [1] The bicentennial *voyageur* would hear the song but see no rolling, and he would understand the varied faces of a powerful symbol. What this symbol represented—in terms of life, liberty, and the pursuit of happiness— would be a question then too ambiguous for him to answer.

Below the dam and into the arch of the Big Bend, the Columbia is lost in calm pools behind more concrete barriers, each bearing the names of dead heroes and a dead geography. There is Rufus Woods Lake, then Chief Joseph Dam, Wells Dam, Rocky Reach Dam, and Rock Island Dam. At Wenatchee, the river gains enough life to leave a hint of its former purpose, and the town itself presents as many subtle reflections of a river community's past as it does the modern conversions of the river's energies. A bicentennial *voyageur* could mark the landing where riverboats served the orchards before the railroad came. Then from the main street he could look across the river to the high hills and let his eyes trace the scar of a huge cross— a full one hundred feet long—burned into the soil with oil and sawdust by Klansmen to whom the early 1920s brought more fear than prosperity. Theirs was for a season a deadly influence, spreading there, as in many parts of the Pacific Northwest, in the form of persecution and discrimination against foreign-born migrant laborers, as censorship of textbooks and teachers, as suppression of social criticism, as crusades by self-appointed guardians of Americanism against diversity and dissent. But it was a short season, now gone and largely forgotten. Though they are yet served by a migrant harvest-labor force which can

1. ROLL ON, COLUMBIA
   Words by Woodie Guthrie
   Music based on "Goodnight Irene" by Huddie Ledbetter
   & John Lomax
   TRO—© Copyright 1957 & 1963 LUDLOW MUSIC, INC.,
   New York, N.Y. Used by permission.

appear sometimes as a menacing rural proletariat, most of the orchardists work as a species of modern yeoman farmers, almost Jeffersonian in their landed identities and their craftsmanship. They tend to their trees with pride, and manage their affairs with considerable independence. With the new chemistry of fruit storage, with the cultivation of hillside vineyards of extraordinary quality, with the opening of a new college, the people of the valley have in recent years known prosperity without confusion and growth without upheaval. To the dismay of Rufus Woods, the great flow of hydroelectricity from the federal dams never favored his city as much as it did the larger urban centers, never wired Wenatchee to the kind of major industrialization which he had all along intended.

Beyond the barrier of Rock Island Dam, the water drifts slowly toward the Snake River where the cities of Pasco, Richland, and Kennewick seem new, lively, and in this landscape curiously incongruous. Born to the new world of plutonium, they are more recently based in a prosperous and diversified economy of nuclear, electronic, and agricultural activities which hold a sophisticated urban population to a desert oasis. The terrors of water which inspired Lewis and Clark to expressions of ultimate physical courage have been lost for decades below the surface of lakes behind McNary Dam, John Day Dam, The Dalles Dam, Bonneville Dam. To the new people, the river is simply a body of cool water necessary to the nuclear technology and happily available for casual recreation.

Below Bonneville, the river moves finally to its natural shorelines as it passes quietly beyond Portland and Vancouver and on to the sea. Edging the river at the Cowlitz confluence, the city of Longview is a symbol of recent aspirations. It was planned and built in the 1920s by Robert A. Long, who then managed the Long-Bell Lumber Company and who wanted his name on a milltown where civic health and pride might stand forever as a deterrent to industrial strife. Before he died in 1934, he had secured the delta lands from flooding and had built a business district, parks, schools, streets, and sidewalks; he had supervised zoning codes, promoted churches, and encouraged residential neighborhoods. He had, moreover, acquired timberlands to feed his own two mills, and here—as at Shelton—the shadow of Mark Reed falls across a timber industry which has changed in ways which probably Reed and Long and the Weyerhaeusers had indeed imagined.

In the 1940s industrialists began to explore the great potential of what they had traditionally regarded as mill wastes—sawdust, chips, bark, debris—and were approaching a technology which could make possible new mills for pulp, paper, chipboard, hardboard, and plywood. As this new wood-products manufacturing became as important to the state as sawed lumber, the augmented industry was depending upon trees and logging practices which loggers had earlier ignored and upon concepts of land stewardship which Reed had so well represented. His shadow was especially evident in 1947 when the Simpson Lumber Company, which Reed had for so many years directed, entered into a pact with the federal government, creating the "Shelton Cooperative Sustained Yield Unit," the first of several pledges between national foresters and commercial companies to join public and private lands into units of inter-related forestry. The companies agreed to replant cutover forests, to accept federal guidance in fire precautions, watershed protection, recreational developments, and wildlife management, and in return for these services to receive first rights, at appraised rates, to timber in national forests. They agreed, moreover, to harvest from the total unit at a rate by which the annual yield would equal the annual growth—a balance whereby the forests could be maintained forever.

It was a splendid conception and a splendid achievement. Environmentalists, however, resisted the law because it opened a door into national forests for logging companies known mainly for their cut-and-run instincts, and some of these companies, for their own reasons, were reluctant to accept federal restrictions. Thus the practice of "sustained yield" forestry has never spread as far as it should have spread when the timber products industry is, in the 1970s, again the state's major employer, and when tree farming has become an exact science. Yet it has become an institution among the major timber industrialists, like the Weyerhaeusers, who are today more firmly fixed to the region than ever before, more ready to contribute to the quality of life in the state by regarding it less as their colony than as their permanent home. Their research into low-waste pulp technology promises to abate a grievous pollution, and their work in "high yield" forestry promises to make "super trees"—to let silviculture do for timber what genetics did for Indian corn.

This is indeed a pleasant prospect, but across the industry there are other, often somber, considerations. "Sustained yield" practice has never spread toward the exploitations of the red cedar of the Pacific Northwest, a species never subjected to precise or extensive farming because a good crop requires two hundred years to grow, yet a species which for a thousand years—in Indian canoes, baskets, clothing, and houses, and in the industrial production of lumber and shingles—has been at the material center of regional culture. In the year of the bicentennial, this wood is disappearing at a rate, which, if sustained until the end of the century, will leave it gone forever.

This devastation is vivid on the Quinault Reservation, where thousands of acres of huge stumps are snarled in an almost impenetrable net of underbrush and debris. A half-century of commercial logging here has left the land practically impossible to develop as tree farms or as healthy watersheds for spawning grounds —a wasteland of cut-and-run which leaves a melancholy scar across the face of the reservation. Nor is the interior world here always comforting, for the Quinault, like most reservation Indians in the state, live with mournful evidence of the cut-and-run across the very heart of their culture. Their share of frontier development was poverty, disease, spiritual confusion, the expectation of a life span low in numbered years yet high in measured desperation.

For a century they had seemed doomed by these circumstances. Yet the reach of time had at least removed them from the murderous Indian wars, and from the next generation, whose white leaders felt compelled to romanticize and thus further to distort the remnants of the history and culture of Northwest Indians. Then the jobs and the conscriptions of World War II brought them closer to the white society from which they could learn at least a few of the devices of self-preservation.

The greatest change, however, occurred during the 1960s when the people of Taholah were moved by forces stirring the energies of native Americans everywhere to take full advantage of the federal programs called the "War on Poverty." With expert guidance, they developed a resource development plan for protecting their remaining fish, timber, and wildlife. A community development plan allowed them to build a cannery and to work toward dramatic improvements in housing, health care, and education.

For a hundred years Indian children from Taholah, if they attended formal schools at all, had been coerced and cajoled, from the best of intentions, and pressured, through shame and humiliation, to abandon their ethnic and family values and submit to a kind of cultural brainwashing which might prepare them to function in the white society—though the results never justified such acts or assumptions. The results, in terms of cross-cultural mobility, were in fact added increments of personal failure and cultural confusion. Most of the individuals who attempted to cross into the world of white ambitions and disciplines never made it, and they retreated not to their homes but to the skid roads of urban areas, where destitute and desolate alcoholics, broken in body and spirit, were unable to lead meaningful lives on any reservations, white or Indian.

In view of this predictable anguish, sensitive educators in the 1960s determined to prepare students for a harmonious life not in Aberdeen or Seattle but at Taholah, not as white people but as Quinault Indians. They began a remarkable attempt to bring students toward an articulate awareness of Indian identities, toward an enrichment of the very values they had formerly been encouraged to abandon. At age three, children at Taholah began to attend classes in which there were usually no more than twelve Indian students, and a teacher, usually white, who was assisted by an adult Indian. In an attractive new building, which became the center of community energies, a bright young faculty was constantly bending the curriculum toward preparing Indians for the intelligent management of their own lives and resources—nutritional studies directed toward Quinault health; biological sciences applied to the river, the forests, and the beaches at Taholah; computations focused upon fish and wildlife inventories and harvest projections; literature and art oriented toward the Indian heritage. There were then reasons to suppose that the Indians of the Quinault might indeed fulfill the goals of the resource and community developments, and that in the year of the tricentennial they might be a people confident in their own traditions and values, rich in space, fresh air, pure water, and sustained yields of fish, timber, and game, rich in terms of opportunities, equalities, and emotional securities—among the most favored of the state's citizens

North of the Quinault Reservation, the rain forests and the wilderness beaches of the Olympic National Park are monuments to a different history—to the accumulation of a natural grandeur all the more profound because thoughtful men and women have protected it from industry and commerce. George Vancouver would today no doubt recognize his passage, mile by mile, from Cape Elizabeth to the rocks of Cape Flattery. Beyond the cape and toward Puget Sound, however, a wilderness becomes the Pugetopolis—the word itself a crude distortion of Vancouver's fine sensitivities —which reveals but a slight resemblance to Vancouver's discovered paradise. In the year of the bicentennial, it projects a confusing sense of positive and negative impressions, a convergence of diversities, which in the late 1960s moved David Brewster to write in *Seattle Magazine* that one could feel here "a sharp contrast between an attractive *private* world and a degrading *public* landscape." [2]

The public landscape then in view was the sludge of Bellingham Bay, the polluted air rising from the entire Puget Sound Basin, the industrial wastes in the rivers, the fertile bottom lands bulldozed into industrial jungles, the sprawling, congested, cluttered atrocities of growth and development which stretched north and south and often wove a ring of white suburbs around an increasingly black urban core.

Yet from the interrelationships of water, beaches, islands, mountains, and a mature urban culture, one could fashion a

2. David Brewster, "Is This the Shape of Things to Come?" *Seattle Magazine* 6 (June 1969): 16–50.

lifestyle rich in subtle possibilities and refreshingly distinct from that of any other section of the state or nation. And it was a lifestyle often adorned with a sense of public grace which could emerge despite the degradations. During the 1960s Lake Washington was rescued from contamination by a remarkable merger of environmental sensitivities and scientific intelligence. A new generation of leadership brought tax monies together and routed urban sewage away from the lake, converting what had become an obnoxious urban cesspool into what it had been at the time of Arthur Denny—one of the world's most pure and beautiful bodies of fresh water. The University of Washington was then the site of research into medicine, fishery science, and silviculture which were yielding insights of the very highest significance. To the south, the range and depth in the Boeing pool of design and engineering talent was an asset of stunning brilliance. Around Puget Sound there were residential neighborhoods of tranquility and of distinguished architecture, and at the heart of the metropolis itself there was an enduring professionalism in the performing arts and a rising vitality in health care which were unusual urban blessings. Dozens of two-year colleges presented educational opportunities for almost anyone who wanted them. The absence of poverty—relative to almost any other American megalopolis—was a symptom of strength and potential. Such measurable distinctions could lead one to conclude that in the year of the bicentennial, the quality of life here and across the state could be of extraordinary eminence.

On this note the reader may recall that we began this essay with a search through the past for shadows of ideals we might need in the present. We have now found such shadows reflected in the free-moving rivers, in the islands and the forests, in the parks, beaches, bays, and headlands, the preservation of which, to future generations, may seem to be among the most spiritual of modern achievements. We could find them also in efforts, particularly obvious since the death of Edwin Pratt, to live with a sense of racial harmony. We could see them in the vitality of political institutions, particularly the "Initiative Measure to the People," which have recently extended the range of environmental protections and individual freedoms. We have seen them in the striving for social stability among people who have been historically torn by geographic disunity but who have nevertheless created order from disorder by grasping certain unique historical advantages: an aggregate of young and vigorous individuals and families whose high level of literacy has given them a high level of affluence; a geographic remoteness which could mean an insulation from the historical tensions and prejudices of other American regions; a sensitivity to history itself which has been deep enough to shape a conspicuous concern for future generations.

We are now close to a moral reckoning for our initial consideration, which was how well people here have secured the rights of life, liberty, and the pursuit of happiness for themselves and for those who may follow after them. There is of course no adequate quantitative measure for our answer, but given the details of a particular historical view, there can be a strong if particular personal judgment. It is this: that while a renewed passion for growth and development in this state, or a revised attraction to stumpfarmer perversities, may quite possibly litter the social landscape with pollutions, corruptions, and inequities which will appall the tricentennial historian, the trend is that they will not. And the shadows which give shape to this trend are sometimes magnificent.

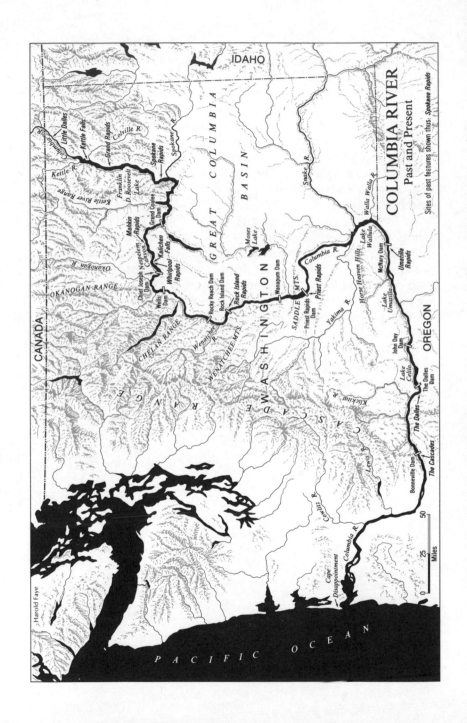

COLUMBIA RIVER
Past and Present

Sites of past features shown thus: *Spokane Rapids*

IDAHO

CANADA

Columbia R.
Little Dalles
Kettle Falls
Grand Rapids
Colville R.
Spokane Rapids
Spokane R.
Kettle R.
Kettle River Range
Franklin D. Roosevelt Lake
Okanogan R.
Malkin Rapids
Grand Coulee Dam
Kalichen Falls
Whirlpool Rapids
Nespelem
Chief Joseph Dam
Canyon
OKANOGAN RANGE
Okanogan Range
Wells Dam
Rocky Reach Dam
Rock Island Dam
Rock Island Rapids
Wenatchee R.
Wanapum Dam
Moses Lake
GREAT COLUMBIA BASIN
Snake R.
Columbia R.
Priest Rapids
Priest Rapids Dam
SADDLE MTS.
WENATCHEE MTS.
CHELAN RANGE
WASHINGTON
Yakima R.
Horse Heaven Hills
Walla Walla R.
Lake Wallula
McNary Dam
Lake Umatilla
Umatilla Rapids
John Day Dam
OREGON
Lake Celilo
The Dalles Dam
The Dalles
Klickitat R.
C A S C A D E   R A N G E
Lewis R.
Cowlitz R.
Bonneville Dam
The Cascades
Cape Disappointment
Columbia R.

50
25
0
Miles

Harold Faye

PACIFIC OCEAN

Suggestions for Further Reading

For the territorial period generally it would be difficult to write anything without H. H. Bancroft, *History of Washington, Idaho, and Montana* (San Francisco: The History Company, 1890). Edmond S. Meany, *History of the State of Washington* (New York: The Macmillan Company, 1909) is sometimes useful, as are Clinton A. Snowden, *History of Washington*, 6 volumes (New York: Century History, 1911) and Edgar I. Stewart, *Washington, Northwest Frontier*, 4 volumes (New York: The Lewis Historical Company, 1957). None of these, however, is really satisfactory for the purposes of social history, and one must range widely to find supplements.

Readers will find back issues of the *Pacific Northwest Quarterly* helpful on specific subjects. In addition, Dorothy O. Johansen and Charles M. Gates, *Empire of the Columbia*, 2nd edition (New York, Harper & Row, 1967) is probably indispensable. A superb and absolutely essential study of the geographic region is D. W. Meinig, *The Great Columbia Plain: A Historical Geography, 1805-1910* (Seattle: University of Washington Press, 1968).

For Elwood Evans there is his own work available now in facsimile reprints—*Puget Sound: Its Past, Present and Future* (Olympia, 1869) and *Washington Territory: Her Past, Her Present, And The Elements Of Wealth Which Ensure Her Future* (Olympia: Public Printer, 1877).

Clifford M. Drury, *Marcus and Narcissa Whitman and the Opening of Old Oregon*, 2 vols. (Glendale, California: The Arthur H. Clark Company, 1973) contains great masses of primary materials that the author lets speak for themselves. There are also valuable and poignant insights in Alvin M. Josephy, Jr., *The Nez Perce Indians And The Opening Of The Northwest* (New Haven: Yale University Press, 1965).

For Governor Stevens, Meany, Josephy, and Bancroft are helpful, as well as Hazard Stevens, *The Life of Isaac Ingalls Stevens*, 2 vols. (Cambridge, Mass.: Houghton Mifflin Co., 1900). However, the best

197

work being done on Stevens is by Kent Richards, who has published "Isaac I. Stevens and Federal Military Power in Washington Territory," *Pacific Northwest Quarterly* 63 (July 1972): 81–86. Our understanding of the Indian wars derives in part from Josephy but also from A. J. Splawn, *Ka-mi-akin, The Last Hero of the Yakimas* (Portland: Binfords & Mort, 1944). There is no adequate biography of Leschi but some information may be found in Della Gould Emmons, *Leschi of the Nisquallies* (Minneapolis: T. S. Dennison and Company), which, though it is fiction, is laced with useful primary sources.

Norman H. Clark, *Mill Town* (Seattle: University of Washington Press, 1970) includes material on Emory C. Ferguson.

Material on the life of James Glover may be found in Snowden, Bancroft, and *History of the City of Spokane and Spokane County, Washington* (Chicago: S. J. Clarke Company, 1912), and in Lucile F. Fargo, *Spokane Story* (New York: University of Columbia Press, 1950).

Industrial and social development around the turn of the century may be explored in such works as Thomas R. Cox, *Mills and Markets: A History of the Pacific Coast Lumber Industry to 1900* (Seattle: University of Washington Press, 1974); Charles Pierce Le Warne, *Utopias on Puget Sound, 1885–1915* (Seattle: University of Washington Press, 1975); and W. Storrs Lee, ed., *Washington State: A Literary Chronicle* (New York: Funk & Wagnalls, 1969). The Lee volume contains the material by Ray Stannard Baker and that from other primary sources. Some material may also be found in the two books by William O. Douglas: *Of Men and Mountains* (New York: Harper & Brothers, 1950) and *Go East, Young Man* (New York: Random House, 1974).

Horace R. Cayton, Jr. has written *Long Old Road* (Seattle: University of Washington Press, 1970) about his father. The main part of May Arkwright Hutton's biography may be found in Fargo: *Spokane Story*. For George Cotterill, readers should see Clarence B. Bagley, *History of Seattle* (Chicago: S. J. Clarke Company, 1916); Murray Morgan, *Skid Road* (New York: Viking Press, 1951); and Norman H. Clark, *The Dry Years: Prohibition and Social Change in Washington* (Seattle: University of Washington Press, 1965).

Labor radicalism may be studied further in Robert Tyler, *Rebels of the Woods: The I.W.W. in the Pacific Northwest* (Eugene, Ore.: University of Oregon Books, 1967), as well as in Clark, *Mill Town*.

Well worth reading on its subject is "Mark Reed: Portrait of a Businessman in Politics," by Robert E. Ficken, *Journal of Forest History* 20 (January 1976): 4–19.

Those interested in the irrepressible Rufus Woods may read further in George Sundborg, *Hail Columbia: The Thirty-Year Struggle for Grand Coulee Dam* (New York: The Macmillan Co., 1954).

Material on Gov. Clarence D. Martin may be found in Stewart, *Washington, Northwest Frontier*.

There is but one book about Boeing—the company and the man— Harold Mansfield, *Vision: A Saga of the Sky* (New York: Duell, Sloan, and Pearce, 1956).

Material on Edwin Pratt may be found in back issues of *Seattle Magazine*, especially 1969.

The Columbia River was described in an early and vivid way in *Journals of Lewis and Clark* edited by Bernard DeVoto (Boston: Houghton Mifflin Co., 1953). Readers may also want to consult James A. Gibbs, *Pacific Graveyard* (Portland: Binfords & Morts, 1964), as well as Robert Cantwell, *The Hidden Northwest* (New York: J. P. Lippincott Co., 1972).

My own reflections on the culture of the state have been stimulated by the thoughtful work of Raymond D. Gastil, *Cultural Regions of the United States* (Seattle: University of Washington Press, 1975) and of David Brewster in *Argus* magazine during the early 1970s.

Index

Agriculture: in Yakima Valley, 4, 70; growth of in late 1800s, 61, 68; effect of recessions on, 104; attention of Gov. Lister to, 112
Alaska-Yukon-Pacific Exposition, 69–70
Allen, William M., 171–173, 175–178; becomes president of Boeing, 171; Puritan ethic, 172–173; high-risk tactics of, 178
Ankeny, Levi P., 94
Antiwar movement, 120–122

Bancroft, H. H., quoted, 5, 15, 38, 45
Bellingham Bay, 53; polluted, 193
Blacks: discrimination against in Oregon, 48–51; and Donation Land Act, 50; employed as cheap labor, 63; in Seattle during late 1800s, 74–75, 78–80; discrimination against in Seattle, 179–185 *passim;* work of Edwin T. Pratt for, 183–185
Blue Mountains, 4, 5, 21, 28
Boeing, William E., 174–175
Boeing Airplane Company, 171–172, 174–178; effect of World War II on, 171, 175; impact of on Seattle, 171, 172, 178, 194; growth of between world wars, 174–175; postwar slump, 175; labor crisis in, 176; production of jets and missiles, 177–178
Bolon, Andrew J., 36, 37, 40
Bush, George and Isabella, 47–52; background, 47; travel to Puget Sound, 47–48; and Leschi, 47, 51; prosperity and generosity of, 49; and Nisqually Indians, 48–49; memorialized by Congress, 50

Camp Lewis, 116
Cape Disappointment, 7–8
Cape Flattery, 9, 35, 40, 193
Cascade Mountains, 4, 7, 38, 53, 73, 119, 157; natural barrier dividing state, 106
Cayton, Horace Roscoe, 74–80; early career of, 74–75; becomes editor of *Republican,* 75; enters middle-class white society, 75–76; crusade against

Seattle's fleshpots, 77–78; becomes middle-class hero, 78; urges Progressive politics, 79; increasingly race-conscious, 80; loses fortune, 80; burial of, 179; mentioned, 99
Cayton, Horace Roscoe, Jr., 80, 180–181
Cayton, Revels, 157, 171
Centralia riot, 125–126, 164
Chinese: pan for gold, 3; employed as cheap labor, 63, 71; influx of into Seattle, 71
Clapp, William, 150, 151, 152
Clough, David M., 134, 135
Clough-Hartley Company, 134–135
Coeur d'Alene Mountains, 4, 119; silver in, 64, 85; gold in, 82
Coeur d'Alenes, The (Hutton), 84
Columbia Plain, 4, 5, 58, 101, 149
Columbia River, 19, 37, 49, 55; described, 3–8 *passim,* 186–189 *passim;* early trade and settlements on, 3–8, 28; attempts to navigate breakers of, 7–8; fished by Cayuse, 21; established as southern boundary of territory, 33; fishing industry on, 101; importance of traffic on, 107; boundary for proposed east-west division of state, 107; and Grand Coulee Dam controversy, 150–152; federal works projects on, 166, 169; dams on, 153, 186, 187, 188, 189; changes in, 186–189 *passim*
Costigan, Howard, 164, 166
Cotterill, George, 90–98 *passim,* 114, 115; importance of as civil engineer in Seattle, 90–92; social vision of, 91–92, 98; campaigns for woman suffrage and municipal reform, 92, 96, 98; spokesman for "moral and civic progress," 93–98; political reform sought by, 93–95, 97; influenced by J. Allen Smith, 95, 96; reform work with Joseph E. Smith, 95–97; as mayor of Seattle, 97–98

Daily Intelligencer, 12
Dams: as sources of hydroelectric power, 150, 153–154, 170, 189; on Columbia

200